Moore & Us

Printed in the United Kingdom by MPG Books Ltd, Bodmin

Published by Sanctuary Publishing Limited, Sanctuary House, 45-53 Sinclair Road, London W14 0NS, United Kingdom

www.sanctuarypublishing.com

ISBN: 1-86074-595-4

Moore & Us

The Rise of Michael Moore and His Quest for a New
World Order

Jesse Larner

Sanctuary Publishing

For Constance Morrill

Contents

Acknowledgements

I am very grateful to the many people who gave me guidance and support throughout this project. I would especially like to thank my editor, Albert DePetrillo, who kept the focus on the real story; my agent, Sydelle Kramer; Maura Spiegel, who gave me the reference; Nathan Thompson, with whom I took a memorable trip to Washington; and most of all my wife, Constance Morrill, whose patience and wisdom have helped me more than I can say.

Introduction
Jester, Rock Star, Preacher, Teacher

It wasn't supposed to be like this. Another four years of faith-based foreign policy, carried out by amateurs with no interest in facts or in the lessons of history. Another four years of sadistic attacks on the poor, of privatisation of social goods, of gifts to the rich. Another four years of creeping theocracy and contempt for the Constitution. Another four years of complacency about an oil-based economy. Another four years in which to nurture a rogue sense of national sovereignty. On 2 November 2004, those Americans who saw through the Bush agenda found themselves contemplating a very dark future indeed.

It must have been worse for Michael Moore. He'd had a hit movie, *Fahrenheit 9/11*, that was supposed to make a difference and, his ego as bloated as his bank account, probably believed that he had single-handedly turned it around, that he was the kingmaker. Had George W Bush lost the election, Moore would undoubtedly have taken credit. He'd staked a lot of personal credibility on this, had confidently predicted victory for the forces of light. At the Republican National Convention in New York in late August of that year, he'd held up two fingers to show the gathered reactionaries that Bush had two months left.

But Moore's movie didn't make an electoral difference. Nothing did. Where does that leave Moore? Where does it leave the rest of us?

Most of those who were delighted at George W Bush's victory don't make much of a distinction between Moore and the 'rest of us' – the 48 per cent of the voters who didn't want a second Bush term. Republicans were quite strategically brilliant in accepting, at face value, Moore's idea of himself as the pre-eminent voice of the American left, such as it is. Right-wing commentator James K Glassman, writing about *Fahrenheit 9/11*, said, 'The sad truth is that the left is so intellectually bereft at this point in its history that the buffoonery of Michael Moore is about all they've got.'[1] In the wake of 2 November, the popular radical-right website www.freerepublic.com positively buzzed with delight at what its members saw as the unitary comeuppance of Moore, the Democratic Party and the left in general. Right-wing commentator David Bossie wrote, 'Mr Moore and these left-wing, Bush-hating groups tried every trick in the book to energise voters with their anger and venom, painting the picture of a divided and pessimistic America. But thanks to their over-the-top rhetoric and scare tactics, it backfired and actually helped the American people see clearly.'[2]

Melanie Morgan, a former television news correspondent who has a right-wing radio show in San Francisco and is now a vice-chairman of Move America Forward, a 'support the troops' outfit that also works to expel the United States from the United Nations and the United Nations from New York,[3] told me, 'I thank God that [Moore] decided to get as politically active as he did. I am grateful to him beyond measure for creating *Fahrenheit 9/11*, because by doing so, with such a lack of scholarship, he ended up motivating our base in a way that nothing else could have. Between the Swift Boat Veterans for Truth and Michael Moore and *Fahrenheit 9/11*, people got motivated on my side of the political fence in a way that I haven't seen before.'

This sentiment was repeated in numerous chain emails sent by gloating reactionaries in the aftermath of the election. George F

Will urged the Democrats to purge their 'Michael Moore faction' and wrote that 'Moore and the hordes of his enthusiasts are a stain on the party',[4] although where Will came up with any great and general enthusiasm for Moore among the executives of the right-of-centre Democratic Party is an interesting question. Will is quite correct, however, to say that many Democrats, like Moore, 'loathe' Bush, and this may have confused him.

Yes, Moore thought himself a kingmaker, and he turned out to be only a filmmaker. But whatever his status since November 2004, Michael Moore – that working-class guy from Flint, Michigan – remains a political phenomenon in North America and Europe. His polemics reside on the bestseller lists. His website is visited by millions. His film *Bowling For Columbine* won the Academy Award for Best Documentary of 2002, and *Fahrenheit 9/11* – love it or hate it – needs no introduction. He is a popular speaker, pulling in big crowds at home and in Europe who come to hear him speak against the corruption, illegitimacy and imperial ambitions of the United States government.

However mainstream Democrats feel about him, Moore has become the face of the angry opposition to the Bush administration. His style of anti-establishment humour has been compared to that of the Yippies[5] of the late 1960s, but there are important differences. The Yippies, after all, were performance-art anarchists who would never have campaigned within the 'system'. In their eyes, merely standing for election de-legitimised a candidate, so they ran a pig for office.[6] Perhaps Moore's style is closer to the earnestness that prevailed earlier in the '60s, the can-do spirit of Kennedy liberalism, without the Kennedy anti-communism and the Kennedy respect for the traditions of American political culture. But Moore delivers a much more radical message than the Kennedys ever did: corporations loot and pollute; racism is an ever-present reality in American life;

government – and, especially, American government – is a conspiracy of oppression and war. Authority is the enemy; working people are never wrong; those in power are never right.

Like all reductionist creeds, this is not completely incorrect, and not particularly helpful in real life. I used to live in Berkeley, California, which to this day cherishes a distant, fading legend about how idealistic young people in the 1960s reclaimed a patch of land from the evil University of California and turned it into a 'People's Park'. For this expression of peace and love, the story goes, they were punished by university president Clark Kerr and Governor Ronald Reagan with martial law and the National Guard, Reagan endorsing the use of a variety of tear gas that was banned by the Geneva Convention. During the ensuing quasi-military occupation, one protester was killed and another blinded by buckshot.

One of the leaders of the movement was still hanging around the campus when I lived in the area. The Battle of People's Park, 1969, was the high-water mark of his life. He's run for mayor of Berkeley several times, on a platform that always involves People's Park and social justice. He always gets a few dozen votes. When I would walk through the campus, in the early 1990s, I would sometimes see this ageing icon, his waist-length hair turning grey, preaching on the steps of Sproul Plaza. He would talk of the bosses versus the workers, of racism, injustice and conspiracy, of the military-industrial complex and Vietnam, of the Free Speech movement and Operation Paperclip as young pre-med, pre-law and anthropology students streamed heedlessly by. Sometimes he would get so frustrated at the distance between him and them that he would scream, 'What's the matter with you? You're going to end up just like your parents!' without the slightest clue that the students' parents' generation was his own.

There are people like this on every campus in America. Some run bookshops, some print up monthly political broadsides and drive trucks for a living while some just work the spare-change racket. They say pretty much the same things that Michael Moore is saying, but none of them is famous. None of them is a factor in national politics. Most certainly (with the possible exception of a few secret trust-fund radicals) none of them is rich.

So why is Michael Moore different? Although his political ideas aren't necessarily more complicated, his presentation is much better. He has a sly sense of humour. He knows how to work with others when he wants to, and he knows how to use the machinery of capitalism to make contacts, contracts and deals. He is tireless, often working on several projects at once and cross-pollinating them. He is genuinely fired up by issues of social justice. He is imaginative. And – one big difference between Moore and the ageing campus radicals, and the paradoxical conceptual weakness at the heart of his populist strength – he goes about his mission with ordinary, non-political, working Americans in mind: people who want to be entertained, not lectured. Moore became famous as something new on the relatively far left, someone who defied its stereotypes. Not a dour sloganeer, not a hippie, not a humourless disciple of political correctness, not a public executive like Ralph Nader or Marian Wright Edelman. An improviser. It's hard to mock him because, in a sense, he is already making a big joke of himself – a serious joke. He invokes the jesters' privilege of saying serious things that wouldn't get heard if serious people said them.[7]

He's also not running for any office, doesn't *want* to run for or hold any office, reports to no editor, no director, no foundation, and thus has no accountability. He's a true independent operator, and if you think about it, there aren't that many of them on the scene. Moore's only job is politics – one-man politics. This is an important clue as to what he can do; short of the law and the market, there are no real restraints.

In the parlance of capitalism, he's got great brand recognition.

We all know by now what a Michael Moore/Dog Eat Dog production will look like. We know it will be funny and irreverent; that it will perhaps include a few cartoons, lest our attention wander; that Moore himself will shuffle through the proceedings, making a point of dressing like a slob; that he will skewer important people on basic questions and make them look like fools. There will be pranks on bad guys – and there will be plenty of bad guys. There will be facts, or – just as often – highly debatable 'facts' relating to social policy.

Moore's career has received a boost from a particular conjunction of phenomena that have tended to discourage subtlety in political discourse and to call forth the broad strokes of populist activism. The two most obvious are closely linked. There is the arrogance and ambition of the political right, put in power by appeals to popular indignation among those whom right-wing politicians do not represent, resemble or respect, but whom – thanks to shrewd market research – they have come to understand quite well. At the same time – and by no means coincidentally – the American news media have been increasingly dominated over the last 30 years by the views of the extreme right.

The attempt to impeach President Bill Clinton put these phenomena in focus. The disputed election of 2000 made them almost impossible to bear. The war in Iraq (more correctly, not the war itself – which many thoughtful liberals can support – but rather the right-wing agenda behind it) made it clear that the stakes are very high.

The war encouraged a populist political style that the reactionary right has been learning to deploy in support of economic and social privilege for the last 40 years. It has not been easy for political liberals to hear the language of social justice being used to explain tax cuts for millionaires and the degradation of the poor, and to see how effective the strategy has been. Is it any wonder that, when someone like Michael Moore comes along to champion a more reasonable set of priorities for working people, his arguments – even when they are sloppy and demagogic – are heard with delight?

There should be many contenders for the role of left populist. There are more registered Democrats than Republicans in the United States, but since 1994 an increasingly conservative Republican Party has outmanoeuvred Democrats and captured both Houses of Congress, the presidency and much of the judiciary. The American left has been on a long, long march into obscurity from its heyday in the time of the New Deal, and it has no one in mainstream politics now among the moderate centrists and right-centrists who are the only type of Democrat in Congress (Howard Dean burned out, Barack Obama's moment has not yet come, Hillary Clinton is not trusted and too shrill). John Kerry's miserable presidential campaign of 2004 ended any possibility of Kerry taking a national leadership role. The late Paul Wellstone of Minnesota was the last Democrat who might have been the next liberal hero, a man of passion, intelligence and eloquence, and with a sense of mission. He died in an aeroplane accident while campaigning for re-election in 2002, a tragedy that, no doubt, encouraged the contemporary notion that God loves conservatives.

It's not just Moore by default; there is a particular rhythm to these political times. What George W Bush – widely viewed (at least in his first term) as a usurper to the throne – has done to reward the rich and to destroy the established international order has brought the liberal mainstream and radical left closer together; and opposition to Bush has drawn in marginal protest groups that do not look to mainstream political leaders. Liberals have been so humiliated by the Republican agenda, so enraged by the arrogance of Bush's rule, that a political clown with an edge – someone who is very calculatedly *not* careful with his words – is a great relief. There is a faction of the left that wants a spokesman who will paint the picture with the broadest possible strokes and offend the greatest number on the right. It is not surprising that Moore's strongest supporters are under 25. Damn the torpedoes!

Yet, while many on the right are delighted to present him as typical of the left, many on the left have serious doubts about Moore. He is good at mobilising outrage, but his presentation of the issues is highly opinionated, usually inconsistent, occasionally paranoid and hardly of any depth. He is not the intellectual heir to the democratic left's glory days of *Partisan Review* or *Dissent*. There are plenty of reasons to doubt him, and even to despise him.

In spite of this, Moore has brought important issues of social justice to the attention of people who would otherwise not know of them. He has agitated for and often achieved (at least, on a local level) significant and positive changes in social policy. He's also hurt some good people on his way to doing this, and he's been susceptible to believing too much in his own showbusiness and political legends, in ways that have hampered his political agenda.

What follows is a detailed look at how Michael Moore's political style influences American culture in a reactionary age. Those who are looking for the predictable hatchet job on Moore will be disappointed with this book. So will those who are looking for confirmation of his heroic status as a defender of truth and justice. It will require a few excursions into some of the major political issues that span Moore's career, and have defined it, to answer the question of why he has become such a phenomenon. Why Moore? Why now? And where next?

Part 1

Class Still Matters

1 Roots

'Moore' is the ninth most common surname in the United States, and its etymology is not complicated: it's from 'moor', meaning a fen or bog, and it implies that the ancestors of the person carrying the name were poor and powerless, confined to the marginal land that the rich folk didn't want. To the extent that the United States is a country with a population primarily of Anglo-Saxon descent, the prevalence of this name says a lot about the roots of its people and about the role of class (along with its inevitable concomitant, the denial of class) in its sociology. An American, regardless of origin, is more likely to identify with the working man than with the aristocrat, and – paradoxically – to insist, against all the evidence, that the accident of birth played no role in his personal fate.

Michael Moore is an anomaly in this regard. His identity seems to be drawn from legends of the New Deal 1930s, a much more radical time when working people were developing a self-conscious culture, one that understood that inequities begin at birth. Moore knows that class is important, if not determinative, in life prospects.

Moore presents himself as just an ordinary working stiff who came close to doing factory work (even if he didn't actually do it), who dropped out of college and doesn't have any fancy degrees, yet who's managed to figure it all out. He's the descendant of Irish immigrants, the son of an auto worker and a clerk, and – perhaps most importantly – he grew up in Flint, Michigan.

To those who still care about things like American labour history, Flint is talismanic. Mentioning the town is a shorthand reference to a whole history of working-class achievements and, more recently, working-class humiliations. If you want to understand Michael Moore, you have to understand Flint – or, more accurately, you have to understand how Moore understands Flint.

Flint has been an American centre of vehicle manufacturing since 1886, the year that local entrepreneur Billy Durant hitched a ride in a friend's horse-drawn carriage. Durant was so impressed with the suspension of the vehicle that he went to see its designers at their plant in Coldwater the next day and bought the rights to manufacture it. The carriage made him a millionaire and allowed him to play the stock market, which made him a multi-millionaire – a billionaire many times over in today's money. The manufacture of horse-drawn carriages had some of the same industrial logic of motor-cars, and in 1903 and 1904 Durant absorbed the Buick Motor Company and its supplier, Mott Axle, to create the nucleus of General Motors, which in the next few years acquired Pontiac, Cadillac and Oldsmobile. By 1911 there was a Chevrolet division, named after Louis Chevrolet, a former race-car driver for Buick.

Charles Stewart Mott accepted 10,000 shares of General Motors stock in payment of a debt from Durant, which eventually made him one of the richest men in the country. Through his Mott Foundation, he also became one of the country's foremost philanthropists, and his public endowments in Flint – an elaborate Cultural Center, the trade school for engineers that eventually became Kettering University, and many others – have been enormously important to the town's economy.

The Mott Foundation became in a many ways a surrogate government in Flint, picking up the slack when the real government's resources ran low. Mott money heavily subsidised Flint's public schools, and it was the Foundation that lobbied for and partially financed the Flint campus of the University of Michigan.

Mott and GM weren't the only auto-industry players in the sociology of Flint. In the heyday of American auto production, in the late 1970s, local and state politics were heavily determined by the policies and internal politics of the United Auto Workers union. The industry was deeply entwined with the existence of the town, on every level.

It was in Flint that the UAW first became a force in American society, through an historic strike against GM that won American auto workers the right to collective bargaining. This right had been legally established by the Wagner Act of 1935, but it had been widely ignored by employers.

In the 1930s, the balance of power presented a real challenge to the working class. Flint was a GM town. The company employed 80 per cent of its residents and its influence was felt in local government, the police and the newspapers. Like all the big auto manufacturers, it quite actively spied on its employees and even on non-employee union leaders, using its large private police force and paid informants. The spying, as well as the lack of job security and Depression-era cuts in wages, was a serious grievance.

By late 1936, emboldened by a successful strike at the nearby Kelsey-Hayes plant that produced parts for Ford, and by the election of Frank Murphy – a New Deal Democrat who had vowed not to send police against strikers – as Michigan Governor, the fledgling UAW targeted GM for a risky strike on important principles of organised labour. The strike was precipitated by GM instructing three employees to quit the UAW, but there were larger issues of representation involved. Under Walter Reuther and his brothers Victor and Roy, who were then emerging as leaders of the union, the strike employed the controversial tactic of the 'sit-down'. Striking workers, rather than going on a picket line outside a factory, would occupy the workplace, preventing scabs from taking their places and denying the company access to its equipment and inventory, with the implied threat that any attempt to remove the strikers by violence would lead to the destruction of company assets.

The strike began on 1 January 1937, and it was the kind of thing that, back when there was a definite working-class culture in the US, used to be commemorated in broadsides and ballads. UAW members seized the Fisher Body Number Two plant, which made bodies for Chevrolet, and refused to leave the shop floor. The company embargoed food supplies and brought in private and city police, who attacked the strikers and their sympathisers massed outside the plant with bullets and tear gas – an encounter that the workers called, with high-labour romance, 'the Battle of the Running Bulls'. When these attacks were repulsed, Governor Murphy called in the National Guard to keep the peace.

The strike spread. One hundred and twenty-five thousand workers went out in solidarity with the Fisher workers, which forced GM to shut down 50 plants, either from the strike itself or from parts shortages caused by the strike. When it reached Chevrolet Number Four – GM's main plant for Chevrolet engines – President Roosevelt personally pressured the company to negotiate.

Ultimately the UAW won recognition as the representative of the workers in the plants that were striking and the right to collective bargaining on their behalf. It was a groundbreaking victory, hard fought, and it showed the way to eventual union contracts with other companies, including Ford, which had most bitterly resisted unionisation by using its 'Service Department', an intimidating apparatus of spies and plainclothes private police. Workers all over the Detroit area were inspired by the strike to form 'locals' in many subsidiary industries. To this day, a monument to the strikers stands in the parking lot of the UAW local on Flint's West Atherton Road, with the original settlement text reproduced on the plaque.

With the legacy of the strike, an industrial economy, union militants who knew their labour history and the influence of foreign-born workers who had been raised in the ideals of labour socialism (Walter Reuther's father was German-born, and Reuther and his brothers had taught tool-and-die making in the Soviet Union in the early 1930s), it makes sense that many of the workers of Flint continued to understand the importance of class. This had various cultural effects, not all of them admirable. Attracted by the idea of class solidarity, radicals of the Weather Underground – themselves mostly of comfortable middle-class background – held a 'war council' in Flint in December 1969 before beginning a decade-long campaign of nihilistic violence.

Nonetheless, the great Flint strike of 1937, and the sense of working-class solidarity and power that it engendered, is on the whole a very positive heritage. The strike was one of the key events that would eventually bring some measure of autonomy and dignity to American industrial workers.

For a long time, the UAW's influence and the deals it could broker benefited both GM and its workers as GM became the world's largest corporation and one of the country's most profitable. The union quite reasonably demanded an ever-increasing share of profits in the form of wages and benefits for its members, but there were plenty of profits to go around. And the unions took care of their members, making sure that they had everything from decent-length vacations to prescription eyeglasses to funeral insurance – a mini-model of the welfare state.

This period of opportunity for the working class, as recalled fondly and frequently by Michael Moore, was a golden age in which his father could raise a family on an auto worker's salary and still maintain his hopes, dreams and sense of self as a human being, as something other than an underpaid, interchangeable and expendable work unit tending the great conveyor belt of production.

Moore knows and honours his roots. His uncle Laverne was a 1937 striker. 'Because of what my uncle and others fought for over the years, families like mine were able to live in homes that we owned, go to a doctor whenever we were sick, get our teeth fixed whenever they needed it or go to college if we chose to – all thanks to the union.'[8]

The subsequent shift in the power relations between the unions and the auto manufacturers is the narrative at the core of Moore's activism: how the union-busting of the Reagan era and opportunities for rootless, irresponsible profit abroad allowed the manufacturers to grievously exploit those loyal workers who didn't lose their jobs altogether. GM moved jobs to Mexico and, throughout the 1980s, laid off 65,000 in the Flint area from the total of 80,000 employed in the late 1970s. The city never recovered. It is now one of the most economically depressed places in America.

Labour, once a powerful force in local politics, was seriously weakened by the early 1980s as much of its sense of class cohesion was lost. Gone was the social orientation of the old UAW under Walter Reuther, which looked not only for money but also for autonomy and dignity for workers – and not only auto workers, at that. The mainstream UAW leadership by this time was eager to salvage its privileges and its relationship with GM's management at the expense of its constituents.

Labour had been weakened in other ways, attacked on all sides by the Reagan administration. To the enormous detriment of the status of working Americans, social issues such as abortion and school prayer had begun to overshadow economic issues and were splitting off blue-collar 'Reagan Democrats' from the rest of the Party. The efforts of the Republican Party and its right-wing think tanks and media were starting to bear fruit in convincing American workers that their economic interests were identical to those of their employers. This was happening despite the decline in the share of profits that went to labour as unions were crushed and taxes were lifted from the rich and from corporations.

This situation might have been easier to fight if social class wasn't such a taboo subject in national politics, even – paradoxically, and perhaps especially – for American working-class people. There's a habit of downplaying class as a factor in economics and sociology. Even in places like Flint that have a proud labour history, this habit is very much part of the American ideology. In the library of the University of Michigan at Flint there's a display case with a book open to a passage from George Wilson Pierson's *Tocqueville And Beaumont In America* in which the author describes how impressed the French travellers were with the democratic society of backwoods Michigan: 'About the practical, religious-minded, solitary pioneer there was nothing rustic, save his log cabin and his temporary surroundings.' As Pierson notes, Tocqueville was taken with the fitness and perseverance of the humble, industrious New England settler: 'Unlike the French Canadian, he proved to have the character, the education, the interests and the ambitions of a civilised city-dweller. Instead, therefore, of finding all the stages in the past history of man recapitulated on a small scale within the territory of Michigan, Tocqueville and Beaumont were forced to proclaim that they had encountered a modern society… Its first cabin, as Tocqueville himself gracefully said, was "the ark of civilisation lost in the midst of an ocean of leaves".'[9]

Tocqueville shows us that his homesteaders' lodgings were rough but his mind and aspirations were the equal of the untitled aristocrats of the land, in no way abashed or limited by humble status. There's a certain unconscious vested interest in the library's endorsement of this romantic view of American social relations – after all, the library, the University and much of the civic infrastructure of Flint are subsidised by the Mott Foundation – but it would be far too simple to say that the vested interest is only on the part of the industrialists. One of the few things that Tocqueville got seriously wrong, and one of the factors for which he is lionised by the right, was his contention that America was a largely classless society. Coming from France, a country still struggling 42 years after the Revolution to fully find its way out of feudalism, Tocqueville could be forgiven for this misconception.

Although there is a long and proud tradition of social analysis that addresses class as a central issue in America – the work of Irving Howe, Daniel Bell, Herbert Marcuse, C Wright Mills, Michael Harrington, Jonathan Kozol, Barbara Ehrenreich, to name only a few – mainstream American commentary has stubbornly held to the myth that we live in a meritocracy, as if people really do start out with equal chances in life and that social justice is therefore merely a matter of individual striving. It's hard to think of an assumption that has been more damaging to the aspirations of working people, and it's a misconception that has deepened dramatically in recent years. Questions of relative income and power between workers and employers have been so neutralised, class so eradicated from the modern American political picture, that no candidate for the presidency dares mention workers. In the 2004 campaign, John Kerry spoke of the 'middle-class squeeze' and was considered bold for promising to raise the federal minimum wage – over three years! – to $7 an hour from its present $5.15. This is what remains of the bold dreams of the New Deal.

Meanwhile, Republicans make the rather surprising yet ubiquitous argument that liberals are 'snobs' who drive special cars and drink special coffees, and that therefore workers should vote Republican. In this model, wages don't matter, unions don't matter, social insurance and health care don't matter, the relative freedom and personal autonomy of employers and employees don't matter; all that matters is that liberals are said to think they know better than Republicans about what is good for people, and therefore they don't. In its utter vacuousness, its reliance on a pure emotional feeling separated from the real world in which corporations wield enormous and dehumanising power over their employees, it is unsusceptible to rational debate, and therefore a brilliant strategy.

But even in these times of resolute working-class conservatism, class consciousness seeps through in strange ways in Flint. The commercial radio stations in the area seem to have very short playlists indeed. How often, really, can one listen to 'My Generation' and 'Free Bird'? Six or seven times a week, apparently, is what the market will bear around here. These songs are from the rock canon, and while hearing them repeated endlessly might be dreary, it's predictable enough. But as I drove around Flint in the autumn of 2004, there was one constant repeat that surprised me.

Reba McEntire's 1990s ballad 'Fancy' was nowhere near the country charts when I was in Flint. It's a song about a working-class girl named Fancy whose family is in such desperate economic straits that her own mother has to prostitute her. But Fancy is no victim; she gets her own in the end, dragging triumph out of humiliation. It's an astonishingly brave and gritty song for McEntire to sing, and it's profoundly unsentimental about class and the burdens of being born into the wrong one. Is it just coincidence that the song is big here? I'd like to think that it hangs on because somewhere, deep down, the working people of Flint know they're getting screwed and want to think of themselves as being strong and resourceful.

Michael Moore, with humour and a certain anti-style, exists to make it clear that class *does* matter. His physical presence is a part of the act, contempt for the conventions of bourgeois society married to the fatman-as-foil tradition that runs from Falstaff to

Oliver Hardy to John Belushi to Chris Farley. There's some history here, some background, and even if Moore himself is now a multi-millionaire who never actually worked on a production line…well, class is more than a matter of income, more even than a matter of occupation. It's a matter of background, consciousness and identity.

Moore's parents, Frank and Veronica, and his older sisters, Anne and Veronica, were not deeply involved in politics, but the family was devout in the religion of the Irish-descended American working class. Frank and Veronica went to Mass every day, raised their children in the faith and were one of the founding families of a new neighbourhood Catholic church. They came from a socially progressive, blue-collar Catholic tradition that leaned on the social justice encyclicals of Pope Leo XIII and Pope Pius XI, and this gave them an awareness of class, the issues of working people and the importance of unionism. They were almost certainly aware of, and influenced by, Dorothy Day and Peter Maurin's Catholic Worker movement. The family took up collections for César Chávez and the United Farm Workers and for Daniel and Philip Berrigan and their religiously inspired, non-violent, anti-war protests. Young Michael himself attended a training seminary while he was in high school, and for a brief period he thought seriously about entering the priesthood. Years later, he proposed a segment for his *TV Nation* television show in which a correspondent goes to confessionals in 20 different Catholic churches and ranks the punishments meted out, calling the results 'A Consumer's Guide To The Confessional'. But even then he was still enough of a Catholic to have doubts about this very funny and sharp idea: 'When the segment was finished, Mike was confident he would burn in eternal Hell if this segment ever ran, so he spiked it.'[10]

Although Moore didn't join the priesthood, he had a clear sense of mission from a very young age and was an active polemicist and populist long before Flint's decline. Yet, although he has wrapped himself in Flint's labour history, he didn't actually grow up there; he was raised in Davison, a bedroom community just to the east of Flint proper, an open and sunny place that, on signs at the city limits, bills itself as the 'City of Flags' and the home town of Ken Morrow, member of the 1980 US Olympic champion hockey team. There is no public mention of a much more famous native son. As a matter of fact, Moore is in the unusual position of being a worldwide celebrity who is apparently banned from his hometown high school's Hall of Fame. His candidacy has been vetoed by Davison school board members who believe it would cost the district private donations. 'Moore has been nominated every year since the Davison High School Hall of Fame's founding in 2000, but he doesn't meet our criteria for being a positive role model that students can look up to who has served his community... There's a kind of silent majority or unspoken rule about Moore around here of people who are irate over the things Moore has done,' attests Don Hammon, one of the selection committee members.[11] Several alumni are now leading an effort to win Moore the honour.

Moore's critics have made much of the fact that Davison is white, comfortable and clean, with many more white collar-workers (middle managers at GM) than gritty, working-class Flint. All of this is true, yet the criticism is still a little off. Davison was an adjunct of Flint, and it was no playground of the leisure class. Its modest suburban charms were well within the reach of the line workers at GM's plants in Flint, among them Moore's father, whose hands made spark plugs for 30 years. Furthermore, Davison – nearly mall-less and mostly an empty subdivision in Moore's youth – has come up considerably since that time, while Flint has gone down precipitously. If Davison has a higher average income than Flint, dramatically lower unemployment and is almost entirely white, at least part of this is due to the aftershocks of GM's withdrawal from Flint, starting in the late 1970s, which separated those who could afford to leave Flint from those who could not. Moore's father had his place in Davison long before this happened. Moore himself had moved to Flint long before this happened.

Before he left Davison, Moore had already established a pattern of outspoken politics that showed the way to much that was to follow. Coming up at a time in which the Vietnam War was boiling through American political life, he was always an agitator. He started his first anti-establishment newssheets in grade school, while in high school he won a public-speaking contest with a speech condemning the local Elks' Lodge for barring blacks. He started a campaign to ban the Homecoming Queen contest, which he considered silly and sexist. Amazingly, he got significant support for this from his classmates.

When the voting age (and office-holding age) was lowered in 1972 from 21 to 18, Moore ran for the Davison school board and won, becoming the board's youngest member. From this position, he set about lobbying the board to fire his principal and vice-principal, whom he clearly despised. The two submitted their resignations soon after Moore's election to the school board, and Moore would later take credit for forcing them out. Why was Moore so intent on getting rid of these men? It's not at all clear. Moore writes of feeling oppressed by deadening routine – not a remarkable memory of high school. In his own words, he has only nice things to say of the principal whose career he damaged: 'I had known this man, the principal, for many years. When I was eight years old, he used to let me and my friends skate and play hockey on this little pond beside his house. He was kind and generous, and always left the door to his house open in case any of us needed to change into our skates or if we got cold and just wanted to get warm. Years later, I was asked to play bass in a band that was forming, but I didn't own a bass. He let me borrow his son's.'[12]

This passage has understandably been leapt upon by right-wing critics of Moore; there's something shocking and unseemly about it, for Moore himself is writing that his knee-jerk anti-authoritarianism trumps any consideration of loyalty or human feeling or the character of his targets. Anyone in a position of authority – or who can be presented as being in a position of authority – is his enemy.

Typically, even the very retail level of politics at the school-board level was for Moore a zero-sum game: teachers (except for the popular anti-establishment ones, who always ended up martyred by the school administration) were the enemy, students the victims of an oppressive system. Moore's instincts were to trust the students always to know what was in their own interests. He did not get along well with the other board members and was precociously litigious, at one point threatening to sue the board for the right to tape-record board meetings, an issue that was probably more provocative than substantive but that was – also typically – couched in the highest language of public accountability. His confrontational style led to a recall effort, which failed.

The Davison school board was too small a stage for a talented social activist, however, and Moore soon expanded his work. He and his friend Jeff Gibbs started the Hotline Center, an emergency line that took calls and made referrals for unwanted pregnancies, drug overdoses and suicide attempts, and soon branched out into broader social issues like police brutality. The Hotline spun off a community newspaper named, in best early-1970s style, *Free To Be*. It was mimeographed and free, and its title was hand-drawn, but there was some real journalistic competence behind it. Moore had been a socially conscious writer and investigator throughout his school years, winning an Eagle Scout badge for a slide-show exposé of polluting industries in the Flint area, and *Free To Be* took on some fine-grained but serious issues, mostly having to do with the politics of the school board and student rights. As Moore gained confidence, *Free To Be* began to address larger matters, such as the case of Ray Fulgham, a black man who Moore decided had been railroaded on a burglary charge and who he made into a *cause célèbre* of local progressives.

Free To Be was the nucleus of Moore's next project, *The Flint Voice*, which first appeared in 1977, after Moore had dropped out of the University of Michigan. While at U of M, he had been majoring – presciently – in political science and theatre.

In that year, Moore had a stroke of luck when he went to a Harry Chapin concert in Detroit and managed to talk his way into the singer's dressing room, where he told Chapin about the Hotline. Chapin, then a big star known for his 1974 hit 'Cat's In The Cradle', agreed to do a benefit in Flint, and in fact ended up doing 11 benefits over the years for the Hotline and the *Voice*. He netted half a million dollars for Moore, which meant that Moore could buy some professional equipment and, with a little discipline, put out a serious monthly paper.

The Flint Voice was a bit ragged, but it became more and more professional over the years that it was published, between 1977 and 1982. In its pages, Moore produced some excellent investigative journalism, as well as sponsoring that of other writers. The *Voice* really dug deep into local and state stories, and looked at things that the conservative *Flint Journal* would never touch. Not bound to any particular news format, the *Voice* could publish in a wide range of styles and tones, and many of the articles – a great many – were written by Moore himself. He was relentless, and everywhere. He rooted out municipal and police corruption. He highlighted GM's demands for local and regional tax breaks with the implied threat of plant closings if it did not get them, a race to the bottom with other towns and counties that carried more than a hint of corporate blackmail. He found cover-ups of corporate chemical dumping. He ran pieces investigating illegal police surveillance and racial discrimination in municipal zoning. He caught Genesee County commissioners going on 'working trips' to Hawaii at county expense while the county was $4 million in debt and laying off hundreds of workers.

Subjects that the *Voice* revisited several times were corruption in local government and illegal use of municipal employees in political campaigns. In late 1979, Moore ran stories alleging that the office of Flint mayor Jim Rutherford was coercing federally-funded city employees to campaign for him on publicly-paid time, that Rutherford had irregularly approved liquor licences, that he had improperly billed the city for services in 1973, when he was the Police Chief, and that Rutherford and Flint Township Police Chief Herbert Adams were part owners of a bar. (Michigan law prohibited law-enforcement officers from owning bars.) In response to the stories, City Ombudsman Joe Dupcza began an investigation, and Moore somehow got hold of and published his report before the official release date.

Six months later, after Dupcza tried to have Flint Police Chief Max Durbin sacked, Flint police obtained a warrant to search the offices of the printing contractor for the *Voice*. The *Voice* later wrote that the police were looking for evidence that Dupcza was the source of the leaked report (vol. IV No 5, June-July 1980); if he had shown it to the press before its public release, Dupcza, who had caused both Rutherford and Durbin grief, could himself be sacked.

Moore of course made brilliant use of the raid, announcing plans to file a huge lawsuit against the city. He attracted the support of the American Civil Liberties Union, the American Society of Newspaper Editors, and the Reporters' Committee for Freedom of the Press, and he got national exposure for his paper and his issues. He also provocatively re-ran all the negative articles about Rutherford.

Rutherford is an interesting guy, a career policeman who joined the force in 1948, got a college degree and rose through the civil service to become Deputy Mayor and Chief of Police. When Flint changed its city charter from the city manager to the strong mayoral system in 1975, he retired from the police force to run for Mayor. He barely won in 1975, but did better in 1979. When I asked him about *The Flint Voice* raid, he is honestly unable to remember it. He did recall, however, that Moore had a problem with authority: 'He was pretty much critical of most politicians. I can't think of any he would say were worth anything, and maybe he was right… What he focuses on is what's wrong and what's going to be wrong. In my elections, Moore was trying to find out anything and everything that I had done wrong. This was his usual use of confrontation.'

It's also what good muckrakers do, and Moore was a good muckraker. 'Moore is very smart,' says Albert Price, a professor of political science at the University of Michigan at Flint who worked with Moore on several projects, including a local TV show called *Roadkill Politics*. 'He was always very focused on class issues, and he's tried to bring political discourse around to social class and the distribution of wealth in our society. He reported on stuff that was serious, and he did at it a serious level. *The Flint Voice* was a far more legitimate source of information than the conservative, establishment *Flint Journal*. Moore simply provided much, much more information.'

He was playful, too. The informality of the paper meant that he could run satirical social criticism like the diary of 'Brian', an individual telling his story from sperm to adult, at first full of optimism, hope, love and humanity, but increasingly distorted through mind-numbing schooling and soul-crushing factory work into a redneck racist slob who hated the world.[13] This story is less grim than it seems in a brief description, if no more subtle. It also reveals quite a bit about Moore's view of human nature: that we are born good, trusting and communitarian, and that it is only exposure to a warped, capitalist value system that trains us to be suspicious, greedy and hateful. This is, of course, the classic left-wing romanticism so often offered in response to the right-wing romanticism of the sacred, selfish individual.[14]

Moore's complete commitment to his causes made him some enemies at GM and in the city administration, but it won over many working-class people. Fran Cleaves, an auto worker, die-hard unionist and activist, ran into him frequently at picket lines and community meetings, and they became close friends. Cleaves was much older, and unlike some in the black community she trusted and welcomed this like-minded white boy. Cleaves grew up in Detroit but moved to Flint in 1964, when Moore was 11, to work for GM. She laughed when I asked if she worked on the line or in an office. (On the line.) She's working class, the real thing, and she was first assigned to 'the hole' – Chevrolet Manufacturing Plant Number Six – where she put in her time on the line, hanging doors. Later she moved to oil pans and rocker arms, then the motor line in Plant Number Four, one of the plants that took part in the historic sit-down of 1937.

Cleaves has paid a very high personal price for being on the wrong side of the American economic divide. Her son Herbert was shot and killed in a drive-by shooting in a rough neighbourhood in Flint shortly before the release of Moore's first film, *Roger & Me*. If you watch the credits roll at the end of the film, there's a dedication to him that warms the heart of his mother.

As Cleaves makes clear, Moore was a dedicated and effective activist long before he had any hope of money or fame. 'He was at everything,' she told me. 'You couldn't hardly be involved in any social issues here and not meet him. He was always respected as a speaker; wherever he was speaking would be packed, and it would be packed with people who had everyday struggles, survival issues, especially people who worked in the plants and the hospitals, homeless people. There was a movement from Tent City; Michael was very involved with that. I can remember picketing one of the banks – just Michael, myself and two or three other people, who picketed Citizens' Bank here to support the people who were trying to organise a union. I remember it well because Michael was covered in snow. He could always be counted on to come up with the right position that would help you teach and educate people. He seemed to have a thick skin and a sense of humour, never retreating from his position but being able to not take it personally.'

Moore made a real difference in his community, too, even helping to stop rampant police brutality in Flint. 'There was one case in particular, a kid named Billy Taylor who was killed by the police, and they tried to cover it up,' remembers Cleaves. 'They said that he was in the middle of a theft – which he was – but Michael was able to show that the boy's hands were up when he was killed by the police. There was a case in which even a black policewoman was shot down and left to die. There was all kinds of evidence, even on the police recorder, where they were making jokes about leaving her dead. Michael exposed all of that in his paper. He got in trouble with some of the leaders of the black community, who would identify him as this kid from Davison who needed to go back where he came from, but Michael had enough support from people in the black community who knew him... He wouldn't debate that kind of stuff; he just kept on doing the work he was doing.'

Moore does seem to have been both careful and sincere in his racial politics throughout his career, to the extent – as some black associates of his have noted – of being unable or unwilling to call out black people on antisocial behaviour. Sometimes his attitudes have earned him ridicule from the right, as when he has intentionally downplayed the effects of black street crime so as to focus on white corporate crime (indeed, one whole chapter in his book *Stupid White Men* is about the evil that specifically white people do). He has nurtured the essentialist view of race in America to the point that he is able to blame the nation's problem with guns in large part on the racially hysterical news media.

But there's no doubt of his sincerity. Once, during a question-and-answer session with a sympathetic crowd in California, I saw a black man stand up to thank him personally for his films and his statements on race, and for his statement in an interview that he would never dream of undertaking any project without having black people involved at every level. The questioner asked Moore how he had come by this attitude, which he considered rare in white people.

Moore sat thoughtfully for a moment (although I would have bet that he had encountered this question before and knew exactly what he was going to say) before answering, 'I was 13 years old. It was Holy Thursday. We were coming out of Mass; it was kind of cold. Someone turned a radio on in his car in the parking lot. He called out, "They just shot Martin Luther King!" And a cheer arose from those people coming out of the church. I was 13, and it was one of those moments in which things suddenly become very clear: "OK, fuck this. I don't want to live in this kind of world. These people have to change…" And that's sort of been my motivation in what I say and do when it comes to race in America.'

Moore went on to talk about how Hollywood has never – not ever – funded a major production by a black American woman, and how he used some of the money he made from *Roger & Me* to start a foundation to give grants to encourage this particular creative group.[15]

With Moore's dedication and political ambition came occasional bouts of insecurity. Sam Riddle is a friend of Moore's and a professional associate with whom he has retained a close bond over the years. Listed on the masthead as a 'founding member' of *The Flint Voice*, Riddle has been an important figure in Flint, Michigan state and national politics since the early 1970s. A high-school dropout who did a stint in the army before getting a college and legal degree, Riddle now operates in the same territory that Moore does, although from a slightly different perspective: the intersection of politics and image, news and entertainment. When I caught up with Riddle, he described himself thus: 'I don't practise law. I'm a political-slash-media consultant, with an emphasis on crisis management. I work in the court of public opinion. I just got calls on three things that are happening now: Memphis, Chicago, Detroit. All three of them are about companies or individuals who are about to have negative dealings with the media. My job is, if there's a real story, to get it right, get it out there, get the truth out so that they can fight back. "No comment" are the two worst words in the dictionary.'

Riddle, a former campus radical who used mass protest in imaginative ways (once shutting down an NCAA basketball game with an organised on-court sit-down), now has political clients all over the country. He has represented politicians in Detroit, Flint, Colorado and many other places; he has worked with Al Sharpton and the Word television network, the largest media operation for black ministers in the country; and he's organised for Ralph Nader, Jesse Jackson, eccentric Michigan politician Geoffrey Fieger and several of the people who have been featured in Michael Moore's films. If there's a racial aspect to be worked, he will work it – not in the cynical spirit of shakedown but because of the plain fact that justice in America is still racial and that, if you expect to get justice where race is involved, you can't ignore race.

Riddle has known Moore since his very early political days on the Davison school board. In his last year of law school, Riddle was working for Genesee County District Attorney Robert F Leonard when the recall movement against Moore was at its height. Leonard – an unusual district attorney for that time and place – was concerned that the recall movement was using illegal intimidation tactics against Moore and sent Riddle to investigate. Moore and Riddle have been friends ever since, and they learned to organise together in Flint.

Riddle points out that Moore did it the hard way, at the grassroots level, where he earned his beliefs about class and politics, all the while with his eye on a larger stage. 'In 1983, he and I decide we were going to change the mayor of Flint,' he told me. 'At that time, the mayor was the former police chief, Jim Rutherford, who had authorised those raids on the *Voice* offices – real Gestapo tactics. November 1983, there's an underdog black candidate, Jim Sharp, a former marine who doesn't have a prayer against this right-wing Jim Rutherford. I said we had to do something to get out the black vote. The *Voice* sponsored a get-out-the-vote rally in Whiting Auditorium in Flint, the same place we would later do Ralph Nader, where we out-drew Bill Clinton. So I fly down to Washington and negotiated a deal where, the day he announced he was running for President – just before the Flint election – his first stop as a major black presidential candidate would be Flint, Michigan, and I delivered the cash to ensure that would occur. Then, to ensure Jesse would be there, I get the jet that Lee Iacocca uses – if you got the money, you can charter anything. We go down and pick up Jesse the day he's scheduled to announce. Except that, when me and Michael get there, Jesse's with Marion Barry at a press conference and Jesse's about to back out; the party doesn't want him to announce. He's trying to make up his mind about whether or not he's going to run.

'I went in and told him – and Michael's all embarrassed about the language I was using – "Look, you motherfuckers, you can do what you want, but I've got two, three thousand people waiting up in Flint, Michigan, at Whiting Auditorium, waiting for you to come there. That's your first stop. That's the deal we negotiated." Jesse glares at me, but he makes his announcement and he gets on the jet. And we get to Whiting Auditorium and they're just rocking. They've been there for three hours, but they're still there! The rally is a humungous success. It motivates the voters to get out. There's a big upset victory, Jim Sharp wins and Rutherford who raided the offices of the *Flint Voice* is out.

'Jesse leaves Flint. He takes the jet and doesn't bring it back! He went down to Georgia and Alabama. Michael's thing is that Jesse is this great black leader. My thing is that he can help us get out the vote, and then get his ass out of town. Sharp won and Michael and I got our picture on the front page, side by side, and Michael said, "This is the kind of thing Sam and I do." With me and him, it's always been action. We *do* shit.'

The role of money, the celebrity weirdness, the secret weaknesses of powerful people, the power of the common people – it's a very American story. It's worth noting, too, that 20 years later Riddle and Rutherford are good friends and speak of each other with respect. Only in America!

Speaking of a recent scandal involving Al Sharpton's personal life, Riddle offers an insight into the culture of American politics that is as profound as any I've heard: 'Our personal lives are what do us in. They're also the foundation for our accomplishments in this nation, depending on the value systems that are implanted in us by our parents. Michael Moore knows how to play golf! He was an Eagle Scout! His family were all very kind. His mother was a great woman. She and his father gave him a value system that is, I think, an inner strength. Some call it stubbornness, some call it bull-headedness, but thank God for his parents or we don't know what he would be, because in many ways Michael could put the "Mac" in *Machiavellian*. He's a strange character, a very complex person. He's driven to get things done, by any means necessary, and I don't hold that against him.

'Michael knows the streets. He helped John Conyers out a lot when Conyers ran for mayor of Detroit. He's worked with a number of black candidates. The difference between Michael and most other Hollywood politicals is that Michael has more field experience of hardcore grassroots politics than the rest of Hollywood combined. He was raised on black issues. He's been around. He knows what it is to work from the ground up. Michael has always had his fingers in the pot of politics, from high school to now.'

The Flint Voice was committed to working-class cultural expression in every dimension, and it had a full slate of literary and cultural reviews. Unlike every other local paper, it let the 'shop rats' speak. Michael Moore, by his own admission, called in sick on his first day on the line at GM, but he encouraged and developed some real talent at the *Voice*.

Moore's big find was Ben Hamper – eventually known as 'the Rivethead' – who was everything that Moore was not, everything he aspired to be as a son of the working class. Hamper was fully conscious of the irony of giving up one's soul just because the blue-collar wages and benefits couldn't be beat. He wrote with a gritty poetry of the nihilistic— no, the *surrealistic* emptiness of a life lived in the plant, of the frustrations of the workers who, in Hamper's time, were never asked to do anything creative.

Hamper is a fourth-generation shop rat; his great-grandfather was making motorised buggies in Flint, and his bloodline carries a faint trace of the days before the Industrial Revolution, some genetic memory of the skilled artisans who were fed into the manufactories. His Catholic parents produced eight children, of whom he was the first. His father drank when he wasn't on the line; his mother worked as a medical secretary and transcriber of medical records. Hamper knocked up his girlfriend, married her and saw his marriage starting to fall apart before he was even a year out of high school. He sought stability in GM's hefty paycheques and benefits, the fate he'd feared all his life but also, with three generations behind him, secretly considered inevitable. Why fight it?

Hamper's 12 years on the line were punctuated by four spells of layoffs to accommodate the vicissitudes of the market, a common feature of Flint life and of the auto industry in general. It was during a period of low-market idleness that Hamper fired off his first piece for the *Voice*: a record review. 'We hit it off well,' Hamper says of Moore, 'both being natural smartasses who didn't care at all for being told what to do. I'd heard of him before we met. He was always popping up in the local paper or on TV creating some nuisance with authority. I was aware that he'd been the youngest elected official in Michigan when he was on the school board in Davison. None of this really mattered to me. I didn't take a keen interest in him until I began reading his newspaper, *The Flint Voice*. Most of the writing in there was pretty bad, ranting hippie shit, but Mike's stuff was usually good. I realised that this was a place where I could get published. The standards appeared quite low, at least on a literary level.' The standard of Hamper's work was higher. Moore was impressed and asked him for more.

At first, Hamper wrote bar and music reviews and was defensive about documenting the life that unfolded before him on the line. He was persuaded to write about his other job after a bad bar review led to a lawsuit; in a memorable and very characteristic turn of phrase, Hamper had written of a brawler heaven called the Good Times Lounge, 'What this place lacks in ambience it makes up in ambulance.'[16] The owners took offence at this and at the headline under which it ran.

What Hamper told me about the incident says a lot about Moore's editorial and political style: 'I don't recall him ever being afraid to run a story. He thrived on confrontation. One time he was set to publish a piece I'd written about this wild bar in Flint, and I pleaded with him not to use the title he'd selected: FLINT'S MOST DANGEROUS BAR. Hell, I liked going to the place, and I knew I'd be unwelcome after penning something with that handle. Mike said he'd switch it, but when the issue came out it still had that inflammatory title. He insisted we had to tell the truth. A few weeks later we both got sued to the tune of ten grand each, though it was later tossed out of court. As usual, Moore was right. As for regrets, I don't think that term is in his vocabulary. He does what he feels is right and proceeds. This hasn't always worked out for him, but I've always admired his adherence to his own beliefs.'

After the legal action fell through, Moore finally persuaded Hamper to write about the line and the characters he hung out with there. 'Once we began talking about the factory, we pretty much stuck to that,' Hamper recalls. 'The yarns were plentiful and Mike had a real curiosity about the way things went down inside a GM plant. He was like a voyeur... The factory stuff was in his blood, his lineage. I always felt there was a small part of Mike that really wanted to give it all up and become a shop rat, surrender to the birthright, like I had. Then again, I don't think he'd have lasted long. The factory was hell on people who thought too much or tried to make some sense of it all.' Hamper's column 'Revenge Of The Rivethead' was born.

Hamper was inspired and angry and he wrote beautifully. In one of his most famous columns, he describes his seven-year-old self visiting his GM-lifer father at the plant on 'family day' and discovering that his father didn't actually 'make cars' – entire cars – for a living, but only attached windshieds: 'Car, windshield. Drudgery piled atop drudgery. Cigarette to cigarette. Decades rolling through the rafters, bones turning to dust, stubborn clocks gagging down flesh, another windshield, another cigarette, wars blinking on and off, thunderstorms muttering the alphabet, crows on power lines asleep or dead, that mechanical octopus squirming against nothing, nothing, NOTHINGNESS. I wanted to shout at my father, 'Do something else!' Do something else or come home with us or flee to the nearest watering hole. DO SOMETHING ELSE! Car, windshield. Car, windshield. Christ, no.'[17]

In *Rivethead*, a collection of Hamper's best pieces that originally appeared in *The Flint Voice*, *Mother Jones* and *The Detroit Free Press*, Michael Moore emerges as more than a hobbyist provocateur. Hamper shows him as a man of tremendous energy who loved his work and had a lot of fun with it, and who was interested in people, really interested in what made them tick, although often reductionist in his Manichaean conclusions about the inherent characters of industrial workers versus those of industrial managers. (Hamper himself had no such illusions. He knew a bullying, soul-corroded burnout when he saw one, regardless of social background.)

Hamper describes Moore coming with him to cover the 'Toughman Contest', a legal, anything-goes fight put on by the bar crawlers of Flint for twisted entertainment. After the combatants mauled each other, Moore sent him to talk to the fighters and get their stories. Hamper was appalled by this degrading spectacle, and for all the right reasons. Moore, however, was excited for all the right reasons: these were real people with stories; they had something to say for themselves. They might surprise you. Moore was serious, but he was always playful. When General Motors started to send a giant cartoon mascot called the Quality Cat around to talk to workers on the line, Moore thought it absolutely hysterical. He tried hard to get Hamper to interview the cat. Hamper refused this humiliating concession to the infantile weirdness of GM's corporate imagination.

By 1986, Hamper's work for *The Flint Voice* and *The Detroit Free Press* was getting some attention and he was featured in a *Wall Street Journal* article by Alex Kotlowitz on blue-collar writers with a line drawing of his face adorning the front page. Television shows were calling him. But Hamper was the real thing: he struggled every day against the deadening absurdity of his line job, but, paradoxically, it gave his life meaning. Although he attacked his typewriter with inspired savagery, there was something deep in his soul that told him that he was a line worker who wrote, not a writer who worked the line. He had some ambivalence about his growing national reputation: 'I was amused by the attention because I realised it was just as much a novelty as anything else: "Look at the shop rat. He can actually spin sentences together!" For me, it was more something to do, something to occupy the time. Moore was the big catalyst. He was the first to suggest that I start to document these stories about the shop. Until then I was just floundering around, searching for an inspiration or niche. There were times when I entertained the idea of being a full-time writer, but I pretty much realised that it was the factory that provided the spark, the adversary, that I needed.' Hamper stayed on with GM until 1988, when his job was moved to Pontiac and the accumulating stress of a dozen years spent serving machines got to him and he started to have incapacitating panic attacks.

If Moore got Hamper some national attention, Hamper also helped Moore. There were timeless truths in Hamper's work that lived on long after everyone stopped caring about the union drives and corrupt local politics documented in the *Voice's* reporting. And because his work was so good, and because it got noticed, Hamper in turn brought national attention to the *Voice* and its editor, who soon found himself in contention for the editorship of a magazine with a national circulation.

The Flint Voice looks like it was a lot of fun to do, and it must have been run by true believers since it couldn't have made much money and was seriously dependent on Harry Chapin and his benefit concerts. This well tragically ran dry, of course, when Chapin was killed in a car crash in 1981, and contributions from Stewart Mott – an heir to the Charles Stewart Mott fortune who was incongruously sympathetic to left-wing causes, and was a friend of Moore's – didn't quite take up the slack. The *Voice* struggled. It was a free alternative monthly paper, although it acquired some advertising and respect.

The Flint Voice's successor, *The Michigan Voice*, was published between 1982 and 1985 and did eventually sell for money. It was glossier and more commercial, ran nationally syndicated columnists and sold all over the state, although it remained true to its counter-culture roots. Its first issue proclaimed that it would not accept advertising that was 'racist or sexist in nature, or from the Armed Forces'.

The Michigan Voice was around for only a few years, and reading it one gets the feeling that Michael Moore was already a little bored. He'd been doing alternative journalism for years before *The Michigan Voice* even got started, and he had a reputation and had branched out a bit, landing a gig as an occasional commentator on National Public Radio by 1985,[18] but he was doing more of the same and just getting by. Moore claims that until he was 35 – until a few years after he left the *Voice* – he'd never made more than $15,000 a year.

Reading *The Voice* now, almost 20 years after it closed up shop, one can clearly see the outline of Michael Moore's future career. All the elements are there: the playfulness, the humour, the unorthodox approach to public policy reporting, the polemics, the undying sense that political action is worth doing only as a crusade, and the assumption that issues are black and white, the good guys against the bad guys, workers against parasites. The naïveté is sometimes inspiring and sometimes irritating, but, although the language is often inflected with the Boomer anger of the 1960s and 1970s, it's not a hippie idiom; Flint is a blue-collar town and the *Voice* was very deeply a blue-collar publication. It is, rather, almost an early-20th-century socialist idiom with its belief in the essential perfectibility of human relations, if only all of that corrupting nonsense of industrial, capitalist life – bosses, police, destruction of individual potential through existential drudgery – could be swept away. It's a pre-Leninist, pre-Stalinist socialism, a socialism of hopeful idealism behind its anger, in which the sunny uplands of post-capitalist society sweep on forever and inevitably, always just over the immediately visible horizon.

But, again in line with the idealists of the early 20th century, getting to this happy place required some uncompromising militancy. The *Voice* published a lot of innovative and probing journalism. In poring over many, many issues of the *Voice*, I never found a retraction or correction. If Moore was ever wrong, he never admitted to it, and perhaps never believed it. And that, too, predicted the style of his future career.

2 New Vistas, New Conflicts

In 1986, a distant age before the internet and online communities and bloggers, the foremost journal of progressive American politics was *Mother Jones*, named after Mary Harris Jones, the Irish immigrant who became a formidable labour activist, feminist, organiser for the United Mine Workers and all-round radical in her 50s. Based in San Francisco, it was, and is, a publication of the Foundation for National Progress, which is funded in large part by the family money of Adam Hochschild, the chairman of the foundation in the mid-1980s. This family money is a legacy of the AMAX mining corporation. Hochschild founded the magazine, together with Richard Parker and Paul Jacobs, when the three of them left the radical magazine *Ramparts* at the same time.

Mother Jones had had some significant investigative coups in the 1970s, reporting on things like the tendency of the Ford Pinto to explode when rear-ended, how the AH Robbins pharmaceutical company put the Dalkon Shield method of birth control on the market when it hadn't been properly tested, and how the Nestlé corporation pushed infant formula as a replacement for breast milk in the Third World. Its circulation was the largest of any liberal political monthly in the mid-1980s but had recently waned, as had the magazine's reputation as a hard-hitting muckraking enterprise. Although *Mother Jones* was slowly making a comeback, there was a sense among its staff that new blood and a new direction were needed.

Change was coming, quite aside from the situation of the magazine. By1986, the editor for the previous six years, Deirdre English, had decided that she wanted to move on to new projects and the magazine was looking for a successor. Michael Moore came to the attention of the board members and of the magazine staff because he'd done some creative and politically important things with *The Flint Voice* and *The Michigan Voice* and they thought, Why not give him a chance at a real national magazine?

Mark Dowie, a seasoned journalist who was at that time the chief investigative reporter for *Mother Jones*, was assigned to do some background research on Moore, to talk to people who knew him, to check out the 'references that weren't on the résumé'.

Dowie had grown up close to his grandparents, who were immigrants from Scotland and were genuinely working class. His grandfather was a travelling apothecary and his mother an industrial worker and union activist who had organised the Edinburgh streetcar workers: 'She wouldn't have called herself a socialist, but the first book she ever gave me to read was the letters of Antonio Gramsci.'

Dowie felt he had a very good sense of working-class values and habits of thought, and of how they differed from those of the educated liberals on the board of *Mother Jones*. '*Mother Jones* at the time was quite democratically managed, and we wanted someone who would fit that culture,' Dowie told me. 'He assured us that he would, but that flew in the face of everything I learned about him. People who had worked at the *Michigan Voice* told me that he was very difficult, not very well liked and not very respected after a while. I collected all these impressions and I took them back to the magazine. I said, "*Mother Jones* is badly in need of working-class sensibilities, and it would be great to have a working-class editor on the board," which had been almost entirely comprised of Ivy League liberals. I recommended that they hire

Michael but that they didn't give him the top job. By this time I had talked to him, too, and I got the impression that he really wanted a national audience. I think that, if he had been told that he could be the blue-collar editor and express working-class sensibilities in the magazine, he would have taken that job.

'I liked Michael. I thought he was very amusing, very articulate. I was impressed with his politics. He's a very personable guy – when he wants to be. He's funny and self-effacing and all the things that you look for in a brilliant, modest person. And he *is* brilliant. But he's not modest.'

Moore was hired as the new editor in April 1986, and moved to San Francisco to take up his duties, reluctantly leaving Flint behind. Five months later, he was fired. His actions in the office – and, even more so, the manner of his leaving it – explain much about how he rose to become one of the most distinct and recognised voices on the American political scene.

Moore's tenure at *Mother Jones* was an odd one. The picture that emerges from the accounts of his co-workers is that he was impossible: moody, abusive, unprofessional. He went on a publicity tour of the Midwest with Ben Hamper and didn't call the office or return calls for more than a week. He had no clue as to how to run a four-colour magazine with a print deadline, and no interest in acquiring one. He was a terrible manager of people. In his first meeting as editor-in-chief, he told the assembled staff, 'The magazine you've been publishing is shit, and we're going to change that.' This is not a good way to build staff morale.

Sometimes Moore was just bizarre. This was San Francisco in 1986, when the AIDS crisis was in full bloom and hitting public consciousness very hard. A staffer pitched a proposal to him for an article about the various conspiracy theories that had sprung up regarding the origins of the disease: a CIA genocide of gay people, a white supremacist plot to wipe out Africans, a government

48

germ-warfare experiment gone awry, etc. How do these things get started? Why do people believe them?

Moore's astonishing response: 'You want a story about AIDS? Here's the story we should do about AIDS: we should find a cure and publish it in this magazine.' He didn't appear to be joking.

He also showed signs of what people who observed him in later years would call manic depression. A senior staffer who worked closely with Moore at the time told me, 'We had a staff picnic in August. Now, if you're the editor of a magazine that has a staff picnic, you go to the picnic and you lead; you have fun. Moore went to this picnic and he found a table in the picnic area off to the side and sat there by himself, staring into space for five hours with this really morose look on his face. He wouldn't talk to anybody. It was the weirdest thing, really bizarre. People were wondering, "What the hell? This is our editor? Our leader?" It was at that point that most people realised, "This guy can't run this magazine; he can't lead us." Some of this stuff would even be excusable if he was coming in on Monday with 30 great ideas, 20 great writers, but that wasn't happening at all. As a matter of fact, he was blowing us away with how stupid he was at running the magazine.'

And at *Mother Jones* there were, embarrassingly, problems that sprang from class-based cultural differences. Moore's virtue as an editor – indeed, the reason why he was hired – was that he would bring working-class perspectives to the scene, but there was a gap. Deirdre English told me, 'Moore's presentation is, "I'm a real man. I love baseball, I love hunting, I'm not working out, I'm not drinking lattés and I'm not drinking chardonnay. I'm the real deal; I'm a working-class guy who wants to raise wages. I'm against going to war. I'm for people power." I think everyone is so nostalgic for that, so bereft of it. And frankly, the liberal elite *is* so out of touch with working-class people that, when one rises up in this way and presents himself as this kind of archetype, he's embraced, for reasons I have a lot of sympathy for.'

On his ability to fit in at the magazine, English told me, 'It was a daring but, in retrospect, crazy risk. We had the assumption that Moore was someone who was going to work well with people. He was going to bring this bracing blast of fresh air from the working-class Midwest into our office, but we also thought that he was going to be collegial and congenial and that he would turn to the professionals at *Mother Jones* to find out how things were done there – not anything that I'd imposed on the culture but how you put out a magazine. We had all kinds of calendars and methods and protocols for how you do things that had been developed over time by me and others. There was a strong feeling of collectivity at *Mother Jones*. There was the belief that we'd be able to educate Moore as to these things that we had learned, and that he would be an inspirational leader. We didn't expect him to tear up the rules.'

If some of the staff didn't know exactly what to make of Moore, Chris Lehmann – now an editor at *New York* magazine – was one of the few people there who felt some cultural solidarity with him. At that time straight out of college, Lehmann came from Davenport, Iowa, a dying industrial town that, like Moore's Flint, was once voted 'Worst place to live in the USA' by *Money* magazine. 'The *Mother Jones* chapter of Michael's career is very rich and very interesting,' he recalls, 'and if you talk to people there you'll get very different points of view – a real *Rashomon* situation. I was one of the few who didn't end up disliking him intensely. We bonded in an odd way: at one of the staff meetings, Michael said, "Anyone who still smokes pot, raise your hand," and everyone's hands went up – except for his and mine. It was a cultural marker of sorts, a left-coast/heartland kind of thing.' But when Lehmann told me this story, it occurred to me that Moore was setting a kind of trap and that, in falling into it, the staff – with the exception of Lehmann – had handed him psychological power over them.

There were less complicated indiscretions. Lehmann remembers Moore circulating a handwritten memo describing how he and Hamper, on that publicity tour from which they had refused to phone home, had thrown burnt pizza out of a hotel window. This didn't go over well with the senior staff, who quite reasonably worried about this childishness reflecting on the magazine. 'It was conduct unbecoming an editor. He was perceived as other than professional.'

Lehmann continues, 'It was a clash of cultural sensibilities. Michael is very confrontational and *Mother Jones*'s culture was very retiring and genteel. Adam Hochschild and Michael are as unalike as two people can get on the planet. Being editor of *Mother Jones* is a very difficult position to fill. Hochschild is on the masthead as a contributing editor, but he has hiring and firing power and if you don't please him – as Michael very much did not – you're not going to get along. If you're talking about "the board", you're talking about Adam. The relationship between Adam and the editor was the central relationship there and, I think, the reason why Michael was fired.'

Moore's introductory column as the new editor appeared in the September 1986 issue and was a very powerful, intelligent, well-written piece on the terrorism that Ronald Reagan was then inflicting on the people of Nicaragua.[19] However, by the time his second piece – the piece in which new editor Moore laid out his vision for the magazine[20] – was in print, in October, he had already been relieved of his duties.

Why was he fired? In his film *Roger & Me*, Moore asserts tthat it was because he brought in a real worker, Ben Hamper, and put his picture on the cover. Hamper doesn't agree; he says the magazine was always supportive of him, and after Moore's departure he got a letter from communications director Richard Reynolds saying that bringing him to *Mother Jones* was one of Moore's best decisions, and inviting him to continue to write for the magazine. Hamper declined, out of loyalty to his former editor. It's hard to believe that the cover had anything to do with Moore being fired, since Hamper's picture had appeared on the first issue that Moore edited and he had gone on to edit two more issues-- both of which included Hamper's column--without any management complaints about that.

But he's said lots of other things, too. Some at *Mother Jones* noticed that, in the years following the abrupt end of his tenure, he tended to tailor his explanation of this event to suit the audience he was addressing. One of his *Mother Jones* colleagues told me, 'If he was talking to New York subway workers, for example, he'd say, "I was fired because I wanted to do an article about how dangerous the subways are, and they wouldn't let me." Or, if he was talking to the Arab-American Anti-Discrimination Committee, he'd say, "I was fired because I wanted to do an article on the Palestinians and they wouldn't let me."'

Here is a no doubt partial list of the reasons that Moore has offered, at different times and to different publications, for why he was fired from *Mother Jones*:

- He wouldn't run an article critical of the Nicaraguan Sandinista government (UPI, 6 September 1986).

- Adam Hochschild wanted a yes man so that he wouldn't have to show up for work (*San Francisco Chronicle*, 13 September 1986).

- He was planning a critical cover story on Governor Mario Cuomo of New York – whom he described as a 'sacred cow' for *Mother Jones*'s 'yuppie left' – and because of a series of articles that were critical of the Israeli occupation of the West Bank and Gaza Strip[21] (*San Francisco Examiner*, 15 September 1986).

- He objected to the dismissal of Richard Schauffler, an advertising salesman for *Mother Jones* who claimed that he lost his job because he had failed to disclose his affiliation with the radical Democratic Workers' Party[22] (*The New York Times*, 27 September 1990).
- Deirdre English had taken his criticisms of the magazine personally and Adam Hochschild 'wanted me gone because I didn't kiss her ass' (*Media File*, October–November 1986).

- He had refused to participate in 'management's numerous violations of its contract with the unionised staff of *Mother Jones*' (Moore, writing in *The Village Voice*, 14 October 1986).

- He had made plans to bring the Palestinian issue into the magazine (awards ceremony speech to the Arab-American Anti-Discrimination Committee, 4 April 1987).

- A number of female employees had complained to him that the then-publisher of *Mother Jones*, Don Hazen, was treating them in a sexist manner (letter from Moore to *Michigan Voice* subscribers, 28 December 1987).

- He had wanted to put Ben Hamper's picture on the front cover[23] (claim made in *Roger & Me*).

- Adam Hochschild wanted him to run an article on herbal teas (*San Francisco Weekly*, 10 January 1990).

- Management wanted him to put movie stars on the cover and make it 'a people magazine of the left' (*Metro*, 11–17 January 1990).

- He had interrupted a discussion about hiring more women and minorities to suggest that *Mother Jones* hire an actual proletarian (*International Herald Tribune*, 17 January 1990).

What is not in dispute is that on September 2, Hochschild suggested to Moore that he ought to depart, and that if didn't, the board would most likely vote to dismiss him. Moore demanded a formal meeting of the foundation's board, which he got, and the board voted to fire him on the unanimous advice of the magazine's senior staff. Moore immediately went to the San Francisco papers, the *Chronicle* and the *Examiner*. In a press conference on the steps of City Hall, he explained that he'd been fired because he wouldn't publish 'lies' about Nicaragua. 'I thought, What are we doing, writing Reagan's next speech for him?'[24] He filed a wrongful dismissal suit and vowed to collect a $2 million settlement.

Moore's own carelessness and his litigious bent created even more trouble for the magazine, and, ultimately, for Moore himself. In his depositions in support of his case against the magazine, he claimed that *Mother Jones* was so badly run, so corrupt, that a freelancer, Laura Fraser (whom Moore had never met) supplied drugs to editors, presumably in exchange for writing assignments. With equal nastiness but no more plausibility, he had let slip to several reporters – including Paul Farhi, the reporter who wrote the 15 September *Examiner* piece – not only that he was fired because he wanted to tackle the Palestinian issue but also that there was a bias among the Jews – including Hochschild himself and several others at the magazine – against any article sympathetic to the Palestinians.

Farhi, as any good reporter would, asked Hochschild about this for the story he was writing on Moore's dismissal, and Hochschild debunked the idea in the column he wrote for *Mother Jones* that dealt with Moore's departure: '[Moore told] several reporters that he had been blocked from doing hard-hitting reporting on the Middle East because of "Jewish" or "Zionist" influence at the magazine. (This might come as a surprise to readers of a number of *Mother Jones* articles over the years, such as Victor Perera's report on Israeli foreign arms sales – "Uzi Diplomacy", July '85.)'[25] Hochschild, who had several times said on National Public Radio that he considered the Israeli occupation to be a crime, wasn't thrilled with being called a censor on behalf of Zionism.

When Hochschild's column came out, Moore was furious. He felt that Hochschild was publicly accusing him of anti-Semitic statements, and sued. He and his wife, Kathleen Glynn, added charges of libel to his wrongful-dismissal suit against Hochschild and the Foundation for National Progress. But when Farhi was deposed on this matter, he said that Moore had indeed told him that there was a Jewish bias at *Mother Jones* and that he had asked Hochschild for his response to this idea.[26] Moore dropped the libel part of his lawsuit.

It's impossible to know what Moore was really thinking in his statements to Farhi, but it's also impossible not to notice that Farhi could easily be assumed to be an Arab or Persian name. Could it be that Moore was once again pitching the story of his firing to his audience of the moment?

Most likely, Moore himself truly never knew or allowed himself to understand why he was fired and that all of the explanations he offered over time seemed equally plausible to him – although, obviously, they couldn't *all* have been true. As he does in his movies, he was most likely lashing out in all directions in the hope that one of his swings would hit its mark.

In conversations with people who worked with Moore, I came to think that the real reason why he was fired was that he was out of his depth as the editor of a national magazine, both in terms of professional skills and political sophistication, and that he could not inspire or get along with this staff. To the extent that the Nicaragua piece played a role, it was because his handling of that matter exemplified these other problems with his work.

Nevertheless, the fact that Moore often put the particular issue of Nicaragua at the centre of the dispute is very important to the way he has cast his cultural role and image. In order to understand what this means, and why Nicaragua stirred such passions, it is important to put Moore's explanation in its historical and political context and to understand what Nicaragua meant to the left at the time.

Feelings were intense on both the left and right about Ronald Reagan's wars in Central America in the 1980s, of which the conflict in Nicaragua was the most prominent and the most controversial. It was a different world then. Even after Gorbachev and Rejkjavik, the Cold War had thawed only a degree or two since the early 1960s. The Soviet Union and the threat that it represented was thought to be a permanent fact of life, and the proxy struggle between it and the United States that was being waged all over the world was used by the political right as justification for every bloodily insane atrocity, every jackboot in the face of democracy and human rights, that was struck by 'our' proxies against 'their' proxies.

Central America in the 1980s was one of the saddest examples of this and one of the most bitter betrayals of everything Americans claimed to stand for. In the name of anti-communism, Reagan was funding a genocidal war in Guatemala, waged by a tiny elite against a vast and desperate Maya majority seeking the most basic human rights. He was propping up a death-squad government in El Salvador, where his client thugs used torture, rape and massacre as political tools. He was sponsoring and training the Honduran Army – accused of serious human-rights violations – as a barrier to the spread of egalitarian ideas from revolutionary Nicaragua. He was training officers of many Latin-American armies at the School of the Americas, where they were taught how to torture captured insurgents.

Prior to the success of the Sandinista Revolution in 1979, Nicaragua was a classic peasant state with a corrupt and deeply oppressive ruling elite. It had a revolutionary tradition going back to the 1850s, and this had provoked numerous invasions by the United States, which managed on many occasions to restore the rule of the rich, who owned almost all the land and were quite comfortable renting it out – along with virtually enslaved labour – to the United Fruit Company or whatever other foreign businesses might want to exploit Nicaragua's bananas, cotton, coffee or labour. The country was even ruled in 1856–7 by an American mercenary, William Walker, who had been hired by the Nicaraguan Liberal Party to defeat the Conservative Party, which he did, and then set himself up as President with the backing of the United States and the intention of annexing Nicaragua as a slave state. By 1979, the country was ruled by Anastazio Somoza Debayle, the last and least of a dynasty that had been set up by occupying United States forces in 1933 and who quite forthrightly made war on his own people.

The article that Berman eventually published in *Mother Jones*, and that Moore found so unacceptably unsympathetic to the Sandinistas, contains an astonishing transcription of the drill chant of Somoza's National Guard:

Who are we?
We are tigers!
What do tigers eat?
Blood!
Whose blood?
The blood of the people![27]

In 1979, the Frente Sandinista de Liberación Nacional – named after Augusto Sandino, a revolutionary leader assassinated in 1933 – overthrew the brutal Somoza dynasty and seized power. They immediately set about confiscating the holdings of the landowning class, setting up public clinics and literacy programmes, making a more egalitarian distribution of the wealth of the nation and repudiating grossly exploitative contracts with American companies. After approaching the United States for reparations for the long and rapacious relationship as a source of resources with which to rebuild the country and getting turned down flat, the Sandinistas went to the Soviets, who gladly sponsored their state-and-society building project.

This, of course, meant that the Sandinistas were the enemies of 'freedom' as understood by Ronald Reagan.[28] Throughout his tenure, one of Reagan's pet projects was the destruction of the Sandinista state. He embarked on a campaign of lies about the totalitarian nature of the new Nicaragua. The fact that the Sandinistas won a presidential election in 1984 and parliamentary elections in 1985, in balloting that was agreed by all observers – except those from the US, but including delegations from Margaret Thatcher's Britain – to have been on the whole free and fair, made no difference. Reagan was determined to overthrow an elected government in the name of democracy and freedom.

Reagan sponsored a group of renegade political elites and international drug traffickers and told them to attack clinics and schools in order to discredit the ability of the Sandinistas to deliver security and a higher standard of living for ordinary people. He told them to mine the civilian harbours of Nicaragua. For these acts, the International Court of Justice at the Hague in 1986 found that the US had 'violated both customary international law and a treaty between the United States and Nicaragua',[29] and in the following year the Court set reparations at $17 billion. Although the Reagan administration had voluntarily agreed to be bound by the decision and had argued its position in court, when that decision was not to his liking, Reagan simply walked away and ignored the judgment that the United States had promised to respect. No reparations were ever paid to Nicaragua or to Reagan's civilian victims.[30]

Nothing so fired up the American left in those days as Reagan's crimes in Latin America. I myself can remember the white-hot fury I would feel on hearing one of his deeply unreal addresses on the subject of Latin America and democracy. But for many on the left, that didn't mean that we had to be blind to the problems of an uncritical view of the Sandinistas.

The fact is that the Sandinistas were far from perfect social democrats. Although there was immensely more freedom of speech in revolutionary Nicaragua than there was in reactionary El Salvador – whose death-squad government the United States was supporting – freedom of speech was definitely limited in Nicaragua. This wasn't entirely inexcusable; after all, the Sandinistas were fighting a war of survival and many of the press outlets that criticised them in this time of war – such as the main opposition paper, *La Prensa* – were supported by the CIA. Still, it was an uncomfortable fact, as was the tendency of Sandinista education and government to work in slogans and to promote a revolutionary orthodoxy. Much worse, it was also a fact that the Sandinistas had mounted a major relocation/terror campaign against the coastal Miskito Indians, who were resisting their control.

While the great majority of the left generally supported revolutionary Nicaragua against Reagan's depredations, there were some who felt that there was no legitimate criticism of the Sandinistas. These were generally the same people who had nothing bad to say about Cuba, about North Korea, about Vietnam, about Mao's China, about the Soviet Union. Either out of a fear of inadvertently aiding the right or out of a conviction that leftist revolutionaries truly could do no wrong, these people would not speak up for democracy and human rights in Nicaragua and feuded with those on the left who did.

The argument about whether the left should acknowledge any wrongdoing by the Sandinistas was playing out at *Mother Jones* during Michael Moore's first few months there. Paul Berman had been commissioned by Deirdre English more than a year before Moore's arrival at the magazine to write a two-part piece about Sandinista Nicaragua. *Mother Jones* had committed to publishing it before Moore took up his duties.

For English, publishing pieces like Berman's that might rouse debate was what should define a vigorous, courageous, liberal magazine. '*Mother Jones* had the largest circulation of any left-wing magazine in the country, and I thought we needed to have room for a variety of different kinds of opinion on the liberal spectrum,' she told me. 'I didn't believe in a party line; yes, a liberal point of view, but an attempt to question our own thinking and bring in writers who would do that. [Berman's piece] was very much an attempt to say, "Let's not look like knee-jerk Sandinista supporters. Of course we're critical of the role that the US has played, and of course we're critical of the US support of the former Somoza dictatorship, and we have an interest in seeing a good socialist party in Nicaragua emerge, but that doesn't mean that we can't be critical of it," just as we would be critical of Carter, of Clinton. Later, when Moore killed Berman's article,

I thought it was a violation of an important principle: you didn't have to agree with Berman, but his piece belonged in the magazine. It was a good article and the left needed to be thinking more critically about revolutionary nationalist organisations like the Sandinistas.'

Berman had learned Spanish for the assignment and spent a lot of time in Nicaragua at all levels of society. The first part of his piece ran in the February 1986 edition of *Mother Jones*. The second part – the part that Moore balked at publishing – was on the whole favourable to the Nicaraguan revolution, but it did not ignore its defects. Berman noted that the Sandinista tendency toward Leninist discipline was necessary to make a revolution but unhelpful in building a truly free and egalitarian society. He was sharp and saw through to the heart of the matter: 'The Sandinistas have made clear that, in their eyes, the Sandinista vanguard is the Revolution, is the Nicaraguan people, is the government. The health of the Revolution and the power of the party are to them inseparable... They consider that they have fought and died for that idea and not merely for the land reform and the medical campaign and the dignity of Nicaragua... No one seriously believes the Sandinistas mean to go so far with democracy as actually to engage in some form of significant power-sharing, not even if the country and the Revolution would be better off for it.'[31]

One type of leftist might or might not argue with Berman on his interpretation of the Sandinistas' position. An entirely different type of leftist might agree with his interpretation but argue that this was an acceptable situation.

Berman's piece was initially accepted by new editor Michael Moore and the editorial board. Moore later asked Berman to cut much of the critical section, then rejected it outright.

What had happened? One thing that seems clear is that Moore

had fallen under the influence of Alexander Cockburn, a leftist hardliner whose work Moore greatly admired. Cockburn is among those who are reluctant to criticise even the most brutal socialist governments. For him the romance of the struggle takes on a life of its own, a life that demands that one choose sides at every point or face condemnation as a traitor. Cockburn has recently gone so far as to attack George Orwell because in 1949 – a particularly grim time in the history of the Cold War when the totalitarian nature and ambitions of the Soviet Union were, or should have been, quite clear in the West – Orwell warned the British Foreign Office against allowing those he suspected of being Stalinist operatives to undertake sensitive work. Cockburn said of Orwell, 'The man of conscience turns out to be a whiner, and of course a snitch.'[32] Cockburn's contempt for Orwell – a dedicated, democratic socialist who was consistently vigilant against the totalitarian tendencies of both the left and the right – is a bit shocking, and it says a lot about his ideological approach.

Cockburn has rarely met a left revolutionary despot or government he didn't like or couldn't defend.[33] Indeed, in a column in *The Nation* that appeared soon after Moore was fired from *Mother Jones*, he defended his previous criticism of tortured and imprisoned Cuban dissident Armando Valladares with this rather amazing statement: 'I don't think Cuba today has thousands of political prisoners being tortured... I do not think there is institutionalised torture in Cuba... I don't think that any evidence has been advanced to show that there is.'[34]

Moore's editorial memoranda to Cockburn suggest that he was quite overawed by the radical journalist, so authentically uncompromising in his revolutionary sympathies, such an inspiration. And Cockburn hated the Nicaragua piece, thinking the criticisms of the Sandinistas unfair and inaccurate, a betrayal by a pampered American liberal of a genuine leftist revolution.

What Moore probably did not know at the time was that Cockburn and Berman despised each other and had been writing nasty things about each other in their respective columns for years.

This is one situation in which Moore clearly comes off as a bit of a naïf. The irony is so obvious as to be hardly worth mentioning: in an argument about the Sandinistas, Cockburn and Moore rushed to enforce the style of totalitarian orthodoxy that they denied the Sandinistas practised. It is telling that Moore repeatedly insisted that the problem with the article was not its point of view but that it was full of 'lies'. He never said what, specifically, was a lie, although there are hints that he objected to Berman's use of the word 'Leninism' in describing at least one element of the Sandinistas' ideology.

Hochschild and the board stood by Berman and the article. Cockburn remained adamant. Moore rather pathetically appealed to his mentor: 'I was wrong – Dracula lives! Did I not drive the stake through at sunrise?? The Paul Berman piece lives. Adam and I in a row. Need your help in building an argument.'[35] Hochschild and the board actually worked out an arrangement whereby Moore would run the piece, in a slightly edited form, and publish it side by side with a rebuttal by Cockburn or Moore himself. But this wasn't good enough for Moore. Others at *Mother Jones* continued to say that they couldn't work with him.

It is also striking that Moore, so confident in his ideological world, was unwilling to see any blemishes on the face of the Revolution. There have always been those on the left who have been uncomfortable at any whiff of the authoritarian, those who see the point of the game as expanding human freedom and opportunity, not as an affirmation of the One True Path that offers a political tribal identity. Moore, apparently, was not among them – or, at the very best, his ability to sense the authoritarian taint was under-developed. He had been to Nicaragua in 1983 and never saw any of the contradictions there that Berman saw. Berman, for his part, continued to write about Nicaragua throughout the 1990s, and later came to a more hard-edged criticism of the Sandinistas' penchant for Leninist, undemocratic rule – as would several of the former Sandinista ministers.[36]

After Moore was fired from *Mother Jones*, Berman was ostracised by many colleagues on the left who, incited by Moore's and Cockburn's position, felt that he had betrayed the Nicaraguan revolution – the last flawed Leninist adventure of the Cold War, the last chance for American romantics to throw in their lot with genuine third-world revolutionaries before the world became both simpler and more complex. It was hard to forgive.

In the long run, the débâcle at *Mother Jones* could not have turned out better for Moore. As Chris Lehmann put it, 'In a way, it was the best thing that ever happened to him. He was motivated almost entirely by revenge, and he went forward and made *Roger & Me* and moved on to better things.' Moore seems to have instinctively known how to set up a narrative of his departure on his own mythic terms: the poor boy from Flint against the publishing Goliath with its sinister capitalist roots. Cockburn was an enormously helpful ally in this, writing in *The Nation*, 'Michael Moore...is learning to his cost the old rule that the rich are different. They think they can get away with anything. Hochschild is heir to the AMAX mining fortune, and although he has devoted substantial amounts of the family income – originally generated by African wage-slaves – to finance the quasi-liberal periodical *Mother Jones*, he can still behave like a 19th-century mill owner.' Cockburn goes on to contrast Hochschild's industrialist background with that of Michael Moore, the working-class boy from Flint whose uncle took part in one of the great strikes in American labour history.[37]

There's a lot going on here. Note the almost autonomic

reversion to the logic of class as binding political destiny – a particularly narrow-minded interpretation of Marx. There is a certain faction of the left that has never had any trouble explaining, say, Franklin Roosevelt as a tool of the capitalist class. Real life, in the case of FDR and others, is usually more complicated, and in real life Adam Hochschild is a man who has devoted enormous effort and resources to advancing the causes of human rights and to unearthing the brutal truths of colonialism.[38] Cockburn's unanswerable ideological device enables him to be as *inherently* right as Hochschild is undeniably rich and to bury any of the real issues, and certainly to bury any of the ambivalence that thoughtful leftists might feel about the Sandinistas. Moore's own behaviour as editor and day-to-day manager of a business could not be part of the picture: Moore is poor, Hochschild a rich colonial!

It was a trick that Moore already knew well, and one that he would use throughout the rest of his career whenever his biography came up: the little guy against the Man; the unpretentious working-class stiff against the fey habits of decadent, too-comfortable 'quasi-liberals' (as Cockburn put it) or outright reactionaries. There's a scene in *Roger & Me* in which Moore, briefly describing his time in San Francisco, jokingly shows his own puzzlement and dismay at the enormous list of specialised beverages available in a North Beach coffee house. That's it! He was too *real* for *Mother Jones*! It's interesting how, in hindsight, Moore's attack on the sophisticates who gave him a chance at the big time anticipates the now-ubiquitous attack tic of the right: the depiction of anyone on the left as an elitist, out-of-touch, *latté-sipping snob*.

Simplistic and deceptive though this storyline might be, it was useful for Moore and enabled him to burnish his iconic image when he launched into his next project, *Roger & Me*, a movie that he was able to begin thanks to a $58,000 wrongful-dismissal settlement that he won from the magazine and used as seed money.

There's an interesting story here, too. *Mother Jones* was usually represented in its legal affairs by the corporate-defence firm of Pillsbury, Madison and Sutro – the very name reeks of a world Moore despises – but the board members felt that, even if they won, taking on Moore with such a firm could be fatal to the magazine's credibility as a voice for the progressive left. Instead, they hired left-wing civil-rights and employment-law attorney Guy Saperstein for one of only a very few occasions in Saperstein's entire career that he has represented the employer in an employment-law case. Saperstein was initially suspicious and told Hochschild and publisher Don Hazen that, if his investigation determined that the magazine was at fault, he wanted the authority to settle, which Hochschild and Hazen gave him willingly, insisting that, if they had done wrong, they would admit it.

When Saperstein deposed Moore, he had some sense of the difficulties the magazine had been having: 'Michael showed up in baggy jeans, worn tennis shoes, a shirt hanging out of his jeans and a baseball cap cocked at an angle on his head... He certainly didn't look like the editor of a national magazine. Michael sat down, turned sideways, crossed his legs and gave the appearance of complete indifference.'

Some of Saperstein's observations seem to foretell the reputation that Moore would later develop: 'He was often funny and had a bit of roguish Irish charm, but he was doing a terrible job of making a case for himself and his tenure as editor of *Mother Jones*... He was full of bluster... I deposed him for three days, and while he was one of the most entertaining witnesses I had ever deposed, he was also one of the worst... His iconoclastic rebelliousness, his obvious disdain for the opinions of others, his quick wit at the expense of thoughtful explanations would sink him in front of a jury.'[39]

Although Moore complained of 'emotional distress' that was

causing physical symptoms, Saperstein concluded that he was incompetent, that the firing was justified and that the magazine should offer no settlement. This, too, is part of the legend; Moore often implies that he had *Mother Jones* dead to rights, and that using its money to start *Roger & Me* and to crusade on behalf of the working class was poetic justice since *Mother Jones* was so corrupted, so effete, so…so…*liberal.*

In fact, *Mother Jones* never admitted any wrongdoing and Saperstein insisted that no part of any settlement would come from the magazine. *Mother Jones*'s corporate insurer calculated the cost of fighting the suit up to the point at which it would inevitably be thrown out and offered Moore slightly less to go away. This amount turned out to be about what Hochschild had offered him as no-fault severance pay.

But doing it that way would have been no fun at all.

3 A National Stage

When he left *Mother Jones,* Moore had no particular reason to be optimistic about his career. He'd had a national platform and he'd been fired after holding it for only a few months. There was no more *Flint Voice*; that part of his life was over. For a little while he worked on seemingly transitional projects, getting some experience in film with journalist James Ridgeway and documentary filmmakers Anne Bohlen and Kevin Rafferty when he contributed to *Blood In The Face*, their documentary on American white supremacists. (Moore appears in one scene of this film, in a shot taken from behind and over his shoulder as he interviews a pretty girl in full Nazi uniform.[40])

Moore won grants from Ralph Nader's organisation and from the J Roderick MacArthur Foundation to publish *Moore's Weekly*, a small Washington, DC-based journal of labour and media issues. Moore put out about 25 issues before the journal petered out in late 1988. By that time, with his *Mother Jones* settlement money, some more grants from the MacArthur Foundation and from Nader, and some technical advice from Kevin Rafferty, he had begun work on a film. If any one project made Michael Moore's career, it was *Roger & Me*.

The film opens with archival footage of prosperous downtown Flint in the 1950s, full of businesses and shoppers, a bustling, healthy community. The scene is astonishing to anyone who has been to present-day Flint. The town does not look like that today.

How GM's abandonment of Flint, with the acquiescence of the unions of city officials, turned the once-prosperous manufacturing centre of Flint into a landscape of boarded-up ruins, crime, joblessness and despair is the theme of *Roger & Me*. The film is held together by Moore's klutzy, shuffling self as he seeks an audience with Roger Smith, chairman of General Motors, so that he can ask Smith to come to Flint and talk to some laid-off workers about the consequences of GM's corporate strategy. It's a playful hook that might owe something to Ben Hamper, who for several years had a running theme in his 'Revenge Of The Rivethead' column on his attempts to get Roger Smith to come bowling with him.

Flint was stunned and stonily unimaginative in the face of GM's pullout in the 1980s. Fattened on cars, city officials and workers alike had long taken GM revenue for granted. Even as it was clear by the mid-80s that the jobs were never coming back, Flint was still giving all the tax breaks it could afford to auto plants, meaning that it had little left over to encourage diversification into other industries. Crack dealers moved in to take advantage of the economic despair, and gangs and drug killings soon followed. At one point, Flint had the highest murder rate in the United States. By the 1990s, the town could not pay its fire department. In 2001, Flint's budget process was so abysmal that it was taken over by the state of Michigan. Mayor Woodrow Stanley was recalled because he could not find enough revenue to keep the city running.

Flint isn't utterly ruined. There are some nice, quiet neighbourhoods along its outer edges, comfortable houses on Chevrolet and Miller Avenues with lawns and driveways, which were lit up in melancholic glory by the autumn leaves of the Great Lakes region during my visit. There is a very extensive arts, culture and sciences complex on Kearsley Street, set up with funding by the Charles Stewart Mott Foundation in the boom years of the '50s. The auto companies and the Flint–Genesee County Economic Growth Alliance are saying that life is getting better in Flint, that it's on the way to recovery, and this is marginally true. The number of auto workers in Flint has now stabilised at around 15,000 and GM has put almost $2 billion of new investment into its Flint plants in the last few years, indicating its intention to stick around at this reduced level. Flint proper has been losing population for years, however, partly from the industry shakeout and partly just as a result of national trends towards suburban residence that have left downtowns struggling all over the US.

But if things are better now than they were a decade ago, Flint must have been a wasteland then. In 2003, unemployment in Flint was a whopping 16 per cent, against a Michigan rate of 7.3 per cent and a national rate of 6 per cent.[41] The northwest part of town – the black quadrant, laid out along the spine of the inevitable Martin Luther King Jr Avenue – looks like a grey dream of the Apocalypse: rotting, boarded-up houses collapse into weed-strewn lots, the streets as potholed as those on Indian reservations.

Along Saginaw, the main street of Flint, there are more empty shops than live ones, and there are lines outside the State of Michigan Employment Office. An abandoned storefront sports a glossy poster touting the town's 'BUSINESS, ENTERTAINMENT, AND LOFT DISTRICT', but there's not much here at all.

On North Saginaw, the bones of former malls stare bleakly out from the littered expanses of their parking lots. The clerk at Brother's Beer, Wine and Whisky dispenses alcohol and cigarettes from behind bulletproof Plexiglass, but businesses that cater to almost all other aspects of human life – hardware stores, bakeries, beauty salons, even auto-parts shops – are abandoned black holes. Even storefront churches and bars are boarded up, signs of a community that has fallen on hard times indeed.

The rapaciousness of General Motors and its abandonment of Flint – all those layoffs in the 1980s and 1990s – is a powerful narrative and one to which Moore returns often in his writings and in his films, not only in *Roger & Me* but also in its sequels, *Pets Or Meat: The Return To Flint* and *The Big One*. But *Roger & Me* is the work that got Moore known on a national stage, made him a hero to some and got others questioning his basic commitment to the truth.

The film was made for a total of $260,000, including Moore's $58,000 settlement from *Mother Jones*. Over the course of the movie's 91 minutes, Moore introduces many memorable characters in his breakout hit: the cowardly and aloof Roger Smith, so addicted to corporate-speak that he uses a seasonal speech to talk about the 'total experience' of Christmas; Deputy Fred Ross, evicting the families of laid-off auto workers from their homes; the buffoonish, insensitive rich people living it up at a 1920s-themed party; Ben Hamper, shooting baskets and talking about cracking up on the line; the Auto World robot; the GM flacks Pat Boone and Anita Bryant, themselves robotically presenting cheerful American banality while insisting that, if capitalism requires human sacrifice, this is all to the good; the 'rabbit lady', Rhonda Britton, selling bunnies for 'pets or meat' because her family is out of work. Britton is shown first cuddling a cute floppy-eared rabbit and then conking it on the head, tying it to a tree and skinning it, a scene that works as a metaphor for GM's relationship with its workers as presented in the film, for executives who talk about one big happy family when workers are needed and then turn them loose without a thought when they are not.[42]

Above all, there's Moore's own overweight, rumpled heroic self, stumbling and bumbling around town while delivering a narrative that just happens to have all the answers about what was going on in Flint in the late 1980s.

The lesson, I guess, is always to be suspicious of the guy who has all the answers.

In late 2004, I sat down at a good restaurant in East Lansing, Michigan, to have a talk with Michael Moore about what was happening in the auto industry in Flint 20 years ago.

Not *that* Michael Moore. This Michael Moore is a professor of labour relations, management and industrial production. He's a serious and impressive man who speaks with great courtesy and precision. His father owned an auto supply company, and he was born to the industry. He started his career at Ford in labour relations in Dearborn, right outside the place where the 'Battle of the Overpass' was held, a famous union fight of the 1930s. He's an academic at the intersection of blue- and white-collar work, and after getting a PhD in Industrial Relations and Human Resource Management he became one of the first faculty members at Michigan State University's School of Labor and Industrial Relations. Since 1996 he's also been a consultant to General Motors on matters relating to the labour and human-resources aspects of the industrial doctrine known as 'lean manufacturing': the concept of making the most of space and human resources while keeping at-hand inventory to a minimum.

This Michael Moore told me a story about Flint, about GM and the unions and about the re-invention of the auto industry in the 1980s that is remarkable, both because there truly was a lot going on here while the filmmaker Michael Moore was making *Roger & Me*, and because the filmmaker missed most of it.

By 1982, the domestic auto industry had lost 25 per cent of its capacity to Japan. That doesn't necessarily mean that GM was losing a lot of money; the corporation had concentrated on making fewer, bigger, more expensive cars with a higher profit margin, the lessons of the 1970s oil shocks already receding. The Americans were hard pressed to figure out Japan's production dominance.

Roger Smith had a deep belief that the Japanese had a secret technology, machines that allowed them to make good cars at a tremendous cost advantage. After losing so much of the market, GM decided – way too late – to do something different.

In 1984, GM looked at auto plants around the world and tried to decide what was the best way to build a car. They picked the Volvo method, something radically new in the automobile industry. Since the 1920s, much of industrial theory had accepted Frederick Taylor's thesis that the worker must accommodate the machine, an idea that has had an enormous impact on the development of American technology, production and sociology. The Volvo method took the opposite approach. It was anti-Taylorism.

At Volvo's plants, workers didn't work on assembly lines. Instead, cars were placed on platforms and moved from one group of workers to another. Workers also did large modules of work, like a two-hour task with 20 people working on a car, putting on the power train or most of the interior trim. They weren't just doing the same thing over and over, like Ben Hamper's father had; they were actually encouraged to think and to solve problems. They were trusted.

GM adopted this idea from Volvo for their new Saturn model. 'After years of kicking the union in the teeth, GM now embraced the union,' Moore told me. 'They had union partners in everything they did, including dealings with suppliers, purchasing, retailers and shop-floor management. Foremen were removed; supervisors became group leaders with less authority but more diplomatic skills. Workers took charge of schedules, quality, timing and output, and they interviewed new members for their teams. It was a tremendous investment in good union–management relations.' There was also meaningful profit-sharing; four years after GM's Saturn plant in Tennessee opened, each worker received a $10,000 bonus.

But Saturn was still never as efficient as the Japanese. Not even close. In fact, it wasn't very efficient at all. Neither was Volvo. The productivity difference was so staggering that GM was forced to try again.

The company responded by building 'Poletown', a factory in the Polish settlement of Hamtramck in Detroit. This section of Hamtramck was old Polish, deep Polish, with lots of old churches and a traditional cultural life, and Detroit mayor Coleman Young found a way to tear it down so that GM could build a plant within the city limits. This plant made Cadillacs, and it operated on a completely different theory from that of the Saturn factory. It was to be the most automated auto plant in the world, and it was not supposed to need workers for much more than turning on machinery. Trouble with the UAW was supposed to be a thing of the past. No workers would mean no hefty benefits packages, no grievances, no strikes. Problem solved![43]

The plant was a disaster. The machines painted each other, attacked each other, broke down more often than the most gold-bricking shop rat. Automation was not the answer.

So Roger Smith, the stolid plutocrat of *Roger & Me*, did yet a third big thing in the 1980s, conducting another billion-dollar experiment: he took the Japanese option. In 1983, holding its corporate nose, GM went into partnership with Toyota, which was a little company then (it's now bigger than Ford). The two companies set up a joint venture called New United Motor Manufacturing, Inc, or NUMMI. To further this experiment, GM gave Toyota one of its plants. Its worst plant, actually.

The GM facility at Fremont, California, had been closed for two years. It had 25,000 unanswered union grievances when it closed, along with a history of low-quality work and low productivity, extremely adversarial union–management relations and a very personal anger between foremen and workers. It was a nightmare. It made no sense to make a car in that plant. That was how much GM wanted the Japanese experiment to succeed.

Toyota did not want to hire a unionised workforce, but GM insisted that they rehire the old workers. Toyota gave in and took most of them, refusing only the ones who had actually been convicted of sabotage. But Toyota was absolutely adamant that no GM manager would be in that plant. The Japanese would manage it. They installed lean-manufacturing principles and management techniques that were similar to the Saturn team approach, with the workers' input valued and creativity encouraged. But while labour–management relations were less hierarchical than they had been at the plant under GM, there was also less emphasis on the union as a partner.

Within two years, the plant began to win awards: Best Plant in North America; Second-Best Plant in North America. The workers showed levels of productivity and quality comparable to Takaoka, one of the best plants in Japan. It seemed that the right management system really did make a difference.

That's where GM finally got wise that the Japanese didn't have secret machines; they had what the management manuals call 'people skills'. They treated workers with respect and gave them training in many areas. They gave them a career path. The workers felt like they had a stake in what they were doing. That made them very productive.

Give Roger Smith credit as a manager – if not as a sensitive human being concerned about his employees – for asking the question three different ways. Within five years he tried *We hate unions*, *We don't need workers* and *We're going to build it all ourselves using technology*. That was Poletown. He tried embracing workers – *We love the union*, *The union is our strategic partner*. That was Saturn. And he tried the Toyota production system, which uses some technology and some team approaches: *We love workers*, *We love efficiency, We'll work with the union on wages and benefits, but we won't compromise on production methods.*

The Toyota system won. Today, every American automobile manufacturer uses it, with greater and lesser degrees of success. GM has it down the best. As investment analyst Maryann Keller has written of GM in this period, the company wasted a lot of money looking for quick fixes to problems that were structural, institutional and 'sociological', but under Roger Smith's leadership it was able to keep looking for solutions and, in the end, was able to see the solution to a problem when one of its experiments paid off.[44]

It is, of course, debatable as to whether there was any real benefit for workers in the new model. David Yettaw, former President of UAW Local 599 at Buick in Flint, led Buick 599 into a loose alliance of hardline union locals known as 'New Directions' that fought for the hard-won rights of auto workers in this new world of pressure from the bosses and from international competition – and, often, from entrenched union accommodationists who wanted nothing better than to go along and get along with the bosses.

Yettaw saw traditional union contracts and rights being shredded at Saturn, where workers got only 80 per cent of a formerly guaranteed pay scale, the rest being in incentive pay. Regardless of what manufacturing and management methods were used, he saw management and union officers colluding to keep the accommodationist faction in union office through the use of a mandatory contribution fund that was funnelled to the political campaigns of mainstream union leadership. The voices of those like Yettaw, who didn't think there was much to be gained by giving in, were eventually silenced. Buick said that they would close their plant in Flint if Yettaw retained his presidency, and Yettaw was voted out. Within three years, anyway, Buick had closed its plant. It was a lesson in where the power lay.

Ben Hamper, too, is sceptical about the new management style. 'I think the Pontiac East plant that I transferred to in the late '80s qualifies as one of these [new-style, lean-manufacturing] plants. It opened the year I transferred there. I didn't see anything that went on there that suggested an effort to treat workers better. In fact, the place was much worse for the workers – a real Gestapo atmosphere with overloaded job duties and very weak union representation. They had a programme there, as they do in many other plants, called "Team Concept", but all it seemed to boil down to was an attempt to get the workforce to police itself via fears of job security and rewards to ass-kissers. From what I hear from former linemates, the plants as a whole are a lot more rigid. The union has really lost a lot of its clout, both at the bargaining table and on the shop floor.'

Still, the overall picture was complex. The enormous changes in the auto industry, in its sociology as well as its technology and economics, were not of interest to filmmaker Michael Moore. He saw only the reality of lost jobs and martyred workers, and these were important realities. The old-style Flint worker had no reason to love GM and many to fight it. After all, no matter how much GM paid the line workers, GM executives and stockholders were getting rich off their labour. The hard battles for unionisation, the sit-downs and the company goons were all remembered in Flint, a town that was proud of its industrial history. The alienation of the shop rat that Moore and Hamper idealised was indeed in some sense heroic.

Here's Hamper on an employee-motivation session in his *ancien régime* plant: 'Hardly anyone tuned in for the technical presentation. It was one long lullaby of foreign terminology, slides, numerology and assorted high-tech masturbation. Why would any of us give a shit about the specifics of the great master plan? We knew what holes our screws went in. That was truth enough. Point us toward our air guns and welders and drill presses and save all the particulars for the antheads in the smocks and bifocals.'[45]

The measure of how little the old GM valued its workers' skills or made use of their full ability can be seen in how easy it was for Hamper and his line buddy to mine potential for efficiency unrecognised by the company – not in the service of corporate profits, but in the service of their own freedom as they 'doubled up' on shifts, each pushing his limits to do his own job as well as that of the other guy for half the shift and spending the other half in one of the many bars near the plant, getting slammed and getting paid for a full shift. The shop rats were brilliant in their own interests, but the company wasn't getting any of that brilliance and wasn't asking for any of it.

That was then; this is now. Auto plants don't work like that anymore; they really *do* demand both more creativity and more responsibility from their workers, which means that workers are both more and less powerful than they used to be in the old-style, smart-enough-to-be-too-dumb-to-care mode. This was just starting to happen when Michael Moore was making *Roger & Me*, but it's so antithetical to his thesis that he could never have been interested in it.

And there is, above all, the cold, hard reality of GM's unwillingness to invest billions in a community that took adversarial labour relations as an historic point of honor. Moore never acknowledges that not all the jobs that GM pulled out of Flint went to low-wage Mexico or Brazil. Some of these jobs went to Lansing, some went to Saginaw and some – like Hamper's – went to Pontiac. They went to places where GM managers thought that new manufacturing concepts would be welcomed, where they wouldn't have to fight the union every step of the way on every change.

For the first time, jobs in the auto industry were transcending Hamper's chilling descriptions of mechanical roles in which lives were wasted in dehumanising drudgery. Changing this grim working relationship was, of course, the secret of the new approach to auto manufacture, but that was entirely beyond the sphere of Michael Moore's consciousness. What Moore really wants of Roger – what he won't forgive GM for not providing – is job security and high wages at the expense of GM's stockholders and market position. He wants a corporation that puts people before profits.

This isn't such a bad idea. It has, in fact, worked to some extent in Japan, where corporate loyalty flows both ways and companies value the respect of their workers, and where there is (or used to be, at least) a tradition that the highest-paid executives make no more than seven times the income of the lowest-paid line workers.[46]

Unfortunately, Moore was selling this idea in 1989. His timing was poor. The American working class had been led to believe that socialism was synonymous with the crumbling totalitarian governments of Eastern Europe, that it was dead and that capitalism was synonymous with freedom. Right-wing intellectuals were declaring Reaganism triumphant and capitalism the end of history, even as Reagan's recession was kicking in. Unions had been weakened by a lack of solidarity, global competition and their manifold humiliations at Reagan's hands. Corporate responsibility in such an environment was a hard sell, even to workers. There were no sit-downs, no riots in Flint in the 1980s.

Yet Moore was a traditionalist. He believed in the power of organised workers in high-paying industrial jobs. But, in a way, he also had little faith in the working people whose misfortunes he was showing in his film, because outside of that scenario he saw working people as essentially lost. Without anything to keep the employer in town, without aggressive and militant backing from their union, Moore goes to some lengths to portray the people of Flint as essentially passive victims with nothing else to do but invest themselves in sad schemes, pathetic in their delusional nature – the Amway 'colour consultant' – or wait for the sheriff to put them out on the street.

Moore, his wife and all of their friends who worked on the project had pretty much expected that he would take it around the country in a van and show it at union halls and working-class recreation centres. It didn't happen quite like that.

After the film was screened to rapturous receptions at the Toronto, Telluride and New York Film Festivals, Warner Brothers picked it up, paying around $3 million for distribution rights. The competition for the film was intense, which meant that Moore could be a hard bargainer. He pressed for some very unusual items in the contract: 25,000 free tickets for unemployed auto workers, $25,000 for the families shown getting evicted in the movie, a seat reserved for Roger Smith at each screening, no distribution in Israel or South Africa.

In the four and a half months that the movie ran in commercial release it grossed $7 million, making it the top-grossing non-concert documentary ever made up to that time, and it was made by someone who was essentially an amateur, an unknown who had no major studio connections. Since then it has probably doubled its gross theatre takings in cable, video and DVD releases.

The movie won Moore a national reputation as the friend of the working man, the guy who would stand up to GM and tell it like it is. More or less adoring reviews appeared in national newspapers *Time*, *Newsweek* and (this must have been especially sweet for Moore, a Van Halen fan) *Rolling Stone*, and Moore embarked on a major US speaking tour.

For a while, *Roger & Me* was touted as Oscar material. GM pulled its ads from any TV or print production mentioning the film, which must have thrilled Moore.

And Moore was suddenly a local hero. His stubborn

authenticity was known and respected. Dave Barber, host of Flint Supertalk Radio AM 1570, who says he has interviewed Moore over 100 times, told me of seeing Moore in his beat-up old Honda – a car that could get its driver's ass kicked in Flint – by the county courthouse soon after he closed his deal with Warner Brothers. 'I said, "Michael. Jesus Christ, man, 3 million dollars. What are you going to do now?" And he said, "Well, I know some things I *won't* do. If you ever see me sitting in a hot tub sipping champagne, hit me with a baseball bat." He's done very well now, of course, but I think fundamentally, philosophically, you have the same guy. I see the same passion.'

Not everyone was willing to go along with the idea that *Roger & Me* was a straight documentary. Starting with work by John Foren in the *Flint Journal*, analysts started to notice that some of what Moore presents as cause and effect doesn't hold true. In a major development for the fate of the film, the critic Harlan Jacobson confronted Moore in an interview in *Film Comment* with some of his disingenuous connections: the layoffs of 30,000 had happened over a decade, not all at once after 1986, as Moore implies, and many of these workers had been relocated or retired with benefits rather than just let go; a visit from televangelist Robert Schuller, which Moore presents as a response to the layoffs, occurred in 1982; the loony plans for reviving the city's economy (also presented as a response to GM's retreat), including an over-investment in a convention centre and the ridiculous Auto World amusement park, had been in the works since the mid-1970s and had gone bankrupt before 1986.

Then there were things that Jacobson didn't catch but others did, such as the fact that the segment that purports to show laid-off GM workers meeting with Ronald Reagan in 1980 is actually footage shot at an entirely different event, which is why the workers' comments are vague and never mention GM or Flint. The big houses of the rich that Moore presents as being in the isolated enclave of Grosse Pointe are actually in Flint itself. The rats that Moore shows taking over Flint were filmed in Detroit. And one of Moore's former associates in Ralph Nader's organisation, James Musselman, said that he had seen Moore interviewing Roger Smith in 1988 at the Waldorf-Astoria in New York, refuting Moore's contention that Smith had refused to have any contact with him – the organising theme of the film.[47] In fact, Musselman and Ralph Nader say that, in May 1987, while he was working on *Roger & Me*, Moore actually filmed a GM shareholders' meeting during which he questions Roger Smith on the tax abatements granted by the city of Flint to GM. Nader and some associates actually supplied a transcript of this meeting to *Premiere* magazine, and in the published version Smith responds to Moore's questions for half a small-print page.[48] But Roger Smith actually taking questions did not fit into Moore's film's agenda, and so the scene didn't make the final edit.

Jacobson's criticisms of Moore's veracity were picked up by Pauline Kael, the influential film critic for *The New Yorker*, who slammed the film on journalistic, aesthetic and political grounds, branding it 'a piece of gonzo demagoguery that made me feel cheap for laughing'. She went on to say that Moore had improvised history and that his approach meant that 'members of the audience can laugh at ordinary working people and still feel that they are taking a politically correct position'.[49]

Moore reacted with fury, never giving an inch. At the time, and in many restatements since, he insisted that everything he showed was true if you use a longer time scale: GM indeed had eliminated 30,000 jobs in Flint and the town was ruined; all the town's schemes were connected with bolstering the local economy, and it was a GM economy – what more do you want? Typically, he took it personally, suggested a conspiracy and impugned his critics' integrity: '*Film Comment* is a publication of the Film Society of Lincoln Center; Lincoln Center had received a $5 million gift from GM just prior to its publishing of the piece trashing *Roger & Me*. Coincidence? Or just five big ones well spent?'[50] In an echo of the Paul Farhi incident at *Mother Jones*, Moore also claimed that Jacobson had flown into a rage during the interview and accused him of making an anti-Semitic film that would inspire pogroms against Jews (because, according to Jacobson, according to Moore, the film contains a brief scene of the Palestinian Intifada, and – even more far-fetched – because a blue-collar audience would assume that Jews are behind America's industrial decline).[51] Jacobson denied that he said anything of the kind.

As for Pauline Kael, Moore said that she wrote a spiteful review because he hadn't allowed Warner Brothers to provide a video cassette for her private viewing.[52]

In these rebuttals, Moore clearly fails to grasp what's at stake. As Jacobson himself says to Moore in their interview, it's true that he's correct about the overall effect of the layoffs on Flint, if you take a long view, but there's a reason why newspapers care about whether a witness's first name is John or Jon: credibility matters, and sloppiness puts credibility in doubt. If the facts are wrong, the entire documentary nature of the project – and therefore the point that Moore was trying to make about GM's corporate responsibility – can be lost. In a very revealing exchange, Jacobson plaintively points this out to Moore in a reference to Lyndon Johnson's manipulation of facts to his advantage in the Gulf of Tonkin incident:

HJ: That's what happens when one manipulates sequence...and that's the core credibility of the documentary... It goes back to the issue of the belief in the integrity of the information.

MM: Uh-huh. Yeah, sure... You are trying to hold me to a different
standard than you would another film...as if I were writing
some kind of college essay...

HJ: No. I hold you to documentary-film standards.

MM: Because you see this primarily as a documentary.[53]

It's a cheap dodge to insist – as Moore does – that the movie is
meant to inform by entertaining and that its entertainment value
requires the fudging of facts. Why? He could have had both.

It also seems almost gratuitously self-destructive. As the editor
of a small paper competing for the trust of a small town with the
conservative *Flint Journal*, Moore could strike poses and write
controversial editorials, but his reporting had to be pretty straight
or people would notice – and it was. As Moore's work has become
better known, as he has become more ambitious – more of a
polemicist and less of a journalist – and as he has become a national
figure without a local constituency that is invested in the issues to
keep him in line, he has taken a frequently casual attitude towards
the facts. This attitude was already starting to come out with *Roger
& Me* and, perhaps even more so, in his response to criticism of
his techniques.

Moore's persistent use of poetic licence in areas where it is clearly
not legitimate seems almost masochistic, a self-sabotaging habit; like
the bank robber who returns again and again to hold up the same
bank, you can speculate that he wants to be caught. Moore's enemies
have never failed to hit him with charges of fictionalising where it
suits his editorial position, and he has given them many opportunities
to discredit not only his material but also his theses. This has
considerably dulled the effect of Moore's voice on American politics,
and on much larger issues than the date on which Auto World closed.

If we can't trust Moore on Auto World, why should we trust him on the relationship of the Bushes with the Saudi royal family? If those big houses are actually in Flint, isn't the class divide in America more complicated than Moore says it is? But this is not the way Moore wants viewers to approach his work, which is meant to be enjoyed, and believed, on its own terms. When his supporters insist that his films are designed to stimulate independent thought, they seriously misjudge his work and its intention.

In his filming of *Roger & Me*, Moore was ruthless as well as stubborn. In Flint there are people who love him and people who don't much care for him, and not all of the latter are corporate fat cats or corrupt cops. Take Larry Stecco.

If you've seen the movie, you've seen Stecco. He's the guy at that party for rich toffs with the 1920s theme, the one where black folk are paid to pose as props in period costume. Stecco is the guy who's so out of it that he talks about what a great place Flint is to live in, even as working-class people are being thrown out of their homes; how there's ballet and hockey, and how everything is great in his privileged little world.

Except that wasn't really Stecco's world and, furthermore, Moore knew this. He knew Stecco personally, if not well. He knew that Stecco wasn't part of the idle rich set and that, in fact, he was on the same side as Moore on many issues. Stecco had helped him out several times. And although Moore never mentions it, the Great Gatsby party was an annual charitable event that raised money for a shelter for battered women, hardly a decadent gambol.

Almost 20 years after the unfortunate interview at the party, I met with Stecco and his lawyer, Glen Lenhoff, at a dark and comfortable bar in Flint. Stecco was a bit greyer but still quite recognisable from the film. Lenhoff was there because Stecco has won a lawsuit against Moore and legal issues still linger, so he monitored our conversation. That was fine with me; Lenhoff's a smart and interesting guy who had a lot to say.

Stecco is soft-spoken, thoughtful and idealistic, someone who supports his town even when things go very bad. He's clearly very decent, clearly nothing like the shallow caricature of a rich jerk that he appears to be in *Roger & Me*. He's a former chairman of the Genesee County Democratic Club, a lawyer who has done a lot of *pro bono* civil-rights work. He's a strong union supporter. For the last seven years he's also been a judge, one who Sam Riddle – a friend of Moore and one of his long-time associates – described as being 'very fair-minded'.

Stecco first met Moore during the time of the effort to remove Moore from the Davison school board. The daughter of Stecco's law partner worked on the Hotline, and Stecco himself had helped with some legal issues there at her request. He donated $1,000 to fight the recall and gave regular if not large sums to support *The Flint Voice*. He and Moore had mutual friends and Stecco supported the idea of an alternative paper. At the time, he felt that Moore 'stirred things up' and that 'there was a legitimate place for someone like that'.

When Stecco ran into Moore at the Great Gatsby party, Moore told him that he and the crew were making a movie in response to *Money* magazine naming Flint as the 'worst place to live' in the US, that it was for local PBS Channel 28 and that it was being produced in conjunction with the Junior League. Stecco knew enough about Moore's rebel populism to find the Junior League connection a bit off, but he agreed to talk for the movie.

'Moore asked questions and I answered them,' Stecco remembers. 'In the film I look like an insensitive fool, babbling about hockey and ballet, but we were talking about raising kids here. I said that times were tough here, but it's still a good place to raise a family. Moore also set it up to make me and the party look racist. There were both African-American and white actors hired to appear in period costume, but Moore shows only the black actors, making the whole scene look exploitative. The black actors sued him for the way they were portrayed.'

So did Stecco. He took Moore to court for presenting his character in a false light – actionable under Michigan law. The trial dragged on for a long time and it was very bitter. In the end, the jury was persuaded that the reality of Stecco was nothing like the guy in the film and awarded him $6,250. Lenhoff explains that Moore had publicly claimed that he gave $25,000 from his movie profits to the four families shown being evicted so that they could buy houses, which sounds like a pretty good sum, but in fact he gave $25,000 in total, so each of the four families got $6,250. The jury thought Stecco should get as much.

The story of Larry Stecco and his appearance in Roger & Me captures many of the contradictions of Moore's career and personality. Moore is genuinely concerned with social justice. He doesn't think it's right that rich people should be partying while poor people struggle to get by on their leavings, and this is an admirable, even noble position. In stating it frequently Moore has no doubt changed the world for the better in certain ways.

But it's a *meta*-position, because the actual people and arguments that Moore uses to make this point are often manipulated and exploited. There are plenty of genuinely callow, shallow, selfish, ignorant, passively racist rich people out there. Larry Stecco isn't one of them, however, and Moore knew it. His portrayal of Stecco in Roger & Me exhibits both tremendous showbusiness talent and a cold, hard core of relentless ideology, an attitude that, as with Leninists of yore, will always put the cause of increasing human wellbeing before the wellbeing of any particular human and will put the meta-truth before the actual, immediate truth of any situation. Like the story of Moore's destruction of his high-school principal, it recurs throughout his work.

Part 2

Roadkill Politics

4 Fun With A Purpose

Michael Moore has never been bound by any one medium. He's been working in print from his earliest school days, and he had a weekly radio show – *Radio Free Flint* – in high school. After *Roger & Me*, he came back to Flint and presented a political show titled *Roadkill Politics* on the local PBS station in which he would research issues of public concern and present them as entertainment.

Television is a natural medium for Moore: ubiquitous, despised by intellectuals, susceptible to populist uses. By the 1990s, it was a medium with a particular appeal to someone of Moore's talents – Jerry Springer had already obliterated a lot of prissy old conventions; Bill Maher was edgily discussing politics – but before Moore there were few on the left who were willing to do a show that was both political and a circus (in spite of the fact that 'ringmaster' Jerry Springer had once been mayor of Cinncinnati).

This shortfall opened a certain cultural niche for Moore somewhere between the present-day *Fear* and *O'Reilly* factors, and his ability to fill this need has always been a key aspect of his success. He hates documentaries – or, at least, the sober PBS style of documentary. He likes to be playful. He needs a gimmick, a hook to draw in his audience – the more outrageous, the better. When he finds one, he can appeal to people who would be moved by the leftist conspiratorial arguments of, say, Noam Chomsky if they weren't too lazy to read him. Moore's diatribes are easy to absorb: pre-cut, pre-chewed and often highly entertaining.

Moore honed his edgy comedic chops on his late-'90s cable TV shows *TV Nation* and *The Awful Truth*. The former was handed to him in 1992, after the commercial success of *Roger & Me* became very clear, by NBC (owned by General Electric), whose executives were – in Moore's telling, at least – thrilled to have him work on a show that would be 'a cross between *60 Minutes* and Fidel Castro on laughing gas' and that, Moore promised, would 'go after [your advertisers] like a barracuda'.[54] Just the kind of show a network could be expected to rush to sign up.

The negotiations for the show generated some serious connections for Moore and did a great deal to forward his career. At that time, Moore had been trying unsuccessfully to raise money for a fictional film with political overtones titled *Canadian Bacon*.

The *TV Nation* pilot tested well with the network executives and in a screening in the blue-collar town of Scranton, Pennsylvania. The response wasn't strong enough to put the concept over the top, however, and the network decided that they didn't want to make the series right away. But then the pilot won commitments from Alan Alda and John Candy to appear in *Canadian Bacon*, and getting the stars on board brought funding for the film.

Eventually released in 1995, *Canadian Bacon* is in fact very much like an extended *TV Nation* segment. Evil elements in the US government and in the arms industry conspire to set up the Canadians as a new mortal national enemy to keep the Cold War military contracts flowing and President Alan Alda popular. The film borrows liberally from Stanley Kubrick's Cold War classic *Dr Strangelove* and anticipates elements of *Wag The Dog* and the *South Park* movie (ie 'Blame Canada!'). But Moore is no Kubrick, and no Trey Parker or Matt Stone, for that matter. The satire is both broad and shallow, and the main lesson of the film is that this kind of thing might work in a ten-minute *TV Nation* episode but gets old somewhere around the 11-minute mark.[55] Commercial audiences agreed.

But the original *TV Nation* pilot was still making the rounds, and it was very helpful for Moore's career. In the UK, the head of BBC2, Michael Jackson, liked it and offered to split the cost with NBC, and the show was back on track as a summer series. In a pep talk to the staff as they began shooting, Moore told them to assume that they would never work in television again, because any future résumé submissions were sure to be met with, 'Oh, you worked on that show that pissed off all the sponsors.'[56] *TV Nation* showcased Moore's talents for both politics and comedy.

The show was truly groundbreaking and nothing on TV since then (except for Moore's *The Awful Truth*) looks anything like it. In several segments each week Moore would harass corporate evildoers and poke fun at the conscience-free in high places, borrowing gimmicks from game shows and anticipating what is now dubbed 'reality TV'. Moore bugs the hell out of receptionists and PR people, standing there with his crew and asking questions while the fifth 'Sir, I'm asking you to remove yourself from the premises right now' rings in the audience's ears, pushing the envelope further than would seem possible (or indeed would be possible, one thinks, with no camera present). The viewer hardly notices that he rarely gets past the front desk of the evil corporations he confronts, or that the people whose day he ruins are those very receptionists and security guards, never their bosses; working-class people just like him, although making far less money.

But if Moore was obnoxious, he was also wildly imaginative. He sent a Mexican mariachi band and the cheerleading squad of historically black Spelman College to disrupt a Klan rally with chants promoting love between *all* people. He sent a multiracial chorus line to serenade the Aryan Nations with 'Stop! In The Name

Of Love' and The Gay Men's Chorus to Senator Jesse Helms' doorstep (the senator's wife thanked the singers graciously). He threw a concert – Corp Aid – to help big corporations that are facing lawsuits. He invented Crackers, the Corporate Crime-Fighting Chicken. When he discovered that Mississippi has never ratified the 13th Amendment, he sent a black reporter to Jackson to purchase white people as slaves and lead them around in chains. He sent a former Soviet spy to find the heart and soul of the Democratic Party. He loaded up a tractor-trailer with Soviet memorabilia and Gus Hall – the American Communist Party's longtime leader – and took 'Communism' on a farewell tour across the country. He went to the former Soviet Union on a mission to find the missile aimed at Flint and disarmed it.

To its credit, NBC (and Fox, a carrier in the second season) rarely stepped in to stop the mayhem. They censored or refused to run only five segments out of 105: a piece on a high-school boy in Topeka, Kansas, who got extra school credit for picketing the funerals of gay people, carrying a placard bearing the legend THANK GOD FOR AIDS; one on a leader of the anti-abortion movement; one in which Ben Hamper searches drugstores for small-sized condoms; and one, oddly enough, on the savings-and-loan crisis of the 1980s.

The Awful Truth, which began running in 1998, continued where *TV Nation* left off; the shows are hardly distinguishable. Moore brought back Ben Hamper, 'the Rivethead', as a correspondent on several episodes, and Moore's attitude about Hamper's role says a lot about the show and Moore's ability to connect to the audience that he was trying to reach.

Hamper was a bit disoriented in New York City, fighting back panic attacks with booze and Klonopin. He was freaked at the hugeness of the buildings and sat in on a production meeting in which a bunch of college graduates argued about whether to engage a real pimp to go down to Washington to bully politicians or to find an actor known for playing pimps; Antonio Fargas – Huggy Bear in the '70s detective show *Starsky And Hutch* – was too old, they decided.

'I really enjoyed Mike's invitations to work on his shows, though they did tend to make a nervous wreck out of me,' Hamper wrote to me. 'I was completely out of my element. In fact, that's why I chose writing in the first place – I didn't like communicating with people in a visible sense... Now here I was being beamed into a few million households. When Mike first brought up the invite to take part in *TV Nation*, I assumed I'd be writing. It wasn't until I got to New York that he informed me that I'd be in front of the camera... At the time I was overwhelmed by the commotion of New York, and my anxiety problems were in high gear. I was drinking heavily and taking a lot of heavy sedatives in an attempt to stymie my fears... During this whole period, Mike was persistent in his encouragement. There were many times I'd call him at his home or show up at his office and tell him that I was quitting...that I appreciated his faith in me but I felt like a total incompetent. Without fail, Mike would talk me back from the gloom and insist that I was just what he was looking for – a real person, a representative of any old couch potato. I admired that about him. Here he could have hired any number of media sorts with actual broadcasting skills and credibility, but he stuck with me because he wanted an average schmoe on board.'

One of Hamper's TV assignments was to find a new job for Bill Clinton. This was in 2000 – Clinton was leaving office soon and Moore was intent on calling him out about those 60 million jobs he was constantly boasting of having created. The fact was that Clinton, although vilified by the right as a crypto- (or maybe not even crypto-) communist, would have been quite at home in the business-loving Republican Party as it existed up until Ronald Reagan made Republicanism a religion, and improving the lot of the poor in America was hardly a Clinton priority; most of those jobs were the result of making it easier for bosses to exploit their workers, not of insisting that they do right by their people. As Hamper put it, they were 'shit jobs with low pay and no benefits and hardly suitable for a family provider, let alone an ex-President'.[57] The show arranged for Hamper to appear as Clinton's emissary in search of a job for the soon-to-be-ex-President typical of the ones that Clinton won for America: at a temp agency, a telemarketing firm, a Domino's Pizza outlet and (they couldn't resist) the New York Sperm Bank.

As with *TV Nation*, the targets that Moore chooses in *The Awful Truth* are, for the most part, genuinely despicable, and he's not restrained by any qualms about good taste. He sends a group costumed as 17th-century Puritans to harass Special Prosecutor Ken Starr and Crackers, the Corporate Crime-Fighting Chicken, to lobby Mickey Mouse at Disneyworld on behalf of Disney's exploited cartoon-character actors. He sends a group of school children to harass another polluting executive while later in the show a group of lingerie-clad models is assigned the same task (you've never seen so many security guards drawn to the scene). He tours the South with a group of queens in a 'sodomite bus', inducing predictable discomfort in the followers of gay-hating fanatic the Reverend Fred Phelps, whose *modus operandi* is sending groups to taunt brutally the mourners at funerals of gay people. He sends Adolf Hitler to Zurich to withdraw all the money that the deceased Führer still has on deposit in Swiss banks, much of which came from the dental fillings of his victims.

Perhaps most satisfying of all, Moore surreptitiously steals DNA from Lucianne Goldberg, Linda Tripp's book agent, who told Tripp to record her calls with Monica Lewinsky. ('I had a ball doing it,' says Goldberg.) Moore had a ball focusing a webcam on her bedroom window, calling her in the middle of the night and otherwise violating her privacy. It's low, but it couldn't happen to a more deserving person. The only sad part is that Goldberg is too much of a narcissist to really get it; when the joke is sprung on her and she realises that a large studio audience (and all those people in front of their TVs) are laughing at the idea that her bedroom window is under 24-hour surveillance on the internet, you can tell that she sort of relishes the attention. It's justice, but it's not the way to get someone like Goldberg to feel anything. 'Why did I do it?' asks Goldberg, speaking of her role in the Lewinsky matter. 'I wanted to do it. I did it. It's done. Now, can we move on?'

Behind the scenes, however, it wasn't all laughs and going after the bad guys. Writing in online magazine *Salon*, Daniel Radosh reported that Moore, contrary to all his supposed class and union loyalties, actually discouraged staff writers from unionising. Moore hit back at Radosh in typically paranoid style: he'd criticised the union policy of bookstore chain Borders, who sponsored *Salon*, so *Salon* was out to get him. David Talbot, *Salon*'s editor, had worked at *Mother Jones* and had protested against Moore getting the editor's job 11 years earlier, so obviously Talbot was out to get him. Radosh had written for *The National Review*, *The Weekly Standard* and *Playboy*, so Radosh was out to get him. Moore threatened to sue *Salon* for libel if the publishers didn't retract the story of his intimidation of the writers. 'One writer remembered Moore telling him and a colleague that *TV Nation* could not afford two writers at Guild rates and that, "If you want to be in this union, only one of you can work here,"' Radosh responded. 'Once they did join the union, they had to constantly file complaints [with the Authors Guild] about Moore's treatment of them.'[58]

Because Moore partakes of both the political and entertainment worlds, it was sometimes not clear where he was coming from, and this could lead to a certain confusion among his staff, in his work and, very likely, in his own perceptions and justifications of what he was doing. A former Moore staffer told Larissa MacFarquhar of *The New Yorker*, 'I have let go of Michael. I have not seen one of his products, his movies, his TV shows, his books. I'm sure they're all good. I'm sure they're spreading the message and enraging all the right people. But I can't accept him as a political person. I can't buy into this thing of Michael Moore being on your side. It's like trying to believe that Justin Timberlake is a soulful guy. It's a media product; he's just selling me something. For the preservation of my own soul, I have to consider him as just an entertainer, because otherwise he's a huge asshole. If you consider him an entertainer, then his acting like a selfish, self-absorbed, pouty, deeply conflicted, easily wounded child is run-of-the-mill, standard behaviour; but if he's a political force, then he's a jerk and a hypocrite and he didn't treat us right.'[59]

Moore, however, does have a political agenda. In the course of Moore's work at *The Awful Truth*, there were times when the intersection of politics and entertainment took on a sinister cast, when the truth was lost to the cheap shot and the quick emotional punch. *The Awful Truth* was light, but it was deceptively light; just because Moore wasn't afraid to be goofy didn't mean that there wasn't a core of steel behind his attempts to stir outrage about outrageous things.

Moore's relentless ideological reductionism is best showcased in *The Awful Truth*'s segment on William Cohen, the moderate Maine Republican who was Bill Clinton's second Secretary of Defense. The segment starts off in a cheerful if slightly ironic tone, most of it spent satirically questioning Cohen's manhood. Moore recalls the sturdy, manly military men of yore: Patton, MacArthur, Schwarzkopf. Then he shows us Cohen, with his shy and genuine smile, the sign of a truly nice guy. We see Cohen dancing awkwardly and vaguely effeminately, handing flowers to a military aide in camouflage. It seems Cohen has written poetry, too. Terrible poetry. Terrible, sensitive poetry. Here's one about how he felt after accidentally hitting a deer with his car, presented against a backdrop of warm pastel tones:

> Forgive me, for I know what I have done.
> I have taken a child of the woods
> In the gunsight
> Of my hood.

That couldn't have won Cohen votes in Maine. And there's more…

> We skipped our laughter into the sea
> And made love in a castle of sand.

We see Cohen getting married – on Valentine's Day! – and dodging the kiss on the lips, going for the cheek. To top it all off, his middle name is Sebastian.

Moore builds his case against Cohen, deeply disturbed that America's enemies will have no cause to fear America with this guy in charge of its military. He gathers citizens of Iraq, Afghanistan and North Korea – as well as a six-year-old girl – in front of the Department of Defense to shout insults. The North Korean uses a bullhorn to yell, 'Your poetry is for wusses!'

But where's Moore really going with this? We find out at the very end of the segment, in a quick but densely packed 40 seconds. He's going for the jugular.

After confronting Cohen in person and calling him a wuss – and getting brushed off in the nicest manner possible – Moore concludes that Cohen must have had a change of heart: 'Like most pansies when pushed into a corner, he had to prove himself to be a man. And did he ever!' What follows is a quick and devastating list of US military actions during Cohen's tenure as Defense Secretary and their consequences, starting with the response to the East African Embassy bombings in 1998 and moving on to actions against Saddam Hussein and the Yugoslav War in 1999: 'First he bombs Afghanistan... Our guy knows how to take out tent-loads of innocent people. Still think Cohen's a gentle man, Mr [Sudanese] Ambassador? Tell it to the people working at your medical facility. He doesn't get mad; he kills Sudanese civilians. Still think Cohen's weak? Well, he's tough enough to smart-bomb Iraqi apartment buildings full of women and children. Now he's blowing up Serbians on trains! And the occasional Chinese embassy! That'll show 'em!'

All of this is accompanied by appropriately gruesome images of victims of war: bodies blown apart, paramedics carrying dazed victims – obviously innocent, very ordinary people – on stretchers, buildings reduced to rubble. After the light satire of the preceding part, it's horrifying, and devastatingly effective. Cohen isn't a nice guy after all, screams Moore's technique. He's a murderer.

Never mind that each of these cases is much more complicated than Moore would have it. Never mind that Americans had been attacked in East Africa by agents trained in those Afghan camps, that Saddam had been firing on US and British air patrols, that Yugoslavia's Slobodan Milošević had been destabilising his country and his region for a decade and had launched wars in which 200,000 people had died, and that Clinton's decision – as executed by Cohen – set in motion a process that ended Yugoslavia's outlaw status. The point is not whether these actions were actually justified; there are arguments on the other side, too – just not the argument that Moore made. When the US bombed Afghanistan, Iraq and Serbia, it wasn't because Cohen was freaked out about being a pansy.

When *Saturday Night Live* has actors portraying George W Bush and Donald Rumsfeld go into a deep kiss – as the show has done – we're not really being told that the President and his Secretary of Defense are lovers, but in the Cohen segment Moore does seem to be saying that the United States *really did* kill people to protect a sissy's threatened sense of masculinity. Because if this *isn't* what he's saying, it's hard to find any point to the episode.

Unlike the vulgar shock of the *Saturday Night Live* skit, Moore's segment on *The Awful Truth* is not funny. This is art meeting demagoguery, and meeting it brilliantly. He manages to make the real issues disappear under his cleverness, his easy style, the wit and humour of his montage. All that's left is a conviction that our leaders are out of control, that war is bad and that it is the result of an over-compensating psychopathology. We don't have any real enemies; it's all about acting tough.

The sympathetic studio audience comes away believing that Moore's insight has revealed a profound truth, whereas in fact he hasn't approached any truth at all. Another word for this is *propaganda*, and Moore has never been more skilful at it – not in *Bowling For Columbine*, not in *Roger & Me* – than he is here. If this is what he does best, we should watch his movies very carefully and thoughtfully because, when you take away the fun and games and ideological agenda, the images aren't necessarily attached to anything in the real world.

5 Take The Gunheads Bowling

Guns are the pathological obsession of the right, and there's really nothing else in American culture that so combines romantic myth, ahistoricism and terrible social policy. To a great many people in the US, guns are still symbols of individualism, independence and rugged frontier character, and they are still thought to be effective for personal crime control and resistance to state encroachments on liberty. They are also considered by many at the peculiarly American confluence of religion and guns to be a near-God-given, absolute right. Warren Cassidy, once head of the Institute for Legislative Action – the National Rifle Association's lobbying arm – put it like this: 'You would get a far better understanding if you approached us as if you were approaching one of the great religions of the world.'[60]

All of these beliefs are highly questionable. Endless objective surveys – most of them in medical and statistical journals – have shown that household guns are far more likely to endanger their owners than to stop intruders.[61] Although gun hobbyists, ably represented by former NRA president Charlton Heston and executive director Wayne LaPierre and scholars like John Lott (whose work is sponsored by the gun industry), may sincerely believe that all our liberties rest on private ownership of firearms, and even that this is the meaning of the Second Amendment, they are provably wrong. Yes – to refute an argument often made by the NRA – Hitler and Stalin took away private guns. So do most of the European democracies. There is an obvious difference in social organisation between fascism (of the left or right) and European social-welfarism, and what matters is not the similarities of regulation but the differences of institutions.

I've always thought that the tautological argument about how tyranny is both a cause and an effect of gun control is deeply insulting to the power and stability of culturally rooted, consensus-derived government, conspicuous by its historical absence from any of the lands that fell to tyranny in the 20th century. People who are governed by consent do not need to encounter their leaders on the battlefield. And if we did, our leaders control machine guns, tanks, chemical and biological weapons, cruise missiles, radar, submarines, aircraft carriers, advanced jet fighters and bombers, and tactical and strategic nuclear weapons. Should all of these things be available to private citizens, in the name of preserving an equaliser?

The Founding Fathers certainly didn't think so. The headquarters of the NRA, in Washington, DC, has half of the Second Amendment engraved in stone by its entrance: …THE RIGHT OF THE PEOPLE TO KEEP AND BEAR ARMS SHALL NOT BE INFRINGED. The association was honest enough to use the ellipsis. Here's what the amendment actually says: 'A well-regulated Militia being necessary to the security of a free State, the right of the people to keep and bear Arms shall not be infringed.' As shown in their individual and collective writings and debates, the Founders had an exceptionally nuanced and careful sense of the meaning of words. That first clause is there for a reason, and in a long string of judgments the Supreme Court has agreed.[62] Even the 1871 founding charter of the NRA implicitly assumes that gun use is properly within the context of militia readiness: '…to promote rifle practice…and to promote the introduction of a system of aiming drill and target firing among the National Guard of New York and the militia of other states'.[63]

Along with the death penalty and lack of a national healthcare plan, it is the American legal sanction for domestic killing tools that really separates the US government from most other advanced, industrial democracies, a secondary historical feature of the country's national myth of individualism and political exceptionalism. Note that I am not talking here about the guns used in deer hunting, an activity that for many Americans is an important part of the home economy and that is vital to maintaining deer populations at sustainable levels now that their natural predators have been eradicated. It's also far, far less brutal than the factory-farming system that produces that neatly packaged steak from the supermarket. But hunting guns are not controversial, because, with their long barrels and single-shot magazines, they're not very effective for killing people.

No, it is handguns and military-style assault weapons that the NRA has to spend its time and considerable resources defending, and in doing so they often mobilise a strain of paranoia that seems to have developed only in America, which (with apologies to Richard Hofstadter) could be termed the paranoid style in American popular culture. It's no accident that *The Turner Diaries* – the pornographic white-racial-supremacy fantasy by neo-Nazi William Pierce[64] that inspired Oklahoma City bomber Timothy McVeigh – is a bestseller at gun shows. This doesn't mean that most people who are regulars at gun shows are vicious racists, but if sales of Pierce's book are any indication it seems that most people who are regulars at gun shows have a paranoid streak, and this tale of secret armed resistance to sinister conspiracy naturally resonates with them.

In a not-so-very-different way, it shouldn't be surprising that a crusade against gun culture would resonate with Moore. It's no great revelation that people often react most strongly against belief systems that have points in common with their own, and the stereotypical gun-lover's creed[65] – distrust of government, faith in community and the people, a call to activism, a willingness to entertain grand conspiracy theories, a pugnacious and tenacious defence of perceived constitutional rights – has many similarities to Moore's own.

Before producing his Oscar-winning movie *Bowling For Columbine*, Moore had shown that he enjoyed taking on the big targets in print, film, radio or television, whether they be GM, the tobacco industry, Ted Turner, major corporate polluters or his own employers, and after *Columbine* he would take on the President of the United States. He has always recognised that the political right is not only, or even primarily, a system of economic and political beliefs; it is a culture. Guns, in the United States, are fundamental to that culture, because an absolutist belief in the right to own them affirms one particular idea of what makes America what it is and what makes it different from other countries. What better subject for Moore's ambitions and contrarian beliefs, or for his agenda? Seen in this light, all of his work on television – his confrontational ten-minute spots that take apart the ironies and insecurities and brutal contradictions at the edges of American social life – becomes a preparation for his attack on this one particular idea.

It wasn't only the question of guns that made sure that Moore's *Bowling For Columbine* would be a focal point for anger on both the left and the right. There's the obvious fact that anything that involves children and how they are raised and educated carries enormous emotional power, and in choosing to look at a particularly horrible recent phenomenon – high-school mass murders – Moore was stoking an ambient social anxiety that most Americans feel but express very differently, depending on their political orientation. To some, these kinds of crimes are symptoms of the breakdown of the family, of a culture that devalues personal responsibility, of lax institutional discipline, moral relativism, parental abdication, lack of prayer in school, perhaps even the teaching of evolution and sexual revolution – not enough guns in private hands. To others, they are the result of insufficient spending on social services, mental health care and law enforcement, of a culture that suppresses human dignity and worships casual violence in movies and video games – too many guns in private hands.

Many or even most of these diagnoses may not be contradictory, and many of them could be simultaneously true and still be insufficient to explain the phenomenon, but they have different and bitterly disputed policy implications. That's why people argue about *Columbine*.

Columbine struck very close to home in Moore's native Michigan. There is a long sequence in the film about a six-year-old boy in Flint who took a gun to school and shot a six-year-old girl, Kayla Rowland, on their way to the computer lab.[66] The boy had been left by his mother in the house of her brother, a crack dealer, and had found a stolen gun and taken it to school. The episode is central to the development of Moore's plans for his film.

I spoke with Art Busch, who is an old friend of Moore from their college days and who, as the District Attorney of Genesee County, was the prosecutor in the Rowland case. He served as an advisor to Moore while he was making *Columbine* and he told me why the film was so important to him: 'I was so committed to what this film was about. The film really stood up for victims, and I think those that watched it are deeply moved by what the victims of crime are doing and what they're saying. Not so much about the NRA as about what's happening to the people of our country… None of [the news coverage] was to the point. Why do we have kids in America today who are living in dope houses with teenage boys and who have to go begging for their food on the main street after they get out of school? I felt that many of the biggest issues in this case were just being ignored, that the problems behind the case were here today and would be here tomorrow after these people were gone. Even as we spoke, the factory down the road from where the shooting occurred, the Fisher Body plant, was being torn down.'

Moore was determined to address pathologies that are very deeply rooted in American society. 'Michael said he'd like to do something with this that has a lasting impact, something greater than the *60 Minutes* format. I talked to him for many hours. Just as we in trial practice begin to develop a theory of our case, he develops a theory of his movie, and his movie is, "Why are Americans so violent? Why do Americans want to have guns? And what's behind all that?" He came to the conclusion that we are simply afraid of one another.'

But, having stirred the pot, what does Moore put into the stew? This is where it gets interesting, and it's also where *Bowling For Columbine* begins to fall apart.

The movie opens, typically, with Moore at centre stage as he opens an account at a Michigan bank and walks out with a rifle as a prize after delivering the scene's punchline: 'Is it a good idea to be giving away guns in a bank?' The scene is set up as candid-camera investigative journalism, but it could not have transpired as Moore presents it. The strength of the scene is supposed to be because it is an everyday event in US gun culture, something that the bank people don't find odd – anyone can walk in off the street and walk out with a rifle – but Moore has changed the rules drastically for his film.

For a start, Moore had to fill in a background-check form in advance and wait for it to clear, which had happened before the scene took place. Normally a customer would not receive his gun in the bank, but Moore's people had called in advance and arranged for the staff to have one on hand in the bank's vault; Moore was insistent that he had to get it right away if he was going to open his account. The staff were also told that he would be a major depositor, and for this reason they were willing to give him special treatment.

When we hear in *Bowling For Columbine* that the bank has '500 guns in the vault', the tellers are referring to the bank's central storage vault, located miles away, but Moore edits this out and allows us to believe that all those guns are right there on hand to distribute to walk-in customers. Moore wants credit for exposing, in gumshoe fashion, a surprising blank spot at the centre of the bank's institutional gaze, but he's already using the tools of the editors' trade to violate the standards of the journalists' trade. His own filmed experience has almost nothing to do with what normally happens when a customer tries to get a gun from the bank.[67]

If the central question of the movie is, as Busch said, 'Why are Americans so afraid of each other?', this is a question about philosophy and sociology but not about policy, and in choosing to go after guns at a philosophical rather than a policy level Moore gives himself a lot of leeway but delivers an unclear and inconsistent message. Most people who saw *Bowling For Columbine*, on both sides of the issue, came away from the movie thinking that Moore is in favour of gun control. He's not – or, at least, not necessarily so. In fact, he starts out in the film with a voice-over explaining that he's been around guns all his life and is a life member of the NRA.

Even here there's a twist: although this is technically true, Moore is using his life-membership status to make a point about his lack of bias against guns, and it's not that simple. As Moore confessed in an interview with the UK's *Guardian* newspaper, 'I was a junior member when I was in the Boy Scouts, when I was a kid, but I became a lifetime member after the Columbine massacre because my first thought after Columbine was to run against Charlton Heston for the presidency of the NRA. You have to be a lifetime member to be able to do that, so I had to pay $750...to join. My plan was to get 5 million Americans to join for the lowest basic membership and vote for me so that I'd win and dismantle the organisation. Unfortunately, I figured that's just too much work for me, so instead I made this movie. But I'm still a lifetime member, until they excommunicate me...which is not far off, from what I hear.'[68] Note the scale of the ambition.

I once attended a Moore event where he said that he'd started out with the belief that stronger gun-control laws would save lives but that he'd begun to think about it differently when he learned that Canadians have even more guns in their homes than Americans[69] yet still don't go on murderous rampages. The same is also famously true of the Swiss. 'So it seems like the NRA has a point when they say, "Guns don't kill people; people kill people,"' Moore pointed out. 'But it's really more like, "*Americans* kill people."'

Here, of course, Moore disingenuously fails to take into account a very major difference between American and Canadian guns: While there are many of them in circulation, Canadian guns are almost all long-barrel, single-shot hunting rifles. Canada does indeed have very tight legal restrictions on private ownership of handguns, the type of weapon suited to committing crimes and which is, overwhelmingly, the type of firearm that is used to commit crimes in the United States.[70]

Having thus casually dismissed all actual gun-control arguments, Moore sets out in *Columbine* to explain *why* people kill people – or, as he puts it, why *Americans* kill people. Moore doesn't think the answer is the easy availability of guns, so has to torture the facts for social explanations. We were bombing Serbia when the Columbine attacks took place. There's a major defence contractor producing missiles in the area.[71] Nobody listened to the Columbine attackers. The Canadian welfare state builds social bonds that Americans lack.

Moore also leans heavily on University of Southern California sociologist Barry Glassner's book *The Culture Of Fear* and expands on Glassner's thesis to make his own argument that the racist media feeds on a racist society's racist assumptions to produce an environment of racial fear and hysteria in which people are trigger happy. Needless to say, none of these theories – at least, as presented by Moore – is exactly good social science, and Moore makes no attempt at objectively proving any of them. He just flings connections around as casually as this one: 'I see bowling as a very American thing, an all-American sport. The other all-American sport is violence. [The Columbine killers] went to their favourite class – bowling – in the morning. I think they just went from one to the other.'[72]

As it happens, the Columbine killers skipped their bowling class that morning; Moore's journalism is here as sloppy as his reasoning is specious. However, specious or not, Moore never questions his conclusions, which allow him to blame American gun violence on an amorphous 'culture of fear' or the war in Yugoslavia while simultaneously pouring scorn on right-wing attempts to blame it on Marilyn Manson's shock rock – an explanation no more implausible than any that Moore offers. In a speech given at the University of Denver in February 2003, Moore made it clear that he believes his generalised argument about a violent society is the *actual* key to understanding the Columbine assaults and understanding America: 'I want everyone to be able to draw the connection between Columbine and Iraq and everything else.'[73]

The film's sequence on racism and the media is particularly instructive as to Moore's methods. Here he shows clips from many cop-reality shows in which black suspects in street crime are tackled by police and wonders why there aren't more white perps or, at least, more white-collar criminal arrests. It's all a racist media conspiracy.

But, of course, street crime in many American urban areas *is* predominantly perpetrated by black individuals, and for reasons that have nothing to do with the inherent proclivities of blacks or whites and everything to do with the historical echoes of crimes committed by whites against blacks. But the police aren't social workers or historians. Neither are the television networks; they seek out entertainment value, not socially responsible narratives, and they'll take it where they find it.

In *Columbine*, Moore interviews Dick Herlan, who produced *COPS* and *The World's Wildest Police Videos*. Throughout the interview, Herlan, who describes himself as a liberal, seems to have a much better idea of the social reality of the United States than does Moore. Herlan looks weary when Moore asks him why he doesn't show white-collar criminals being brought in: 'I love the idea… I just don't think it would make very interesting reality TV. If we can get those people to get in their SUVs and drive really fast down the road away from the police…if you can get [a corporate criminal] to take his shirt off and throw his cellular phone at the police as they come through the door, and try to jump out that window…then we'd have a show.'

It's a little surprising that Moore included this clip because Herlan has him here, and in an interesting way. The media angle is no help at all to Moore's racism argument because, in fact, it's not racial; one gets the sense that Herlan would show white people smoking crack, jelly wrestling with prostitutes and carving their bloody initials on their grandmothers if he could find the footage and if it helped his ratings. But this media angle is actually a great help to Moore's anti-capitalist argument since it shows the utterly exploitative nature of profit-driven showbiz.

The problem for Moore is that he can't have it both ways. If it's racism – if Herlan could keep his ratings up by showing white-collar crime arrests but chooses not to – there's something else going on here besides the pursuit of profit. But if profit is all that matters, capitalism is motivated only by mindless, almost impersonal greed. This would normally be a tasty morsel for Moore, but he can't use it here without contradicting himself because it nullifies the racism argument.

Moore resolves the paradox brilliantly by bounding to the higher generality of asking why Canada has a lower murder rate, somehow managing to *suggest* both theses simultaneously to the viewer without having to take responsibility for either one.

And yet the racism angle is not as completely far out as some on the right have made it out to be. Right-wing commentator Dave Kopel has gone to some lengths to pour scorn on Moore's linkage, in *Columbine*, of the origin, goals and ideology of the NRA and the Ku Klux Klan,[74] and in the limited historical circumstances Kopel addresses, he has a point. But listen to Art Busch, who was on the front line of law enforcement in Flint for a dozen years: 'Shortly after [the Kayla Rowland shooting] started, I was all over the news media as a spokesman for our city. Michael and Kathleen were talking to me throughout this incident, and I was sharing with them the hate mail that I was receiving, which was bizarre. I had done an interview with Katie Couric in which I started to describe the boy who shot Kayla as a "little guy" and said that we needed to wrap our arms around him and love him and realise that he's a victim as well. That really stirred a lot of nutty people across our country; it stirred up the racist people because it didn't take them long to figure out that he was black and she was white, although no pictures of him were ever published, since he was a juvenile.

'So the racist people of the world decided that they would begin to write me letters, notes, threats. What amazed me was the anger of these people as I began to talk about guns. You see, the context of Kayla Rowland was the assault-weapons ban in Congress, the 2000 election cycle and the fact that we were having all these school shootings all at the same time. I pointed out that the gun used to shoot Kayla was stolen in a burglary, and I began to talk about how this was a huge problem, that guns were being stolen from people's houses and used in crimes. People get these guns and they think that they're safer, but just the opposite is true. Well, that stirred up the gun nuts. They were writing me letters comparing me to the prosecutor who was prosecuting Byron de la Beckwith[75] down in Mississippi. I didn't take the comparison as an insult.

'It was pretty disturbing to see people writing stuff like that. My life doesn't involve gun nuts, usually, and I was struck by how these two – the racists and the gun nuts – came together in one package.'

While making *Bowling For Columbine,* Moore's path intersected that of his old friend Sam Riddle, not once but twice – an interesting coincidence that says a lot about American media, American politics and those who manage both.

Riddle was the media representative for Isaiah Shoels, the only black student killed by the teenage berserkers Eric Harris and Dylan Klebold. 'Our position is that hate pulled the trigger,' Riddle told me. 'It wouldn't have mattered if they'd had billy clubs or rocks or knives. They were bent on killing. It was a state of mind.' That's clearly true enough, but Riddle's implication that Shoels was *especially* hated because of his race seems as questionable as the claim – frequently made by evangelicals in the aftermath of the massacre – that student victim Cassie Bernall was 'martyred' because she refused to renounce Jesus. The possible deployment by the killers against Shoels of the most powerful word in the English language doesn't necessarily prove anything; people filled with hate will use any hook that presents itself, and Shoels's blackness might have been convenient for them rather than determinative. But we can't ask Harris and Klebold what they were thinking, so we'll never really know.

Riddle also represented the mother of the boy who shot Kayla Rowland. The section of the film that addresses her situation is the closest Moore ever comes to real policy engagement, and although it is a digression from his main themes, the fact that it is grounded in particular facts – very poignant facts, at that – with actual solutions makes it one of the most moving and effective parts of the film.

We learn that the boy's mother was kicked off public assistance by Michigan's draconian welfare-to-work laws. Without resources to care adequately for her child, she was forced to leave him with the crack-dealing uncle and to commute for hours every day to a fast-food restaurant in a white suburban mall, where she worked for the standard low wage provided by such jobs. Before Moore, the national media usually took the blame-the-monster-mother approach.[76] It took Moore's movie to raise the question of the consequences that follow when a society that professes to be concerned with 'family values' cuts loose its most vulnerable members and leaves them with only bad options.

In this part of the film, Moore truly raised some important points; and he also left himself vulnerable to even more reactionary attacks. The usually careful Dave Kopel, in his article cited above, makes an atypically specious argument that lets the state of Michigan off the hook. And Michael Wilson, the director of the film *Michael Moore Hates America*, says that he was inspired to go after Moore by this very sequence in the film: 'My mom worked two full-time jobs when I was growing up and she went to school full-time. And I never shot anybody, you know? We were poor. I grew up in Missouri in a house that was right between the projects and the trailer court. My mom worked really long hours, but she put her job as a mother first, you know? And to me, that's what you do as a parent: you make choices; you're accountable.'[77] In saying this, Wilson – probably from pure naïveté, untainted by political malice – shows an enormous lack of understanding of the realities of class, realities that are so much at the heart of Moore's work.

Bowling For Columbine is a strange mix of facts, ideology and assumptions, a hodgepodge in which no particular positions or statements hold centre stage but are thrown out to the viewer almost at random, without any structure or attempt to build a consistent thesis. It's no wonder that its critics have not been kind.

David T Hardy and Jason Clarke, the authors of *Michael Moore Is A Big Fat Stupid White Man*, definitely don't like Moore and don't like the political left in general. They are not fanatics or ravers, however, and their book has much value. They spend a lot of time going over how Moore plays with chronology in his films, making the confusion of cause and effect serve his thesis. They show how, in *Bowling For Columbine*, Moore has refined the technique of deceptive editing that he developed in *Roger & Me*: he cuts and edits short snippets from two different speeches given by Charlton Heston more than a year apart, puts the edits together entirely out of order, presents them in such a way that the viewer assumes they are part of the same speech – one given at Denver just days after the Columbine massacre – by using cutaway edits to distract from Heston's apparent mid-speech change of clothes, and uses all of this to indicate that Heston is a callous fool who doesn't care or doesn't realise that the people of Denver and its suburbs have just been traumatised by a terrible crime. In fact, as Hardy and Clarke point out, far from being blusteringly defiant, Heston and the NRA cancelled every event associated with their Denver meeting out of respect for the victims of Columbine, with the single exception of their officers' meeting – which had been planned two years previously and which, as a chartered association, they were legally obligated to hold at that time and place, unless they could notify their millions of members of a change in plan in the few days remaining before the scheduled meeting, clearly an impossibility.

Hardy and Clarke also spot some of the setups in Moore's sandbagging interview with Heston and prove, through a careful examination of the camera angles, that Heston could not have still been on the scene when Moore makes his ridiculous, exploitative plea on behalf of the murdered little girl.

Bowling For Columbine's problems as a documentary didn't prevent it from accruing honour, fame and riches. In addition to its Oscar, Moore took home the Cannes International Film Festival's special 55th anniversary Palme for *Columbine* in 2002 – the first time in 50 years that a documentary had been in contention – which set the stage for his 2004 Palme d'Or for *Fahrenheit 9/11*. *Columbine* won awards at international film festivals from Amsterdam to São Paulo, Australia, Sweden, Norway, Vancouver, Toronto and many other places where the film's thesis about the basic anti-sociability of Americans found a warm response.

Bowling For Columbine won plaudits at home as well as abroad, scooping awards all over the United States, including the Dallas/Fort Worth Film Critics' Association Award. Made for around $4 million, in six months it grossed over $21 million in the United States and over $35 million abroad. That's not even counting DVD and video rights, where most movies make their real money. This was absolutely astonishing for a documentary. It was unprecedented.

But, of course, what really cemented *Columbine*'s place in American culture was Moore's behaviour at the Academy Awards. Everyone who has any interest at all in politics or films knows what he did. In March 2003, with the bombs falling in Iraq, Moore took to the stage in tuxedo and baseball cap and didn't abide by the unwritten law of the tightly scripted, harshly time-limited Academy ceremony: thank your actors, your parents, God, and be gone.

Clutching his golden man, Moore addressed the elephant in the public room. With other documentary filmmakers on stage with him, Moore famously said, 'I've invited my fellow documentary nominees on the stage with us. They are here in solidarity with me because we like non-fiction. We like non-fiction and we live in fictitious times. We live in a time when we have fictitious election results that elect a fictitious President. We live in a time where we have a man sending us to war for fictitious reasons, whether it is the fiction of duct tape or the fiction of orange alerts. We are against this war, Mr Bush. Shame on you, Mr Bush. Shame on you. And any time that you have the Pope and The Dixie Chicks against you, your time is up.'[78]

In an irony little remarked upon, the rich movie people in the audience cheered while the working-class technical people booed. On the bonus features disk that accompanies the DVD release of *Bowling For Columbine*, Moore, speaking with theatrical humility to the camera in a back yard 'somewhere in Michigan', explains his unorthodox acceptance speech: 'They had just honoured me for my film, a film that was about guns, violence, American violence, American violence exported to other countries...so my comments were very much in keeping with this film...If I'd made a film about birds or insects, then maybe it wouldn't have been appropriate... I try to live my life in an honest and sincere way, and at the end of the day, I'm Michael Moore. What else am I going to do?'

The speech was a supremely calculated grab for national attention, whether for Moore's movie, for opposition to the war in Iraq, for Moore himself – it hardly matters. Indeed, most commentary on the incident, from both left and right, seemed unconcerned with the distinction. The speech and the accompanying publicity may well have improved box-office takings for both *Columbine* and Moore's forthcoming *Fahrenheit 9/11*, but it also spawned endless right-wing screeds and internet rants – far too many to begin to attribute here – on how Moore was a traitor who worked against the troops and the President in wartime and, more diabolically and significantly, someone who *represented the left and all opposition to George W Bush*.

There were people close to Moore who understood the danger here. His wife, Kathleen Glynn, was reported to be unhappy with his outburst. Sam Riddle told me that a week before the incident, when Moore's film was in nomination, he'd emailed Moore and told him, 'I know what you're thinking of doing. Don't do it.'

And Moore understood who he was dealing with: 'I forgot that the right wing and the conservatives don't really believe in free speech. They were not going to give me my 45 seconds uninterrupted and then boo if they wanted to. Their job was to try and stop me from saying another word.'[79]

Moore's speech was an easy hook on which the right hung the following non-sequiturs: to question Bush's legitimacy is to hate America, to be a whiny ideological has-been, an elitist Hollywood slob (the right was certainly not above bringing Moore's weight into the equation, and the fortuitous Hollywood location gave the right's billionaire-and-corporate-funded attack machine yet another opportunity to go after the 'liberal elite'). For many Americans, both left and right, this was the moment that Moore became indelibly associated with the left and with opposition to Bush. It was a controversy that would linger and bloat in the blogosphere.

It hardly mattered that nothing Moore had said – with the possible over-estimation of the powers of the Pope and The Dixie Chicks – was factually incorrect. He had offended some deeply rooted American sense of propriety, one that, for many, transcended political loyalty.

Bowling For Columbine's success meant that Moore was free, as an artist and as a political activist, to do whatever he wanted. As with Mel Gibson after his *The Passion Of The Christ* broke box-office records for an independently distributed film, there would now always be a sufficient number of studios that would court Moore to assure him that those concerned about the controversy would never be able to turn their backs and prevent him from working. But the success of *Columbine* also had a certain slow-motion, built-in drawback.

The film captured very well the fears and concerns of many Americans regarding gun culture and violence, but its flaws would be noticed, and noticed anew, when Moore took on even larger causes. The film is emotionally satisfying in many ways, but there is nothing in it that stands up to statistical analysis or even deductive logic, and several viewings can reduce it to a joke.

It's more than likely that, in the cold light of day, as the problems with *Bowling For Columbine* as a documentary began to be widely known, this fact contributed to a certain wariness towards Moore on the part of many who were in a position to make institutional judgments and, combined with similar questions about his next blockbuster, seriously contributed to keeping *Fahrenheit 9/11* out of the running for the 2004 Academy Awards.

Part 3

Spokesman For The Left

6 Ascendancy

On 6 November 2000, the day before the American presidential election, Michael Moore was a successful documentary filmmaker who'd worked in television and had written a left-populist, lowbrow book of political entertainment. He'd stirred up a lot of people and gained a fan base with his first film, *Roger & Me*. He'd made a bit of money, and this – along with his television exposure, his book *Downsize This!* and his films – gave him something of a platform. He'd created the Michael Moore brand. But could he really be said to be influencing the way Americans think, or a major figure on the political scene? Certainly few on what passes for the left in the United States would have identified him as a national spokesman for progressive causes, although perhaps he could be counted on, in general, to be in tune with the left agenda.

One factor in Moore's rise is the political background of his times. Commentators like Rush Limbaugh and his many imitators had been changing the tone of political discourse for many years and had already been greatly successful in turning political commentary into a sort of national cockfight, drawing blood for savage entertainment value. Rush, however, is merely the end result of a very long-term and very successful right-wing plan to dominate American opinion.

Motivated by Lyndon Johnson's crushing defeat of Barry Goldwater in 1964, American conservatives fell back, regrouped and developed a comprehensive plan to move the centre of political discourse farther to the right. Central to the development of this plan were right-wing activists such as William F Buckley, Richard Mellon Scaife, the Coors family, conservative strategist Paul Weyrich – a former journalist and founder of the Heritage Foundation and a member of the boards of many other right-wing institutions – and the Trostskyist-turned-reactionary Irving Kristol. They realised that the key lay with access to the media.

These activists were helped by a young reporter named Kevin Phillips – at that time a conservative – whose 1968 book *The Emerging Republican Majority* laid out the blueprint for absorbing Southerners alienated from the Democratic Party by civil-rights laws and racial integration. Although Buckley has occasionally made noises of disdain for the more loony, John Birch-type elements of the Republican coalition (Robert Welch, the founder of the John Birch Society, wrote that President Dwight Eisenhower was 'consciously serving the Communist conspiracy...for all his adult life'),[80] and for the out-and-out racists on the fringes of the right, he has also written against desegregation and against civil rights.[81] The conservative movement that Buckley shepherded from its intellectual founding in the heat of the Goldwater campaign to its triumph in the election of Reagan and the electoral coup of George W Bush has never been shy of extremism; it has embraced radical anti-government agitators like Grover Norquist of the innocuously named Americans for Tax Reform and Stephen Moore of the Club for Growth, and it has quietly encouraged the racist fringe.

Scaife, a generous funder of an enormous web of far-right institutions, has personally contributed millions of dollars to the cause over the years, funding organisations that promulgated rumours that Bill Clinton and his administration were involved in murder and drug dealing. Scaife also donated several million dollars to the right-wing magazine *The American Spectator* while it was engaged in what it called its 'Arkansas Project', the attempt to dig up personal and political dirt on Bill and Hillary Clinton in Arkansas. This investigation first brought Paula Jones to the nation's attention, with results that we now know all too well. In 1981, when questioned about his largesse to the right by reporter Karen Rothmeyer, Scaife famously replied, 'You fucking communist cunt. Get out of here.'[82] So much for the chivalry of conservative values.

Media matters have always been a central part of the right-wing agenda. The resurgent conservative movement was greatly helped by libertarian right-winger Edith Efron's 1971 book *The News Twisters*. In this volume, Efron compiled disputed statistics that purported to show left-wing bias in the news and concluded that the network news under the prevailing 'fairness doctrine' was biased against conservative opinion that she considered mainstream – as well as against radical left-wing opinion far out of the mainstream. She argued that merely expanding the range of opinion would be inadequate, and that the only real solution was complete privatisation and deregulation of television news, which would allow the American public to get the news it wanted by a 'dollar vote'. Note that Efron's proposed solution gives no value to any attempt to find an objective truth, only for the most popular preferences about subjective truth; note also that it hands a distinct advantage in public debate to the private broadcasters with the deepest pockets. Private, unregulated television news did not exist when *The News Twisters* was published. The subsequent success of Fox News – an extremely conservative outlet whose reporting is often challenged on the facts, but which nevertheless wins Efron's popular 'dollar vote' – should be read as a cautionary tale by anyone who questions both Efron's proposal and her motives

These have been the marching orders of the radical right ever since, and in a campaign massively funded by elitist billionaires like Scaife (heir to a banking and oil fortune), the Olin family (armaments and chemicals), the Buckley family (oil), the Coors family (brewing), the Koch family (oil), the Bradley family (automobile parts), the Smith Richardson family (Vicks Vapo-Rub) and the foundations that the above individuals and families have endowed, the right has been massively successful.

Right-wing radicals now oversee a vast network of 'think tanks' like the American Enterprise Institute, the Cato Foundation, the Heritage Foundation, the Hoover Institute, the Manhattan Institute and many others that nurture ideology-driven scholarship and publish it in non-peer-reviewed journals, then place their 'experts' as 'legitimate' commentators on mainstream news programmes. Scaife and these other angels of the right make a practice of subsidising these 'scholars' – Michael Novak, Dinesh D'Souza, Robert Bork,[83] William Bennett and Newt Gingrich, to name only a few[84] – with cushy grants that allow them, ironically, to write and make a very good living free of the realities of the market. The right-wing foundations then buy in bulk the books that their writers produce, giving them away or selling them below cost to conservative book clubs, thereby both expanding their readership and propelling them up the bestseller lists – again, free of market realities.

Political radio, too, is a vast wilderness of right-wing rants. A network of right-wing websites and 'news' digests – many of them also funded by the right-wing foundations – feed right-wing rumours to right-wing talk-radio and television stations, whence – anxious lest they be scooped or, even worse, accused of a liberal bias – the 'respectable' media often pick them up, after a little fact-checking.

The US cable networks aren't much better. Here, hard-right hosts and guests greatly outnumber even tepid liberals in both roles, and when there is a 'liberal' side to the debate it is usually a professional journalist with a considered and balanced, factual approach who is paired with a political ideologue supplied by one of the right-wing foundations. With the repeal of laws regulating media monopolies and of the federal 'fairness doctrine', there is little recourse against this type of thing.

US right-wing media 'watchdogs' have so intimidated the network broadcasters that the same patterns prevail there. The real conundrum is that liberalism, by definition, requires a hearing for both sides of any political argument: *The New York Times*'s op-ed page runs two regular far-right columnists (David Brooks and John Tierney), two middle-of-the-road liberals who often praise right-wing ideas (Thomas Friedman and Nicholas Kristof), one unpredictable stylist who has written scathingly of both George W Bush and Bill Clinton (Maureen Dowd), one political liberal who is an ambivalent economic liberal (Paul Krugman) and two all-round liberals (Bob Herbert and Frank Rich).

Conservatives also greatly outnumber liberals on the op-ed page of *The Washington Post*, which runs both George F Will and Charles Krauthammer in syndication. William Kristol, the son of Irving Kristol and major force in right-wing politics, and Grover Norquist appear frequently on National Public Radio. Even *The New Yorker* has been known to run commentary by William F Buckley, most recently an essay on the work of Westbrook Pegler, a prolific journalist most active in the 1930s and 1940s who in many ways pre-figured the political positions and attitude, if not the style, of Rush Limbaugh. It is inconceivable, however, that Buckley's *National Review* would ever publish an equivalent erudite Grand Old Man of the left – Gore Vidal, say (even if the personal and legal feud between Buckley and Vidal did not exist).

Buckley's magazine would not do this because conservative media has room for only conservative ideas. Yes, Alexander Cockburn was once the house leftist of *The Wall Street Journal*, but that was years ago and there's a great deal of room for suspicion of the *Journal*'s motivation in hiring him.[85] Compared to the space that the supposedly liberal *New York Times* gives to conservatives, the number of column inches that the *Journal* is willing to give to non-conservative points of view is minuscule, while no commentator to the left of Oliver North will *ever* grace the pages of *The Washington Times* under its present management. Two of 'liberal' New York's conservative papers, the *Post* and the *Sun*, routinely insert right-wing political commentary into their news stories. Imagine what their editorial pages are like.[86]

The situation is particularly tragic in the United States because there are no effective public media. The UK has a fiercely partisan for-profit media sector, but it also boasts a public media sector, the BBC, which is funded by annual licensing fees for media access and overseen by a non-partisan Board of Governors[87] in the public interest – a mechanism that results in one of the most impartial and respected news organisations in the world, where all sides are heard. In contrast, the American environment – in which a tiny, underfunded and only partially publicly funded National Public Radio and Public Broadcasting Service[88] are constantly under attack from conservatives and intimidated by them – in practice imposes a near-blackout on any medium that could be effective in getting out any point of view that contradicts that of the right. In such an environment, independent media – with its small distributional networks and its lack of resources for fact-checking and institutional checks and balances – naturally flourishes, and so does a hunger for alternative points of view.

Michael Moore had a tremendous opportunity here, and he took it. A big part of the Moore phenomenon is that he has been able to break out of the 'alternative' news ghetto, to short-circuit much of the media monopoly because his work makes money and corporations like Disney and Miramax want to make money. That is, as he says in an interview in the film *The Corporation*, 'the enormous hole in their capitalistic model that I can drive my truck through'. He fills a market niche that would otherwise be a vacuum only partially filled by obsessive bloggers and local protest sheets, and he's proven that he can show a return on investment. Since he's the only one doing both of these things, he has an enormous audience.[89]

The language of populist opposition has been a staple of American discourse since at least the days of the Revolution. It has always depended upon the articulation, as Michael Kazin puts it in his book *The Populist Persuasion*, of 'four clusters of beliefs: about Americanism, the people, elites and the need for mass movements'.[90] In different political ages, the polarity of populism has shifted from the political right to the left and back again and has often borrowed from the bedrock beliefs of both. In a classic contradiction that captures much about American political character, populist rhetoric has often insisted on self-reliance and a right to success that is limited only by one's individual merits, while condemning excess and the concentration of wealth within a social and economic elite.

In recent times, Republicans have captured populism and used it to advance the interests of the most privileged. It was no accident that Connecticut senator's son George HW Bush ate a lot of pork rinds in public (although he never really seemed to like them, and people noticed). Republicans have made a point of conspicuously enjoying NASCAR racing.[91] The right-wing syndicated columnist George Will enjoys the amusements – baseball, jazz – that were devised by a class he despises in order to ease the burdens imposed on it by the class for which he advocates.

Republicans, many of whom know better,[92] will even sink so low in their pursuit of populist appeal as to go along with the most regressive currents in American intellectual life. The Republican Party in Kansas and Georgia is at the forefront of efforts to discredit the teaching of evolution in public schools, thereby crippling the professional and intellectual prospects of any students who wish to study biology; and George W Bush himself has said that 'the jury is still out'[93] on evolution, which no doubt ensures him the votes of evangelical mass-media genius James Dobson's millions of followers. As Thomas Frank has described so well in his brilliant book *What's The Matter With America?*, these small tokens of fake solidarity have enabled the rich people who run and benefit from the Republican Party to convince working-class people to vote Republican and to militantly *demand* that the party cut taxes for their bosses and bust their unions.[94]

Republicans have somehow pushed these measures as 'revolts against elitism', while their leaders have been the most elite individuals and families in the nation: the blue-blooded, old-money William F Buckley; the aristocratic Bush family, which has been at the intersection of high finance, industry and politics in the US for 100 years; Richard Mellon Scaife; the Coors family; Malcolm Forbes, Jr, folksily known as Steve – these are the people who benefit from low taxes and reduced government services, and from taxing work rather than investments and capital gains, as the Republican Party is now bent on doing.

To this end, Republicans have worked hard to redefine the extreme right as encompassing 'normal' American values, although throughout much of American history the working-class has quite sensibly regarded the executive class as its adversary. Newt Gingrich, when he became Speaker of the House in 1995, frequently referred to Democrats as 'the enemies of ordinary Americans'; right-wing MSNBC commentator and former Reagan and George HW Bush speechwriter Peggy Noonan described Republican gains in 2002 as 'the triumph of the normal'.[95] The identification of the American working class with the interests of the plutocrats and businessmen who run the Republican Party is perhaps the best possible example of what the Italian Marxist theorist Antonio Gramsci called 'false class consciousness': the tragic and apparently universal human tendency to identify with the oppressor.

Erstwhile conservative activist Kevin Phillips understood well, and early, that the battle would be won on 'cultural' issues. Back in late 1972, when Nixon had just won a second term in a landslide election, Phillips bemoaned the fact that right-wing victories in 1968, 1970 and 1972 merely repudiated a left seen as violent and un-American but did not signify a national embrace of the right-wing agenda. How to get the people to give a real mandate to the right? '…the fulcrum of ideological gain is not adherence to classic conservatism, but rather hostility toward the emerging liberal elite of amorality activists and social-change merchants…'[96]

Phillips went on to say that practical matters that hinged on real differences of economic philosophy, such as wage and price controls, were the wrong approach. He recognised long before Newt Gingrich and Karl Rove that the appeal to moral righteousness was the way to achieve the right's objectives in the class war.

No matter whose interests the rhetoric actually served, American populism has always emphasised distrust of the high and mighty and faith in the humble striver, a prejudice that perhaps can be traced to the Calvinist influence on the American ideology. The trick consists in being exclusive enough to motivate with a sense of mission while being inclusive enough to have a shot at power. The Populists of the 1890s thought they'd got it right with their appeal to a broad coalition of 'producers' – farm workers and labourers – that also included movement radicals such as the various types of Christian socialists and adherents to the temperance and women's suffrage movements. The realities of power-seeking in America have usually meant that the rough edges of direct appeal to class or race or industrial sector are eventually filed down, but populist legitimacy still springs from a sacramental reverence for an idealised labourer – the rough, honest producer of the necessities of life – and, via association with this character, from true patriotism, unspoiled by privilege or station.

The politics that flow from this are by no means as predictable as one might think. The self-righteous polemics of Michael Moore and Bill O'Reilly are, in slightly different ways, both descended from those of the self-consciously working-class newspapers of the 1830s, in which Jacksonian editors like Horace Greeley of *The New York Tribune* and James Gordon Bennett of *The New York Herald* drew glowing moral lines between hardworking 'producers' and sinister elites. The split between modern left and right populism can be traced back, through many twists and turns, to the abandonment of the progressive economic agenda by religious reformers after the success of the broad social coalition that worked for the passage of Prohibition and, before that, to the split between the religious and economic constituencies of the Populists of the 1890s in the wake of that movement's political defeat.

The newfound (for Americans, anyway) reality of terrorism has made it easier for the right to appropriate the language of populism, which thrives on the political use of an external enemy to divert attention from matters closer to home. The patterns are drearily predictable. Michael Kazin, in *The Populist Persuasion*, directs us to Richard Hofstadter. Speaking of the very first fully American populist age – that of Andrew Jackson – Hofstadter wrote: '...class struggles did not flourish in states like Tennessee until the frontier stage was about over. The task of fighting the Indians gave all classes a common bond and produced popular heroes among the upper ranks.'[97]

To get a fuller sense of what Moore is up against from the right, take a look at Kazin's description of the contemporary cult of Andrew Jackson, which resonates eerily today: 'Jackson's reputation as an uncompromising foe of the Indians, a man of action who scoffed at negotiations and legal formalities, was of immeasurable aid to his political career, especially in the South and West, where "removal" of the "savages" found overwhelming support. Jackson's journalistic backers…praised him as an "untutored genius" who cut to the heart of the Indian problem and solved it swiftly. They contrasted Jackson's candid, blunt approach with the outraged opposition to Cherokee removal voiced by John Quincy Adams and Chief Justice John Marshall, whose university learning and sense of racial guilt allegedly paralysed their manly faculties.'[98]

Populism's dark side comes out in other ways, too. There is a negative, brooding strain of American populism that has never been politically successful in the long run. Given the industrial and labour history of Flint, it is probably no accident that one of the most influential radio personalities of the 1930s, Father Charles Coughlin, found a comfortable broadcast home in Royal Oak, Michigan, half an hour's drive from Michael Moore's home town. The story of Father Coughlin offers some very interesting parallels with that of Moore, although these parallels are much more analogous than exact.

For much of his career, Coughlin preached politics in a classic populist style, condemning the machinations of the world's bankers and the 'money power' that conspired to steal the hard-earned living of the working man and keep him humiliated and subordinate. Coughlin's ideas grew out of the Catholic Church's social doctrines and its responses to the Industrial Age, but were seldom restrained by them. He shared his Church's hatred of communism and socialism so that, while he inveighed against the bankers and plutocrats who kept the working man down by controlling his access to capital, he was forced to a certain vagueness as to how this situation was to be remedied.[99]

As he made political miscalculations and found himself

increasingly marginalised, Coughlin's paranoia grew and he began to ride a legitimate proposition to sinister conclusions. Starting in the mid-1930s, his attacks on an international banking elite gradually gave way to attacks on communists, and then on Jews. Karl Marx was not merely an ideological foe but a 'German Hebrew', and even poor Alexander Hamilton was a Jew who had founded the federal banking system. By 1938, Coughlin's newspaper *Social Justice* was excerpting *The Protocols Of The Elders Of Zion*.

In 1941 Archbishop Edward Mooney of Detroit told him that it was enough; his broadcasts were to stop. Several months later, after Pearl Harbor, Mooney conveyed a message from Attorney General Francis Biddle: publication of *Social Justice*, too, would stop. Coughlin's demons had finally ripped the mask from his populism, exposing the twisted need in his soul that had produced many powerful speeches. The world saw, and the world turned away.

In articulating the potential damage of the right-wing agenda, Michael Moore sometimes draws on the sunny 'producerist' populist style and sometimes on the negative, paranoid populism that shares roots with Coughlin. His tendency to romanticise the lives of working-class people – as when he talks about the social solidarity of the union meeting – is an example of the first type and usually works better for him than the second type, which includes his tendency to sketch sinister conspiracies and to talk about how stupid Americans are. When he goes negative, he is a man only his die-hard fans can love (although, admittedly, there are many of them); when he is positive, he seems to be straining for a type of banal communication that someone like Michael Wilson, director of the film *Michael Moore Hates America*, has completely mastered.

Knowledge of the right's domination of the media and the desperate need for someone who could get around it, along with his populist media skills, meant that Michael Moore appeared as a saviour in certain quarters. But two things in particular – two things squarely in the realm of action, not of thought or commentary – pushed many on the left into Moore's capacious embrace.

The first was the Republican attempt to unseat a sitting Democratic President on specious grounds involving his personal life. This pathetic morality play had two affects: it made non-conservatives very aware of the lengths to which conservatives would go to seize power, and it made some of them seriously consider playing by the same rules.[100]

Call the Lewinsky case the prelude. More than anything else – more than the war in Iraq – the event that primed non-conservatives for bare-knuckled political brawling was the election of 2000. Many Americans believed at the time, and still believe, that that election was stolen.

In order to understand the anger against Republicans and conservatives, in order to see how Michael Moore's polemics could come as a relief, we have to look at some of the facts in that election. The tale of the 2000 election can be told as a conspiracy theory, one that is not so far-fetched. Consider:

- The election was determined by Florida's 27 electoral college votes.

- George W Bush's brother was Governor of Florida.

- Bush's cousin, John Ellis, was a Fox News analyst who called the election for George W before all the votes were in.[101]

Bush's Florida campaign manager, Katherine Harris, whose job it was to help him to win the election, was also the Florida Secretary of State[102], charged with running a fair and impartial election. Harris had spent the two years prior to the election purging the voter lists of felons, who are not eligible to vote under Florida law. In the process she had kicked thousands of legitimately registered Democrats off the rolls, using a 'scrub list' supplied by Texas contractor ChoicePoint, a company whose officers had made heavy donations to Republicans. The net percentage of voters improperly deleted from the rolls was significantly higher in solidly Democratic districts than it was in solidly Republican districts. Although repeatedly and explicitly told that her methodology was flawed and that it was disproportionately disenfranchising Democrats who were in fact legitimate voters, Harris refused to stop or re-examine the purge (although counties had the right not to participate, and several, appalled at the inaccuracy of the data, did not).

When it came time to vote, affluent white counties used voting technology that had a low rate of invalidation of ballots, so that in Leon County, for example, only 1 in 500 ballots was 'spoiled', whereas in poorer, blacker, more Democratic counties such as nearby Gadsden County, one in eight ballots was rejected.

Bush won the state by only 537 votes – well within the statistical margin of error – and this triggered an automatic recount. When Miami–Dade County's recount started to show Gore gaining, a threatening demonstration was staged outside the county offices that intimidated the officials into stopping the recount. Although the demonstrators claimed to be a spontaneous grassroots crowd, it later turned out that they were a group comprising Republican Congressional staffers and at least one Republican Congressman.[103] John Sweeney, a representative from New York, was heard to shout, 'Shut it down!'[104] – that is, shut down the recount, a legal process put in place by the institutions of democracy.

As the recount battle dragged on, the Republicans sent lawyers who successfully argued that the recount must allow the legitimacy of votes to be judged under the strictest standards in Democratic districts and under the loosest standards in Republican districts.

It happened that military absentee ballots for Bush had glaring irregularities: some ballots had no postmark, some were incompletely filled out or requested by someone other than the voter, some were filed after the deadline, and so on. Democratic vice-presidential candidate Joe Lieberman generously proclaimed that, while some of the military ballots might have been questionable, it looked too bad to go after the military vote, so the Democrats dropped that line of challenge.

Although Gore had originally wanted to recount only ballots in strong Democratic counties, the Florida Supreme Court ordered a statewide hand recount of *all* ballots. The Bush campaign, however, couldn't accept this and Bush brought suit at the Supreme Court, demanding that all recounting stop. In *Bush vs Gore*, five justices – all of them appointed by Republican Presidents – ruled that irreparable harm would be done to Bush if the statewide recounting team was given a few more weeks to count every vote carefully. They said that Bush's 14th Amendment right to equal protection (an ammendment which these same justices had refused to enforce in many other contexts, especially when asked to go against state courts – as they were in this case – ruling that it was an unconstitutional interference with states' rights) was somehow at stake, even though it was the Republicans who were demanding different counting standards in different districts. The Supreme Court stopped the recount, in effect making Bush President.

The five justices who decided the case in Bush's favour were known, or quite reasonably presumed to be, Republican partisans in their personal lives. Justice Sandra Day O'Connor, on first hearing that Gore was apparently the winner on the close election night, had been overheard to remark, 'Gore won? That's terrible!' Justice Antonin Scalia's son Eugene was employed by a firm that worked for the Bush campaign, and he had already nailed down a job with the incoming Bush administration in the Department of Labor, if Bush were to become President. Justice Clarence Thomas's wife, Virginia Lamp Thomas, was employed by the conservative Heritage Foundation to review résumés submitted for appointments in a possible Bush administration. All three judges refused to recuse themselves and all three ruled for Bush.[105]

After the election, a consortium of news groups examined the ballots and found that, if one counted ballots in which voters had both punched Gore's name and written it in (surely the 'intent of the voter' is not obscure in this case), a statewide recount would have shown a Gore victory.

Jake Tapper, Greg Palast, Jeffrey Toobin and many others have done some excellent reporting on the 2000 election, and there are good books on the Supreme Court decision by Vincent Bugliosi (the LA district attorney who prosecuted Charles Manson) and Alan Dershowitz. Moore himself did a pretty good job of explaining what happened in his book *Stupid White Men*, whose section on Florida, 2000, was a brief foray into seriousness and coherence and a far better summary of the subject than the one Moore presents in *Fahrenheit 9/11*. Of course, there have also been many books and columns from the right disputing these conclusions, but they've never shaken the evidence gathered by Tapper and Palast and the many people who have documented what went on behind the scenes of the election.

The outrage lingers and can't be assuaged – certainly not by the protests at Bush's 2001 inauguration, which I observed and which Michael Moore discusses in the opening sequence of *Farhenheit 9/11*. In that film, Moore describes Bush's armoured limo being hit with eggs and forced to stop and says that Bush was not able to make the traditional walk for the last few blocks of the route. This last part is not true; Bush did get out and walk, but not very far, and only when he was in the safe, restricted zone among his ticket-holding supporters.

I remember that the fury was like a living thing. There was applause from the Republican stands when Bush and Dick Cheney took the stage, but the boos and calls of 'Thief!' from the crowd were quite audible on the steps. Chief Justice William Rehnquist got the biggest applause from the Republican bleachers, which struck me as candid acknowledgment of what had happened. There was a *pro forma* line in Bush's speech thanking Clinton for his service to the nation, and the new President looked startled and confused when this line got big applause from the crowd.

The police had to delay the parade because a group of protesters had burst through the police lines at 14th and Pennsylvania and were blocking the route. Finally, when the motorcade rolled, there were really loud boos and taunts as the cars turned onto Pennsylvania Avenue. Bush must have heard it. I can testify that, just as Moore showed it in *Fahrenheit 9/11*, the street was very densely packed with signs reading HAIL TO THE THIEF!, ILLEGITIMATE!, GORE GOT MORE! and BUSH CHEATED! He must have seen them. It wasn't just in one place along the route, either; it was all along it. In some places, the protesters were the very large majority, and they were loud.

They were in no mood for finesse, either. Michael Moore might be a loudmouth who occasionally makes unjustified, even scurrilous attacks on Bush, but many of those who knew that Bush stole the 2000 election thought, 'Well, more power to Moore.' The election showed that it was no time for fine-grained reason and delicate, balanced argument in political debate. What was wanted was a return to democracy itself. Yes, and revenge. The blunter the instrument, the better. A significant part of the broad opposition to Bush was ready to coalesce around a star.

7 A Debate About Reality

On 28 July 2004, there was a showing of Michael Moore's *Fahrenheit 9/11* in Crawford, Texas, the adopted home town of George W Bush. The showing was arranged by the Crawford Peace House, the Waco and Dallas branches of the Friends of Peace and John Young, a columnist at *The Waco Tribune*.

Waco is the nearest town to Crawford that is large enough to have movie theatres, but *Fahrenheit* wasn't playing there – not because the cinemas refused to play it, as some locals thought and as Young suggested in his columns, but because the Wallace Theaters chain, which owns all the screens in Waco, was having a dispute with Lion's Gate Films over how to split the take from a previous Lion's Gate release: an adaptation of Marvel Comics' *The Punisher*. Conspiracy made a better story, though, and there certainly were upstanding citizens of Waco who were trying to keep the film unseen and out of their town.

John Young and the Peace House thought that people should have a chance to see it, and the symbolism of showing it in Crawford was certainly not lost on them. Michael Moore himself promised to show up, inviting George W Bush to join him. (Moore likes nothing better than to write open letters to Bush, and may well believe that Bush reads them.) Bush had no comment, and in the event neither man showed.

Lots of other people did turn up, though. The movie was shown on some portable equipment set up by the Alamo Draft House of Austin in a nearby park and was viewed by a few thousand people, most of whom didn't like Bush. Although the $8 admission charge was supposed to be waived for card-carrying Republicans (the organisers said that they did not want to preach to the converted), most of the Republicans who wanted to see the film were asked to pay.

Galvanised by the prospect of disrespect towards their leader, Republican Party activists of McLennan County had mobilised several hundred protesters. Rather than allow any of what they considered Moore's propaganda to wash their brains, most of the Republicans stood and heckled from the sidelines rather than watch the film. Near the end of the evening, perpetrators unknown dumped several tons of bagged manure on the parking lot of the local middle school – the place where TV anchors do their standups when Bush is in town – and sped off, making a pungent statement of contempt for the media. Local police officers had to clean it up. If the perpetrators are ever caught, Crawford Police Chief Donnie Tidmore told me, they will be charged with illegal dumping.

I guess it was the shit that got me out to Texas. Since I was writing a book about the political and cultural significance of Michael Moore, I couldn't pass up this sort of mudslinging. A week later I was heading west out of Waco on Farm Road 185, into the heart of darkness, seeing the billboard for the Brazos Electrical Co-operative that reads, SUPPLYING POWER TO THE PRESIDENT AND FIRST LADY – and, in much smaller letters, AND OTHER RESIDENTS OF MCLENNAN COUNTY.

For a man whose just-folks act won him a lot of Texas votes, Bush is treated around Waco with an almost royal reverence. Huge pictures of him and the First Lady mark the road at both ends of town; Bush wears an expression that is not too thoughtful, not too smiley: that of a simple but honest son of the soil who means what he says and says what he means.

After stopping off at the Yellow Rose of Texas gift shop, which displays slogans suggesting that we will win the war on terror in spite of the obstructionism of the liberal elites, it's already clear that Crawford has fully bought into the 'red state' mythos: Westerners are real Americans, straightforward folk who prize their own everyday competence, are incapable of irony and don't need anyone else's help in this world, certainly not that of effete Eastern establishment latté-sipping intellectuals. This is complete nonsense, of course. The American West is much more dependent on the East than vice versa, but this mistaken belief in Western independence is no doubt comforting.[106]

I was going to see Cathy Horton, a local Republican woman who describes herself as 'an activist and an environmentalist'. We met at the Coffee Station, at the only real crossroads in this small town, where Bush has been known to drop in to chat and where partisan feeling runs so deep that not only is the entire place covered in Bush–Cheney paraphernalia and anti-Clinton and anti-Kerry signs (FLUSH THE JOHNS IN '04!) but the only ketchup served is Hunt's (wouldn't want to add to the [Teresa] Heinz [Kerry] fortune).

Horton is intense. She asks me directly about my politics but is not fazed when I tell her I'm a Democrat. Her sister is, too, she tells me, and they get on but don't discuss politics. Her startlingly light eyes flash as she tells me what a great job President Bush is doing. She is one of the people who organised hundreds to come out and protest the Moore film, calling everyone she knew and everyone on her list of McLennan County Republican volunteers, using mass email, alerting the media. She tells me that she is well informed and gets her news and views from a diverse range of sources: from *Hannity & Colmes* to Bill O'Reilly, even though 'it's really hard to find conservative sources in the media. You have to

really dig for the conservative point of view. I watch *Hannity &
Colmes*. They give both sides. They're balanced. You can flip over
to CNN and see what they say, too.'

When I suggest to her that the media is dominated by right-
wing propaganda, she recoils from me in astonishment. 'I'm just
amazed that you could think that,' she says.

Our conversation drifts to a discussion of September 11 and
her plans for an elaborate McLennan County monument to the
vistims of the terrorist attacks, freedom and America's wars. She
tells me how, on that memorable day, she drove the rural route to
her son's school and pulled him out of class, there in the rolling
landscape of central Texas. There was no way of knowing what
was going to happen next. Horton's plans for the monument feature
a 'liberty tree' and a granite slab commemorating the victims. There
will also be slabs for each of the many fire and police departments
that responded on that day. And still more slabs, one for each of
America's wars since World War I. There will be a Texas flag that
was flown over the state Capitol on the 2002 anniversary of the
attacks, and an American flag that was flown over the national
Capitol. Horton tried to get pieces of the World Trade Center itself,
but these were no longer available. She did, however, get a piece
of the wreckage from the Pentagon.

It turns out that she did not attend the screening: 'I have no idea
what happened there. It was their chance to voice their opinions.
They have the right to do it. I didn't need to be there. I have my
own agenda.'

Of all the Republicans I asked about the film and their protests
of it, only one had actually seen it. MA Taylor, chairman of the
McLennan County Republican Party and a former member of the
Texas legislature, told me he hadn't seen it and probably never would,
but that it was important for Republicans to get out and protest. 'I
think what you saw here was that there were a great many people

who were looking for an opportunity to get out there and support the President.' Many people like Cathy Horton did just that. Like her concern for the symbolic content of a largely imagined polity, there is much power in a shared belief about the world.

At the Crawford Peace House, on the other side of the train tracks from the Coffee Station, the ambience is quite different. I sat on the porch there and spoke with Joshua Collier, a sharply intelligent and articulate young man who for the last four years had been living in Ecuador, where he'd gone to study Spanish and Women's Studies, staying on to teach world history at a private school and to work as a production assistant at the International Women's Dance Festival. He's the resident assistant at the Peace House, which means that he greets visitors and the press and provides a welcoming atmosphere for this lonely outpost of opposition to Bush in Crawford.

Collier insists that the Peace House is not just anti-war but pro-peace, that they are in the business of providing real alternatives to war. When I press him on this, however, the alternative he offers is 'creating a more diverse discussion' about the war rather than uncritically accepting the government line as presented in the mainstream media. He tells me that the point of bringing 9/11 to Crawford was not to promote the film but to promote discussion, to get people to see each other as 'people first, and then people who have politics'. He walked me out to where the film was shown, in a lovely little tree-ringed field near a swimming hole and a picturesque waterfall, watching me carefully the whole time with a sharp and quizzical eye – never confrontational, never less than friendly. He hadn't quite made up his mind about me.

When I came back the next day, there was an event that might have been right out of 1969, without the anger, drugs or violence: earnest young people in tie-dye, strumming guitars and proclaiming that 'peace is possible'; poems read in honour of the life spirit of the universe; a vegan buffet. Collier gave an intelligent and insightful talk on the rush to war with Iraq, in focused counterpoint to the surfeit of vague brotherly love. The event as a whole struck me as being exactly as relevant to the real problems of international relations and of war and peace as Cathy Horton's odd mélange of patriotic signifiers.

To its credit, the Jewell 16 multiplex in Waco did eventually show *Fahrenheit 9/11*, even though the management had received hundreds of letters urging it to suppress such 'propaganda'. I'd seen the film in New York, where the audience (I think I'm on safe ground when I say that there were few Republicans present) loved the film, were deeply moved by it and saw it as a decisive and irrefutable blow against Bush, so I wanted to see it in Texas. I asked a teenage employee of the cinema who'd seen the film several times what he thought of it. After making me promise to protect his identity ('We're not supposed to say a word about this to the press'), he said, 'I think Moore's a brilliant propagandist, but the film is nonsense. He gets Bush totally wrong and twists all the facts.'

What you take away from the film is what you bring with you.

Waco is an endless landscape of shopping malls and car dealerships amid highways, thrown down without any apparent plan, relieved only by the elegant but very small umbra of Baylor University. It's not surprising that people there would look to their churches for fellowship; there is apparently very little other public space, few other public institutions.

Outside of Waco, the countryside is lovely, with rolls of harvested hay sitting in the fields, gently rolling hills that cradle expanses of ranch. Driving around in this bucolic landscape, looking at the cows as George W Bush supposedly loves to do, I found it instructive to listen to the radio programme of the evangelist James Dobson's Family Research Council. A woman's voice speaks to me in the most dire tones: 'A scientific study released recently by the Beverly LaHaye Institute[107] shows that John Kerry's policies are so unfriendly to families that the institution of the family may be entirely unrecognisable after four years of a Kerry administration, if it even exists at all.'

I felt as if I'd entered a parallel universe where none of the rules of logic or induction that I know apply. It occurred to me that this is what arguments about *Fahrenheit 9/11* are all about – not whether or not Michael Moore manipulates the facts (many people who despise Bush think that he does) but about the very nature of reality and the rules that we use to assess it. That's why things that didn't matter quite so much in the past – an election, a movie – suddenly matter a great deal more. No less than we do when we debate whether or not Saddam really had weapons of mass destruction, we're arguing about what is real and what is an illusion.

Fahrenheit 9/11 got noticed. It won awards even before hitting the theatres. Its premiere was a cultural and sociological event. Leonardo DiCaprio was there. Salman Rushdie was there. So were Spike Lee, Tom Brokaw, Lauren Bacall and Martha Stewart.

If some were excited about the film and happy to see it, others took a different view. Citizens United, a right-wing political organisation led by commentator and Clinton investigator David Bossie, filed a complaint with the Federal Election Commission about the film, claiming that advertisements for it violated federal election laws. Another group, Move America Forward, tried to stop the film from being shown at all, writing to cinema managers and asking them not to show 'Michael Moore's horrible anti-American movie'.[108] Clearly, there was serious political opposition to the film.

Louis Menand wrote a scholarly piece in *The New Yorker* in which he explored the historical evolution of the idea of the objective documentary, tying his observations to *Fahrenheit 9/11*.

The volatile cultural critic Christopher Hitchens, meanwhile –
currently of indeterminate political orientation – wrote a blistering
riposte that introduces his subject thus: 'To describe this film as
dishonest and demagogic would almost be to promote those terms
to the level of respectability. To describe this film as a piece of crap
would be to run the risk of a discourse that would never again rise
above the excremental... *Fahrenheit 9/11* is a sinister exercise in
moral frivolity crudely disguised as an exercise in seriousness.'[109]

In a pre-release screening in May, the film won the Palme d'Or
at the Cannes International Film Festival, and the screening was
followed by a 20-minute standing ovation. Moore was somewhat
more gracious on this occasion than he was in accepting his Academy
Award for *Bowling For Columbine*: 'I've forgotten to thank my
actors! Thank you, George Bush. Thank you, Dick Cheney. And
above all, thank you, Donald Rumsfeld for the love scene!'

The White House, unsurprisingly, was less happy. George W
Bush's campaign staff referred to the award privately as the 'Palme
de Bitch Slap', a term that originated with a correspondent on Jon
Stewart's *Daily Show*.[110]

The popularity of the film was helped along by a shrewdly
manufactured controversy in the United States. The Disney
Corporation refused to distribute it, and Michael Moore got a
good deal of free publicity from claiming on his website, in TV
interviews[111] and in the press, that this was a last-minute betrayal
of an existing agreement, an attempt at political censorship aimed
at appeasing Disney's right-wing constituency. But Moore had in
fact been told a year before the film had been completed that Disney
would not distribute it, as he was later forced to admit.[112] Buoyed
by this sort of calculated conspiracist outrage, in its first week of
a limited American release the documentary grossed more than
the light comedies *White Chicks* and *Dodgeball*, both commercial
releases aimed at the core moviegoing demographic.

Fahrenheit 9/11 was proving to be more than a movie; it was a perceptual test, a magnetic pole of ideological attraction or repulsion charged by the brutish certainties and edgy uncertainties of a crucial moment in American politics.

There is no doubt that Moore is a talented filmmaker. The apparent sloppiness of his work is highly calculated, part of how he gets his audience to trust him. He seems to be taking the viewer aside and marvelling at a secret, lifting the curtain on special information that is all around us but that somehow we never knew about. How did Moore get all that film of the Bushes clowning with powerful Saudis, of Bush looking like an idiot whenever he's not primed by his handlers? How did Moore discover those connections between the Bushes and the bin Ladens?

Moore, like Bush, is certainly no intellectual, and he doesn't hide his own excitement at his discoveries. 'See what a guy with a high-school education can find out if he puts his mind to it?' he seems to be saying. 'All this stuff that *they* don't want you to know!' But those who really struggle to find the truth are left to ask, 'What is real in all of this?' If you care about that question, it's complicated.

There is some good stuff in *Fahrenheit 9/11*. When Moore leaves his undisciplined commentary behind, the film can be revealing. His most damning material is more personal than factual. There's something profoundly off about Bush shooting a bird and saying, 'Somebody say, "Nice shot!",' getting the praise he asked for and then saying, with fake modesty pitched to be charming, 'Thank you.' It reveals a great deal about a man of privilege who never questioned his luck, never doubted his right to the praise of sycophants and hangers-on. There's that painful moment when Bush gets halfway through a standard adage about 'Fool me once…', and it's clear from his face that he has no idea how it ends, so he improvises: 'Well, you don't get fooled again!' Look at him playing golf, making an announcement condemning terrorism – and, contrary to Moore's detractors, it really doesn't matter whether he's actually talking about al-Qaeda or Hezbollah – and then saying, 'Now watch this drive!' without missing a beat. Look at him preparing to make a speech about the nation going to war and fooling around like a six-year-old, profoundly unaware of the seriousness of the moment but no doubt aware that when he goes live, in a few moments, he will have to *appear* that he is aware it is a serious moment. It is in these scenes, when Moore – almost accidentally – peers into the soul of a little boy playing at being President, that the film has real power.

Ultimately, there is some truth here – the truth about Bush – and it is separate, or can be separated from, the means Moore uses to tell it. The truth is in the lives of Americans like Lila Lipscomb, and the segments of the film that focus on her and her family and the loss of her beloved son to Bush's imperial ambitions are deeply felt, as are those on the marine recruiters zeroing in on poor kids who have very few options in life.

Moore's interview with Sergeant Abdul Henderson is also very powerful. Henderson is clearly a man who thinks more than he speaks – an attractive and unusual quality – and he says softly, 'I will not let anyone send me back over there to kill other poor people.' Sergeant Henderson's quiet dignity, his clear-sighted sense of the ultimate meaning of class warfare, could not help but remind me of a certain epigram, often attributed to Lenin but more likely originating with Engels: 'A bayonet is a weapon with a worker at both ends.'

But when Moore tries to present his heavily annotated version of political reality, he runs into trouble. Serious trouble.

Louis Menand, in his *New Yorker* piece on Moore,[113] traces the history of the idea of objectivity in the documentary. He goes back to the film *Nanook Of The North*, released in 1922, and describes how filmmaker Robert Flaherty took liberties in that piece with what we would nowadays call the objective truth of the Inuit way of life. Flaherty had his subjects stage hunts for the camera and re-enact obsolete traditions. Although he thought he was doing ethnography instead of entertainment – or as well as entertainment – in 1922 no one found these practices to be a problem.

Menand discusses Frederick Wiseman, whose classic documentaries *Titicut Follies*, *High School*, *Hospital*, *Juvenile Court* and *The Store* are objective in the sense that they make no explicit commentary, but – as Menand points out – Wiseman's art gives them enormous editorial power.

In making these historical observations, Menand seems to be suggesting that objectivity is always, and inevitably, open to question in the documentary, and that Moore's work is a documentary in the same sense that these earlier works were documentaries.

But Menand is far too gentle. The problem with Moore's films is not the same kind of problem that Menand identifies in *Nanook* or in Wiseman's work; it is not the question of the legitimacy of a staged but in some sense authentic ritual; it is not the editorial dilemma of what raw footage to run and what footage to cut, and of how these decisions build in a point-of-view bias, a bias that may still be called honest because it is unconscious. When it comes to making an editorial point that is not supported by an underlying reality, Michael Moore has no shame. There's nothing unconscious about it. To his credit, when pressed, he doesn't really deny that he is advancing a particular point of view rather than adhering to strict standards of documentary neutrality.

In *Fahrenheit 9/11*, Moore is up to the same old tricks he used in *Roger & Me* and *Columbine*, but he's so committed to his vision of America as conspiratorial evildoer that he hardly bothers to build a case that will stand up to scrutiny; instead, he just lets fly with the version of events that best suits his world view. He claims that the war in Afghanistan was fought in order to build a Unocal pipeline and that Enron would benefit from this pipeline, when in fact the project was abandoned in 1998, after feminist groups made clear to Unocal and the Clinton administration that there would be a domestic price to pay for investing in gender-apartheid, Taliban-ruled Afghanistan, and after Unocal executives realised that the security situation in Afghanistan just wasn't workable.[114] The pipeline planned after the fall of the Taliban is entirely different than the one envisioned by Unocal in the 1990s. And Moore says that, just five and a half months prior to 9/11, Taliban representatives were 'welcomed' to the US by the State Department when in fact their request for diplomatic recognition was rebuffed, although they did meet with State Department officials.

Moore builds a conspiracy out of the fact that the Bush and bin Laden families both have business ties to the Carlyle Group without mentioning that the billionaire sponsor of Democratic and progressive campaigns, George Soros, also has such ties. In both cases, so what? The Saudis also have extensive investments in Disney, the studio that financed the production of *Fahrenheit 9/11*. By his own logic of guilt by association, Michael Moore is himself a 9/11 plotter. And if American policy is vetted in Riyadh, why did we go to war against the wishes of the Saudis in both Afghanistan and Iraq?

Bush can and does condemn himself with his childish antics, but Moore tries too hard to do it for him, and when he does this, he stumbles badly. When I saw *Fahrenheit 9/11*, I was amazed at a scene of a Bush speech, in which the president, gazing out over a privileged crowd, says, 'This is an impressive crowd of the haves and have mores. Some call you the elite; I call you my base.' He's admitting it! He's *boasting* of representing the plutocracy! There was no context, I thought, that could make this right. This scene was used in television ads for the movie, and that made sense; what more damning slip could one ask for if one was out to show the sheer blundering nastiness of Bush?

My take on this scene changed when I read a short piece in the obscure journal *Catholic New York* that provided the context. The event was indeed a fundraiser, but not a political one. It's the annual Al Smith Dinner, which benefits Catholic medical services in New York State. The dinner is bi-partisan and comes with a long tradition that speakers poke fun at themselves and their reputations. This particular dinner took place in October 2000, in the run-up to the presidential election. Al Gore spoke just before Bush, saying, 'The Al Smith Dinner represents a hallowed and important tradition, which I actually did invent.' Referring to his oft-repeated plan to put Social Security funds in a 'lockbox', he promised to put 'Medicare in a walk-in closet'.[115]

Although the mood was self-parodic, it is of course true that Bush and the Republicans represent the interests of the rich and not of the poor and the middle classes, and even a casual examination of their record should make this very clear. But Moore's point in showing this moment is that Bush is proud of his ruthlessness, proud of his plutocratic associations and agenda. Indeed, he might be, and in fact probably is, but there's a double-wrapped irony in his dinner statement, meant as a joke about how his party is perceived and not of how Bush himself perceives it. To Moore, the *essential* truth of the moment justifies the distortion of the context. But this usage is not fair, and to use it in this manner is to degrade democratic debate.

This out-of-context usage reveals something about Moore's technique and about its impact not only on his audience but also on our culture's evolving ability to evaluate evidence. In fact, it points out something that Moore and Bush have in common.

Both men would probably roll their eyes at a conversation that turned to the subject of academic post-modernism, with its radically levelling thesis that all interpretations are equally valid, all evidence equally corrupt. This is the territory of intellekshools, not something that these carefully scripted public characters, Union Joe and Tex, care about greatly. But *Fahrenheit 9/11* and Bush's foreign policy are both deeply post-modernist artefacts. Both insist that there is no truth out there, only a contingent reality defined as whatever serves the preferred political narrative; both use pastiche and abuse context to present a highly massaged 'truth' that has earned its scare quotes; and both end up insisting that reality is what the author says it is, and that questioning or deviation from belief is a betrayal of the cause.

Both Moore and Bush offer a highly faith-based political doctrine. It should be no surprise that their adherents respond with the passion and righteousness usually reserved for those defending a theological position.

The parallel realities are that viewers of Rupert Murdoch's highly partisan Fox News Network are much more likely than other Americans to believe that Saddam actually had weapons of mass destruction, that there were substantive links between Saddam and al-Qaeda and that Saddam was involved in the 9/11 attacks – all false positions that the Bush administration has been very active in disseminating.[116] As many times as Moore has insisted that the terrorist threat is a fabrication, Bush has insisted – against all evidence – that we are winning the war in Iraq, that his strategy is designed to bring freedom and self-determination to the region and that it has weakened, rather than strengthened, the position of international Islamic terrorism.

Moore is equally facile. His propositions that Saddam wasn't hurting anyone (to which he seems committed *except* when he is discussing US support for Saddam in the 1980s) and that Iraq was a happy place under Saddam's rule are not only bizarre but truly callous. Moore's portrayal of Iraq under Saddam includes no mention of rape as a weapon of terror, of the omnipresent web of surveillance, of tongues cut out and victims disembowelled on suspicion of speaking ill of Saddam, of the Thursday hangings in the stench of shit and entrails at Abu Ghraib, of one in six residents of Baghdad having at least one relative who had been killed by Saddam.

Bush has mostly got a free pass on his constructions; Moore has not. The journalist and professional contrarian Christopher Hitchens, who has spent some time in Iraq, wrote a devastating attack not only on the facts in *Fahrenheit 9/11* but also on the good faith of its director.[117] In the ongoing argument about reality, no one did a better job of exposing Moore's shattered and inconsistent approach.

Hitchens starts with Moore's various and contradictory positions on the Saudis and moves on to his contention that Saddam Hussein never posed any threat to Americans or America, and then to the conduct of the war against bin Laden. He simply takes Moore's world view apart, leaving not only his thinking but his character in tatters. There were few writers on the left who were willing to challenge Moore on his facts and even fewer who bothered to challenge him on his intentions. Hitchens did both. His article destroys the image of Moore as John Berger's 'people's tribune' and renders Moore's moral universe shabby and contingent.

Like so much of Moore's other work, *Fahrenheit 9/11* gave the right much ammunition with which to attack him, liberals and the left, along with openings to advance their own fantastic takes on truth. There are greater and lesser degrees of honesty in the right's response to the film, but even the conservative Dave Kopel – who very thoughtfully and honestly deconstructs Moore in his '59 Deceits In Michael Moore's Fahrenheit 9/11' – fails Philosophy 101. Because *Fahrenheit 9/11* is sometimes wrong, it does not mean that the opposite is true. Because Moore comes up with a fantastic, simple-minded conspiracy based on connections between the Bushes, the Saudi princes and the bin Laden family, it does not mean that the real connections between the Bushes and the Saudis are not sinister and that they do not damage US national security. Because Moore plays down the real dangers of militant Islam, it does not mean that there were compelling connections between Iraq and al-Qaeda. Because some of the soldiers portrayed in the film resented Moore's use of their statements, it does not mean that the sacrifices of soldiers should give greater weight to their opinions on the war or that opposing the war is unpatriotic.

In the polarised environment of American politics, the Michael Moore version of reality allowed the partisans of the right to smear all liberals as America-hating propagandists while taking the focus away from their own grievous battles with truth and their propensity for propaganda. Fact-checking Rush Limbaugh is an industry in itself.[118] Sean Hannity and Michael Savage both insist that liberals and terrorists pose an equal danger to America. Dr Monica Crowley, a regular on New York's far-right WABC AM talk radio, once said, 'These academic elites, almost all of them are absolute pacifists who don't support war under any circumstances whatsoever.' David Horowitz, once a radical ideologue of the left and now a radical ideologue of the right, has come out with a book claiming that Bush's critics are sympathetic to Islamic terrorism. Ben Stein and Phil Demuth claim that Bush's critics hate America. Ann Coulter, viewed by many as a crazed coquette of the right, believes that Democrats love radical Islam, and that, by the way, good old Joe McCarthy was a national hero maligned by the evil Communist Democrats.[119]

Other reactions to Moore went deeper and roved farther afield, historically. To a great extent, Moore invited these attacks by making some rather ill-considered statements. Take this one, posted on his website soon after September 11: 'They did not deserve to die. If someone did this to get back at Bush, then they did so by killing thousands of people who DID NOT VOTE for him! Boston, New York, DC and the planes' destination of California – these were places that voted AGAINST Bush!'[120]

The implication that anyone who voted for Bush deserved to die is genuinely offensive, although, one hopes and suspects, it is more satirical than serious. But take a look at what can be done with this.

The right-wing 'think tank' the Cato Institute is staffed by political advocates who are committed to the idea of market forces as an absolute good, even when they do objective damage to the people they supposedly serve. In their ahistorical faith, the staff at Cato approach economics as a religion rather than as a mechanism of human interaction. They are much farther on the economic right than, say, Ronald Reagan, although, unlike Reagan, they are libertarian on social as well as economic issues. David Boaz, the executive vice-president, thundered in print against people like Moore and Italian playwright Dario Fo, who claimed that Western crimes of colonialism and economic domination were the parents of September 11. Boaz makes a rather striking accusation: '[Moore and Fo's writing] sums up the criticism of America that unites the Islamic terrorists, the anti-globalisation street protesters, the resentful right and the literary left: They hate the culture of markets and liberalism. They hate the Enlightenment and modernity. They hate reason, science, technology, individualism, pluralism, tolerance, progress and freedom. And to be more specific, they hate Wall Street, Hollywood, McDonald's, Starbucks, Microsoft, Ralph Lauren ads and the casual joy of American freedom.'

Boaz concludes with this non-sequitur: 'One consequence of the evil acts of September 11 was to help us all remember what is good about America. And another was to give a few people an opening to reveal to us what they really think about America – they don't like our freedom, our openness, our tolerance, our prosperity, our exuberance.'[121]

When I spoke with Boaz, he took some pains to point out that he was not intending to lump anyone who believes in regulated markets or anyone on some vague 'literary left' (a phrase he justified by its alliteration) into the category of those who hate America and make common cause with Islamic terrorists. He was kind enough to exempt specifically mainstream, market-orientated centre-leftists, mentioning Michael Kinsley, Nadine Strossen, the editors of *The New Republic*. But he did say this: 'Does Michael Moore hate reason? Absolutely. He used the emotional medium of film to distort, manipulate and mislead… Does he hate individualism? Well, since he seems to be pushing socialism, I'd say so… Capitalism is part of modernity, and if you're resentful of capitalism and "conspicuous consumption" and things like that, then I think you don't like modernity.'

There's a lot to work with here, all catalysed by a particular interpretation of Michael Moore's positions. Note Boaz's conflation in his article of things that many on the left would consider quite reasonable objects of criticism if not hatred – Wall Street, McDonald's and Hollywood (criticised on the right as well) – with things that no one on the democratic left dreams of criticising: reason, science, technology, pluralism, etc. Here, Boaz has himself made a classic lapse of reason. Note, too, that there is a difference between criticising what people do with science or technology (a type of criticism that is sometimes made by the left) and criticising science itself (a type of criticism that is never made by the left, although it is heard often on the evolution-denying, religious-fundamentalist right).

In using the moralistic language of good and evil, no matter how appropriate it may be on an immediate level, conservatives like Boaz deny the legitimate point that Fo – very clumsily – was trying to make: that there actually were historical causes of September 11. In this lack of historical perspective, in this complete lack of concern with cause and effect, Boaz and the many conservatives who talk and write like him are at least as unreasonable as Michael Moore.[122]

More importantly, Boaz has little understanding of the values of the Enlightenment that he is professing to support. The Enlightenment was a movement concerned with discussing what we know about the world, how we can know it and how we can use this approach to improve the human condition. The work of Karl Marx is every bit as much a part of that intellectual heritage as that of Adam Smith.

Ultimately, Boaz can legitimately criticise Moore for many particular things in *Fahrenheit 9/11*, but he can't really claim to have anything over Moore when it comes to respect for reason.

In the wake of the success of *Fahrenheit 9/11*, Moore had a national platform as the elections approached. He was just where he wanted to be.

He was even at the Republican National Convention, courtesy of the newspaper *USA Today*, which thought it would be cute to hire him to write a daily column on the goings-on there. They also hired right-winger Jonah Goldberg, of *The National Review*, to cover the Democratic Convention in Boston.

Actually, *USA Today* hired Ann Coulter first, but she proved a bit too much for them. Her first column opened, 'Here at the Spawn of Satan Convention in Boston…' and spiralled downward from there. She didn't much care for those 'corn-fed, no-make-up, natural fibre, no-bra-needing, sandal-wearing, hirsute, somewhat fragrant hippie-chick pie wagons they call "women" at the Democratic National Convention'.[123] *USA Today* was in the market for political trash talk, not nastiness for its own sake, so they took a pass. Goldberg was hired to replace Coulter and wrote boring, predictable and empty pieces about how boring, predictable and empty the Convention was. He was mostly right about this, though, and he didn't get too personal.

Goldberg and Coulter have a bit of a history, and this history instructs about the standards of right-wing journalism, the charged atmosphere of post-9/11 political commentary and the level of seriousness of what *USA Today* was trying to accomplish in hiring Moore and Coulter, then Goldberg.

Before September 11, Goldberg and Coulter were both featured columnists at William F Buckley's *The National Review*, where Goldberg was also an editor. Coulter's provocative, far-right rants had attracted attention since long before 9/11. Her friend Barbara Olson died on American Airlines flight 77, the hijacked plane that was flown into the Pentagon. Like Coulter, Olson was a telegenic political commentator, and the author of numerous hate pieces aimed at the Clintons. Two days after the attacks, Coulter wrote a piece in *The National Review Online* that started as a tribute to Olson ('she was really nice') and to Olson's relationship with her husband, Ted, who'd helped to make Bush President after the 2000 election by arguing the Republican side of *Bush vs Gore*, before the Supreme Court and was rewarded with the office of Solicitor General of the United States.

Then Coulter famously had this to say: 'This is no time to be precious about locating the exact individuals directly involved in this particular terrorist attack. Those responsible include anyone anywhere in the world who smiled in response to the annihilation of patriots like Barbara Olson... We should invade their countries, kill their leaders and convert them to Christianity. We weren't punctilious about locating and punishing only Hitler and his top officers. We carpet-bombed German cities; we killed civilians. That's war. And this is war.'[124]

The National Review ran this, but Coulter followed up with a column that helpfully suggested, 'Congress could pass a law tomorrow requiring that all aliens from Arabic countries leave… We should require passports to fly domestically. Passports can be forged, but they can also be checked with the home country in case of any suspicious-looking swarthy males.'[125]

This was a bit much even for William F Buckley's calloused old patrician soul and editor-in-chief Rich Lowry's class-warfare-waging blue pencil, and the column was spiked. Coulter then had a temper trantrum so extreme and unprofessional that a consensus developed at *The National Review* that she had to go.

Goldberg broke the news in a piece in which he tried to blame Coulter's departure not on institutional intolerance of psychotic right-wing raving but on bad writing. Defending Coulter against charges that she hates Muslims, he wrote, 'But this was not the point. It was NEVER the point. The problem with Ann's first column was its sloppiness of expression and thought. Ann didn't fail as a person, as all her critics on the left say; she failed as a WRITER, which for us is almost as bad.'

Goldberg insisted, correctly, that giving Coulter the boot was not censorship, and lest we miss the point that *The National Review* has no intrinsic fear of looking like a haven for ranters, only of looking like a haven for ranters who can't write, he concluded, 'In the same 20 days in which Ann says – over and over and over again – that *The National Review* has succumbed to "PC hysteria", we've run pieces celebrating every PC shibboleth and bogeyman. Paul Johnson has criticised Islam as an imperial religion. William F Buckley himself has called, essentially, for a holy war. Rich Lowry wants to bring back the Shah, and I've written that Western Civilisation has every right to wave the giant foam "We're Number 1!" finger as high as it wants.'[126]

Ann waded back in and called Jonah, Rich, Bill and the rest of the crew at *The National Review* girlie-boys, and that was that.

Anyway, Coulter and Goldberg's paths crossed again in the summer of 2004, when Goldberg took over her forfeited Democratic Convention gig with *USA Today*. Goldberg had the virtue – for the purposes of *USA Today* – of being no more of an actual journalist than Coulter or the Moore of his post-*Voice* years. He is a young reactionary whose work is awesomely unoriginal. If there's a right-wing *thème du jour* – the perfidy of the French; the suddenly urgent need to fight the politically correct secularisation of Christmas; the reasons why gay marriage will mean the end of Western civilisation – he can be counted upon to enter the bray. Goldberg once speculated, with a weird satisfaction, that John Allen Muhammad, the black Muslim 'Washington Sniper', would turn out to be gay – something that would have given the right-wing propagandists a chance to accuse three different disfavoured groups at once: a 'three-fer', as he put it.[127]

Moore was much better behaved at the Republican Convention than anyone expected him to be, at least in print. When he got away from putting the main focus on himself, his articles were remarkably restrained. He wrote about how what Republicans think are Republican values are actually, mostly, American values. He praised George and Laura Bush for having been good parents to their girls. He also wrote a lot of criticism of the war in Iraq and of Bush's economic priorities. But, on the whole, Moore's pieces are less carping and small-minded than Goldberg's complaints from Boston about the Democrats.

Moore had a good time with the Republicans, possibly a better time than he had at the Democratic Convention. It's interesting that Moore was not welcome at either. The Democrats pointedly did not invite him; John Kerry wouldn't come anywhere near him. He slipped in under the rope as a guest of the Congressional Black

Caucus, which honoured him for pointing out in *Fahrenheit 9/11* that they were the only ones who seemed to care about democracy in the wake of the stolen election of 2000. Moore attended the Democrats' gathering with no less than five bodyguards in tow, and he managed to delight Republicans and fuel their propaganda machine in all sorts of predictable ways when Jimmy Carter inexplicably invited him to sit in his VIP box.

At the Republican Convention, Moore didn't have to please anyone. He must have been very gratified that John McCain referred to him in his speech, although not by name. McCain got as far as saying 'a disingenuous filmmaker' when he was interrupted by a roar of boos directed at Moore that went on for a minute and a half and finally broke into a robotic chorus of 'FOUR MORE YEARS'. McCain, playing to the crowd, eventually got a chance to repeat 'disingenuous filmmaker' and to add, in a perfectly fair accusation, 'who would have us believe, my friends, that Saddam's Iraq was an oasis of peace, when in fact it was a place of indescribable cruelty, torture chambers, mass graves and prisons that destroyed the lives of the small children inside their walls'. As McCain spoke, Moore was up in the *USA Today* press area, in a secure bubble, protected from the many thousands of people in Madison Square Garden who would have liked to have torn him limb from limb.

In one of his columns in *USA Today* on the Republicans, Moore gives us his take on what happened during this speech. He starts out with a justified astonishment that McCain is working for Bush, considering that the Bush campaign slimed McCain in a particularly nasty way in the 2000 South Carolina primary, when McCain was running against Bush for the Republican nomination.[128] Now McCain goes around saying that Bush deserves not only our vote but also our admiration: '[McCain said] some gibberish about my movie. Everyone then sees me, I start laughing my ball cap off, the crowd goes bananas... Thousands of Republicans turned to me chanting, "Four more years." ...As for McCain, he had to beg the mob to be silent and listen to the rest of his speech. He must have wondered why a party that promises to protect us from terrorists booed my name more loudly than Saddam's or Osama's.'[129]

Moore disingenuously avoids McCain's quire reasonable accusation, but he asks a good question. It turns out that McCain, like many Republican critics, boasts of not having seen Moore's film. In the video of the Convention moment (the cameras go back and forth between Moore and McCain), Moore looks absolutely delighted, glowing with the thrill of public recognition.

Valerie Duty, an alternate from Crawford with the Texas delegation who was in Madison Square Garden every night of the Convention, has a different view of what happened between Moore and McCain. 'I looked and there were all these people pointing and staring, saying, "Michael Moore is right there," and I saw him. There he was, no farther away than that column over there' – she pointed out a column about ten yards away from where we were talking in the lobby of the New York Hilton. 'And we decided that McCain wasn't going to have to look at him. We got all these Bush/Cheney signs and held them up high, totally covering his secure little area. So McCain was talking about him but never knew he was there. We didn't want Moore to make that moment about himself.'

Valerie is a small woman with dark hair and a charming, slightly shy smile. She runs a Republican-themed gift shop back home in Crawford, selling shirts and mugs and buttons urging George W Bush's election in 2004. Her personal website features a memorial to 'Spot Bush', one of Bush's dogs, recently deceased. She was one of the organisers of the *Fahrenheit 9/11* protests in Crawford, and she stayed and saw the whole thing but was not moved by Moore's arguments, having inoculated herself in advance by reading Kopel's '59 Deceits in Michael Moore's Fahrenheit 9/11'. She's clearly a kind and decent person, and she clearly believes that George W

Bush is the same, speaking of him in the language of evangelicals; she knows his 'heart': 'What angered me most about Moore's movie was the idea that Bush was willing to send kids off to war without a second thought, without caring about them. I've seen him in person and I can tell you, that's not how he is at all. He's a caring and thoughtful person, and he would never have just sent our soldiers into harm's way unless there was no other choice for our country. I know it hurts him. I've been with him in church. I've prayed with him. We used to have a politician in Texas who talked like a Christian but it was all for show; he didn't really live it. You can tell the difference. George W Bush is for real.'

Valerie would have liked to have talked to Moore, to have asked him why he does what he does, why he wanted to show his film in Crawford and why he didn't show up. When she spotted him at the Convention, she handed up her card in his direction and saw that someone gave it to him and that he did not throw it away. She had some hope that he would call her cell phone number. I told her that this is not very likely.

'But he knew it was me. I saw him looking at his card, and then the person who had handed it to him, and then over to me. And he put up his hand like this…' Valerie holds her right thumb horizontally up by her forehead while extending her index finger straight up.

'What's that mean?' I asked.

'L for "loser". Somebody told me. I didn't know.'

Valerie and her husband are not rich. She's here in New York on her own dime; the Party doesn't pay expenses for delegates. She had nothing, went into debt to start a business, worked hard and made a go of it. The several thousand dollars that Bush's tax cuts saved her over the years made a big difference to her and her family.

I could have made my standard counter-argument: Are you really better off with a few thousand dollars in your pocket than you would be with that money in the national Treasury, joined by the billions of dollars that others would have paid, with that money spent on projects that benefit us all – schools, roads, law enforcement, hospitals, the military, the environment, medical research, paying off the national debt, etc, etc, etc? But looking at Valerie's kind, hopeful face, seeing her so glad to be here in New York, even though most New Yorkers emphatically did not welcome her or her party to town, this seemed excessively theoretical. Bush helped her family; that's her experience, what she knows. I felt that I was winning on points but that, even so, I would have to concede this round.

I must say that a few days later it became harder to sympathise with Valerie, or any Republican, although I still struggled to see her as a well-meaning, hard-working individual and not merely as a representative of her party. Over the next few days, as the Convention dragged on, I had to watch turncoat Democrat Zell Miller and then Dick Cheney make speeches steeped in the most astonishing demagoguery; I had to hear Rudy Giuliani claim that, amid the chaos of 9/11, he had turned to Police Commissioner Bernard Kerik and said, 'Thank God George W Bush is our President,' going on to say that the US as a nation 'owes' it to the victims of September 11 to keep George W Bush in the White House.[130] I had to hear about Republicans passing out 'Purple Heart band-aids' in mockery of a man who chose to go to Vietnam rather than use family connections to get a safe haven in the Texas Air National Guard. As I watched in disbelief, I imagined myself a part of an emergent community of Americans who, perhaps for the first time, were glad that there was someone like Michael Moore preparing to respond to this. Partisanship in the face of this assault seemed normal and natural. Suddenly, the polarisation of American politics began to seem inevitable, and therefore not regrettable.

I wondered how Valerie reacted. Her online journal of her experiences at the convention is full of glowing praise for everyone she meets, for all the speeches, for all the Republican functionaries. She expresses no doubts whatsoever.

This kind of American attitude is what Moore loves to attack when he goes on tour in Europe, where he will pander to his audience by describing Americans as the 'stupidest people in the world', deaf, blind and, especially, dumb: blind to the devastation wrought by the Imperium; deaf to the cries of the world's oppressed; dumb about anything outside Americans' very narrow field of vision. If *Fahrenheit 9/11* is a debate about reality, Michael Moore and Zell Miller truly need each other. How could each know that his preferred version is correct without the other – or some stand-in – at work to prove that it is not?

8 Fahrenheit Vs Celsius

Michael Moore invented his own way of doing populist, tendentious, political film, and his style became part of popular culture. But nobody owns popular culture, and the Moore attitude has been widely copied. Populist insurgency develops spontaneously and from the bottom up. You don't need $10 million to make a film or a political advertisement nowadays. Digital and broadband changed everything; the sheer availability of information in our society is quite different from anything that has gone before. In many ways, this is good; it is good that there was a built-in corrective to the abuses at Abu Ghraib prison, in the form of the cheap digital cameras and the worldwide distribution network to which everyone – including soldiers and civilian contractors in war zones – has access nowadays.[131]

The flipside of this is that anyone who can lay hands on some relatively cheap equipment, clip and image archives and a distribution network – preferably a national cinema distribution arrangement, but an internet server will do – can get public attention for any partisan pastiche. There's no real oversight, no mandatory fact-checking in a still mostly free society, and this is as it should be.

This scenario does, however, pose some problems. Just as many high-school students nowadays don't seem to realise that a 'news' item found on an internet blog isn't necessarily a good citation, a large swathe of the public seems to use only its own political prejudices as a filter, leaving it (and the political process) highly vulnerable to the most skilled demagogues. Many on the right have seized on the methods Moore pioneered, and while they might not have made as much money as Moore, the propagandistic documentary slapped together with little fact-checking has been heartily adopted by conservatives, and to great effect. It is a tribute to the format's power that, in the wake of the success of *Fahrenheit 9/11*, there were almost immediately some frenzied efforts to produce a right-wing version of it, and taken together these efforts say a great deal about where American political culture is at present. As right-wing activist David Bossie put it, 'I will credit Michael Moore with [opening] up a new genre in politics... Whether you agree with it or disagree with it, he did make people open their eyes to that. And delivering political messages through that medium is now going to be commonplace.'[132]

Bossie was right. One great example is a film titled *Celsius 41.11: The Temperature At Which The Brain Begins To Die*, produced by Bossie's own organisation, Citizens United, which exists to attack Democrats while pushing the most childish conservative causes ('Boycott France!'). Citizens United has advocated in defence of the 'under God' qualification in the Pledge of Allegiance taken in American classrooms, for Dick Cheney's 'right' to hold secret communications with for-profit energy corporations in setting energy policy, and in support of Texas legislation criminalising gay sex. During the 2004 election, it also energetically created and disseminated material attacking John Kerry's war record, which it advertised on its website, along with anti-Kerry petitions.

Bossie himself is a frequent contributor to *The Washington Times*, which makes no pretence of objectivity in its news stories, much less its editorial pages, and proudly employs convicted right-wing felon

Oliver North as a columnist.[133] Bossie has been a volunteer fireman for fifteen years. His work is highly cognizant of where working people are coming from politically, and although the conservatism of his Virginia firefighting brethren is for me tragically ironic, it never seems to occur to him that they vote against their own interests.

Bossie used to work for the House committee investigating the Clintons' Whitewater affair, and is convinced that he discovered great wrongdoing on the part of the Clintons, even though Special Prosecutor Kenneth Starr, after spending millions of dollars investigating the Clintons, declined to recommend any Whitewater-related charges against them. Bossie's experience with Whitewater gave him an insider cachet that allowed him to write several books attacking Bill Clinton, Al Gore and John Kerry, accusing them of every sin of corruption, cupidity, stupidity, irresponsibility and dissoluteness under the sun.

Bossie has written that Bush cares deeply and Reagan cared deeply about democracy and human freedom and that Reagan was a brilliant man. He has co-authored, with Christopher M. Gray, a lengthy faux-scholarly disquisition on why Osama bin Laden and his followers hate the United States that includes excursions into Islamic theology, the life of Muhammad, the Crusades, and Sayyid Qutb but makes no mention whatsoever of the history of European colonialism, American support for repressive Arab governments and for Israel, of Ronald Reagan's support for and encouragement of Islamic fundamentalists as a way to resist to the Soviet Union's invasion of Afghanistan, and of historical European and American attempts to block the development of democracy in the Arab world.[134] Bossie considers any attempt to look for historical explanations of terrorism in US policy as 'blame America first'; he has even gone so far as to write that the Iranian people, and not the United States, were responsible for the overthrow of Iranian nationalist Muhammad Mossadegh in 1953[135] —a bizarre attempt at freelance history that is not supported by a single reputable Iran scholar, nor, in fact, by the CIA itself.[136]

With the election looming, Bossie became the executive producer of *Celsius 41.11*, which is truly a gem of a propaganda piece. Its writer and producer, Lionel Chetwynd, had done previous work on the adoring (and highly fictionalised) *DC 9/11*, which portrayed Bush as a great and resolute leader in the aftermath of the attacks.

Unsurprisingly, the Republican Party made the trailer for Bossie's film available for free viewing on its website, and – also unsurprisingly – so did 'fair and balanced' Fox News. Purporting to be the truth behind Moore's lies, it actually spends little time refuting his specific charges and a lot of time showing no-context pictures of carnage, exploitative clips from September 11 and the most idiotic and unrepresentative statements of anti-war protesters: 'With a dictator, there are pros and cons. A dictator that provides universal health care – I *like* that dictator!'

One section of *Celsius* features 'terrorism expert' Mansoor Ijaz speaking at length on the mistakes of Bill Clinton's anti-terrorism policies, but the film never mentions that Ijaz is the chairman of Crescent Investment Management, a group that had extensive contacts with the Sudanese government, or that he and Crescent donated very large amounts of money to the Democratic Party and that he could have reasonably expected to get some Sudanese oil money to invest when US sanctions were lifted on that country. Ijaz was bitterly disappointed when, instead, Clinton tightened sanctions on Sudan for sponsoring international terrorism. It's not at all inconceivable that he has an axe to grind.[137]

The film completely distorts the facts about the election of 2000 and completely misrepresents the scope of the Patriot Act. The right-wing columnist Charles Krauthammer solemnly presents his own ahistorical opinions as fact and a parade of 'experts' from the American Enterprise Institute and other right-wing institutions tell us about the threat of terrorism, but again completely ignore the historical context.[138]

For good measure, *Celsius* throws in the usual accusations about how John Kerry would fail to protect the United States while replaying many of George W Bush's charged statements about the war on terror, some of them merely highly questionable, emotional rhetoric, many of them proven to be untrue. This is topped off with an iconic, highly manipulative sequence of Bush throwing out the first ball at a baseball game, looking just as sincere and American as can be. Say what you will about the right: its partisans understand where Americans are psychologically vulnerable.

Citizens United sent tape-recorded messages in Bossie's own voice to phones across the country saying in part, 'It's the answer to *all* the lies in Michael Moore's *Fahrenheit 9/11*, as well as exposing John Kerry's *dismal* record on the war on terror. If you care about defending America, if you don't want the liberals anywhere *near* our national security, if you were as offended as I was by Michael Moore's propaganda, then you need to go see *Celsius 41.11*. Unlike *Fahrenheit 9/11*, we have the *truth* on our side…' These messages even went to California, where Bossie knew perfectly well that Bush was not going to win; he just wanted to get up liberals' noses with his movie. In a similar spirit, Bossie rented the two largest billboards near the Kodak theatre in Hollywood on which he expressed his thanks to Moore and the Hollywood liberals for contributing to Bush's 2004 election victory.

While *Celsius*, in its concern with propaganda at the expense of truth, has a great deal in common with *Fahrenheit*, the Moore-debunking vehicle *FahrenHYPE 9/11: Unraveling The Truth About 9/11 And Michael Moore* is in a somewhat different category. It is a bit more respectable on the facts and it is very good at calling

Moore out on his more grandiose conspiracy theories and on his lack of concern for any truth that doesn't serve his purposes.

There are powerful sequences that take apart the war-for-oil idea, the Carlyle conspiracy and the particular nature of the Bush–Saudi connection. The film is honest enough to point out that the ties between the United States and Saudi Arabia are very seriously not good policy, but it quite fairly makes the point that these ties do not begin and end with the Bush family. Like *Celsius*, the film misrepresents the 2000 election results, however, in claiming that the recounts and the media-consortium investigation both unambiguously showed that Bush won. Neither of them did that, and this statement avoids the larger issues of fraud that took place before anyone stepped into a voting booth.

FahrenHYPE also rightly castigates Moore for his insistence that terrorism is just a mirage, an irrational fear that Bush uses to consolidate power, with no real policy implications or significant human impact. But it is precisely on the question of terrorism that it crosses a very subtle line into propaganda, and it is here that Moore's role as a cultural provocateur is important at a time when the war on terror, and misinterpretations and misrepresentations thereof, are shaping US society. Moore gets the war on terror wrong, but so, in some ways, does *FahrenHYPE*.

The film spends a good deal of time taking sentimental testimony from those who witnessed 9/11 or who lost loved ones on that day. In doing this, like many other post-9/11 American cultural artifacts, it elevates the event to an unfathomable evil while conferring on its victims the status of holy suffering – a uniquely American suffering. This is sadly predictable; the idea of extraordinary victimhood has been used again and again in human history as a call to unite under the caller's banner. The film indignantly insists that US citizens were attacked but purely innocent, absolved from history, a good and decent nation fighting an irrationally hateful foe. We see Bush sombrely intoning on September 11, 'Freedom itself was attacked this morning by a faceless coward. And freedom will be defended.' This is the very view of history that is so unhelpful to fighting and winning the war on terror.

FahrenHYPE enlists some sketchy characters to make this point. Former Clinton adviser Dick Morris, Bush speechwriter David Frum and former Democratic mayor of New York Ed Koch weigh in to insist that anyone who questions Bush on strategy does not understand the threat, and imply that any disagreement with Bush is tantamount to advocating appeasement. So does Steven Emerson, the author of *American Jihad*, whose questionable research has been supported by Richard Mellon Scaife.[139]

Morris makes the astonishing claim that, even if the US had had advance notice of the attacks of September 11, it would legally have been impossible to stop them without the Patriot Act – and that this was Bill Clinton's fault. Ann Coulter repeatedly uses the word 'liberal' to mean 'those who don't want to fight terrorism'.

The film keeps returning obsessively to the terrorist threat, even in sections that have nothing to do with the plots of al-Qaeda. Zell Miller, the Democrat who spoke such nonsense at the Republican Convention, talks about how he once found a nest of poisonous copperhead snakes on his ranch: 'I didn't ask permission from the town council, from my wife, from foreign governments or anyone else. I took a hoe and chopped their heads off. And we're in a war with a bunch of poisonous snakes.' Ironically, by dwelling so righteously on the obvious – that terrorism is a threat that must be fought – the film almost gives the impression of upholding Moore's thesis: that the fear of terrorism is a ruse by the right, an induced hysteria used to exert political control.

There's another pro-Bush film that deserves a special mention just because, for anyone who is not a hardcore evangelical, it is so very weird. The coyly titled *George W Bush: Faith In The White House* was released at around the same time as *Fahrenheit 9/11* by Grizzly Adams Productions, an evangelical-owned outfit that makes commercial family films for the television market, not all of them religious in nature. It was billed as an antidote to *Fahrenheit 9/11* and was pushed hard at the 2004 Republican National Convention in New York City.

The film is a blatant hagiography of Bush. Not only is he a strong religious believer, it seems, but he's a kind man who wants only to serve and to help others, never asking anything for himself. The man who admitted to trading on his father's name during his presidency,[140] who doles out no-bid contracts to Halliburton and who engaged in insider trading at Harken Energy, the man whose Vice-President met with many members of the energy industry in order to hear their thoughts on energy policy and environmental regulation, is supposedly appalled at even the slightest suggestion of corruption in politics or business.

The narrators present what they believe to be inspirational messages about Bush's faith, messages that might almost have been calculated to terrify non-evangelicals. When Bush is shown answering the question 'Who is your favourite political philosopher?' with 'Christ, because he changed my heart,' Christians whose faith suffuses every aspect of their lives might be impressed, but the rest of us are appalled, not merely at the idea of Jesus being an adviser on important issues of State but also at the possibility that Bush – a politician for much longer than most people think and the son of a sophisticated politician – is using religion as a political tool; or perhaps that he has not read or cannot think of anyone else; or, most frightening of all, that he is completely sincere.

The film sets out to prove that Bush's faith is genuine, that faith has always been a necessary part of American political leadership and that Bush is doing brilliantly *because* of his faith. It also takes for granted that, as Rabbi Daniel Lapin of the American Alliance of Jews and Christians tells us, 'there is a struggle going on inside America, and it's a struggle between those who regard Judeo-Christian values as vital to our nation's survival and those who view those values as horrible obstructions to progress. The future of our nation depends upon the outcome of this struggle.' As Lapin speaks, the film shows images of marchers with signs calling for safe and legal abortion and ominous music plays. Lest the point be lost, Bush biographer Tom Freiling follows up with '[Bush] has given strength to Christians who are in the middle of fighting a culture war, whether it be the issue of abortion or same-sex marriage.'

The film dwells on the story of Bush's former drinking life and his redemption in Christ, a sentimental narrative that has been tremendously helpful to Bush in his political endeavours – and one that he and Karl Rove have exploited shamelessly – because it is the surest mark of sincerity in Christ that he has to offer to his followers.

Faith In The White House blithely asserts that 'a majority of churchgoing Americans believe that George W Bush is the right man at the right time' and that only Washington, Lincoln and George W have had to lead the country during a time of attack on its own territory. Franklin Roosevelt, the father of the New Deal, who rallied the nation in the wake of the attack on Pearl Harbor without explicit appeals to Jesus, is strangely absent from this version of history.[141]

The film is also adept at couching its most ridiculous assertions in the form of careful rhetorical questions: 'Is it possible that George W Bush, by his faith-based example, is leading the nation in a re-awakening of the principles on which it was founded?'

Although it is scathing about the 'propaganda' of Michael Moore, and quotes the deeply religion-averse Christopher Hitchens' view that Moore's work is 'an exercise in moral frivolity', *Faith In The White House* unabashedly recycles some of the most offensive White House propaganda about Iraq, repeating as if it proves anything Donald Rumsfeld's assertion that 'America is not interested in conquest or colonisation.' It also perpetuates – as many right-wingers have – the canard that Bush's forceful actions in Iraq and Afghanistan brought Muammar Qadaffi of Libya to his senses and were the reason why Qadaffi gave up his nuclear-weapons programme when in fact Qadaffi's decision was the result of long negotiations begun with the Clinton administration, negotiations that had almost been completed when Bush came to office.

Faith In The White House was clearly produced for a very specific audience, and its message was probably not intended or expected to resonate much beyond those who already believe that America is rightfully and properly a Christian nation. If everybody who does not consider Jesus to be his personal saviour and that of the United States had seen this film before November 2004, it is hard to believe that Bush could possibly have won. This is primarily a film about religious faith, not about acts of governance or war, but there is enough comment on public affairs to hold the film to journalistic standards, and here it fails dismally. When it takes on Michael Moore's contentions, its contempt for him is palpable, but it uses his methods to further its thesis. No right-winger who accepts this abuse of the facts has any right to object to Moore's own idiosyncratic presentation of reality.

There is one film about Moore, however, that really is different. Michael Wilson's *Michael Moore Hates America* stands alone in this category because it is less overtly tendentious – despite the provocative title – and because its hook is that it's about America and truth rather than about politics. Wilson doesn't want to destroy Moore; he wants to help him find the long-neglected core of decency in himself that Wilson earnestly believes is there, deep within every American, every human being. It's *Roger & Me* in reverse, as Wilson tries endlessly to track down Moore so that Moore can explain himself, and Moore's dodges look increasingly cynical, hypocritical and unfair. The film is brilliant propaganda, and while it never rises above banal sentimentality, nothing in it is actually untrue.

Wilson opens with his own biography, a conscious emulation of Moore's introductions to *Roger & Me* and *Bowling For Columbine*, and just as Moore does, he uses his life story to establish his working-class *bona fides*: father worked in construction, was laid off when Wilson was young, moved, was laid off again but never gave up hope, never stopped believing in America. Now Wilson has a small daughter of his own: 'I was the one responsible for making sure she had a shot at the future she deserved. Michael Moore had told her that she couldn't do it, that she was enslaved by corporations and greedy politicians.'

The film is divided into two themes: seeking to show how Moore sets up situations dishonestly and showing the sunny, optimistic side of Americans and American society that Moore short-changes. On the debunking side, Wilson is dogged and comes up with much good stuff discussed earlier in this book, from Charlton Heston to the gun in the bank to Moore's penchant for conspiracy theories. He does a good job of showing Moore's unscrupulousness in the service of his cause. But the heart of the film is the ordinary Americans Wilson interviews, who talk about working hard and fulfilling their dreams and not giving up.

Sometimes Wilson seems innocent to the hilarious bathos of what he learns from America. At one point in the film, he is talking to a sandwich-shop owner who has pulled himself up by his bootstraps when a dissatisfied customer breaks the store's front window. The stoic owner faces it like the brave American he is. He will rebuild! 'It's just a bump in the road. I guess that's what separates us from all other countries.'

Wilson then goes to Washington and finds an affirmation of the indomitable American spirit in the fact that there are people playing street hockey in the section of Pennsylvania Avenue that was blocked off after the Oklahoma City bombing of 1995. Innocent or not, he knows his audience will eat this stuff up.

Wilson is never nasty (although he does briefly indulge in some mild Francophobia) and he walks through the film with a sort of wide-eyed wonder that only a liberal elitist could find irritating. The moral crux of the film comes when he interviews the mayor of Moore's home town, Davison, and misrepresents what he is doing because he is afraid the mayor will clam up if he hears the name Michael Moore. Wilson says he is doing a film about small-town values and the American dream. It's less of a lie than even Wilson knows, because these things exist in the sentimental imagination – which is also whence Wilson's film springs – and they're all mixed up together. But it's still not right, and his cameraman says he will walk off the job if Wilson doesn't get straight. Wilson has a crisis of conscience, writes to the mayor confessing all and asking to be forgiven. The mayor is disappointed but gives him permission to use the footage as long as he doesn't run down Davison.

Wilson is right; he's a better man for doing the right thing, and the film is a better film because of it. Indeed, it is this sequence that makes the film, and Wilson is sharp enough to know it. He truly has a point about how Moore works and how it compromises him. Wilson also quite legitimately makes much of Moore's repeated refusals to give him an interview and borrows a page from Moore's playbook in showing the runaround he gets from Moore's staff, endlessly calling the office, endlessly being told on speakerphone that Moore would certainly give him an interview if he could; it's just that it's impossible right now.[142]

This should be an existential question for Moore: if he refuses to talk to his critics, how can he continue to self-righteously demand interviews with public figures whom he clearly despises and claim to have shamed them when they refuse? On *The Awful Truth*, Moore once made a big deal about how millionaire industrialist

Ira Rennert got a restraining order against him – made it the focus of the segment, in fact, with Moore dramatically hiring a guard to ensure that he, Moore, did not yield to temptation and come closer than the marked-off, legally allowed distance. Moore shouted questions and answers up to Conan O'Brien's set at the Rockerfeller Center for an interview because O'Brien's show is in the same building as Rennert's offices. But what did Moore do when former *Awful Truth* employee Alan Edelstein began to follow him around with a camera to ask why Moore had fired him? He got a restraining order and filed criminal charges, saying that Edelstein had threatened him and his family. Edelstein refused a plea bargain. Moore seems to have lost interest in the case after that, and dropped the matter.

Wilson has some truly wise and good quotes from some unlikely public figures. Penn Jillette, half of the illusionist duo Penn and Teller, says, 'When you start thinking that you're so right that you can twist things a little, it's a wonderful warning.' Respected documentary filmmaker Albert Maysles says, 'The essence of tyranny is the denial of complexity,' and 'I don't think that you think clearly, or film clearly, when it's hate that motivates you in the making of a film.' Asked what he would say to Moore if he could ask him anything, Maysles says, 'If you worked more the way I do, to set out to discover things, let the chips fall where they may…do you think you'd be unhappy about that?'

Wilson's final narration unfolds against the background of a small-town parade. His calm, soothing voice intones, 'Most of us are looking for that quick fix: "Take the red pill! Take the blue pill!" – anything to make our problems go away – but that just doesn't exist. If it were that easy, I don't think anyone would appreciate the satisfaction of working hard for what we have and realising that we solved our problems on our own.' Wilson's understanding of the American idiom is masterful and far beyond anything Moore can do. Moore's style may provoke, may win him fans and riches and acclaim and enemies, but Wilson's style is what wins American elections. Neglected among all the optimism and decency is the possibility that Moore's exploitative corporations, greedy bosses and evil politicians might share the American reality with Wilson's plucky strivers.

Wilson's movie has the potential to be a real breakout hit, and with the new fashion for right-wing film festivals he'll have plenty of places to show it. One such event, the Liberty Film Festival, was held in Hollywood in late 2004 and featured such films as Evan Maloney's *Brainwashing 101*[143] and Elinor Burkett and Patrick Wright's *Is It True What They Say About Ann?*, a Coulter-friendly documentary. Several films were explicitly anti-Moore, such as Citizens United's *Celsius 41.11* and right-wing talk-show host Larry Elder's *Michael & Me*. The focus was not predominantly on Moore, however, and the Festival had broad scope and included many other films for a right-wing audience, including some non-documentary, sentimental favourites like 1942's *Dark Victory*, starring Ronald Reagan, and *The Ten Commandments*, starring Charlton Heston.

In Dallas, meanwhile, there is the Renaissance Film Festival, set up by Jim and Ellen Hubbard, who seem to have a fairly narrow idea of what appeals or should appeal to the American moviegoing public: 'We were in law school and we took a study break and visited our favourite art-house theatre and noticed that *Frida* [a widely respected biography of the radical Mexican artist Frida Kahlo] was playing, and *Bowling For Columbine*...was also playing. And we just looked at each other and said, "Where are the films for the rest of us, for real Americans?" So that's how the idea got started, from that time when we realised that we needed to do something about the lack of films that existed for people like us.'[144] The populist appeal is assumed, the identification of anti-Moore beliefs and an anti-international cultural position with 'real

Americans' complete.

The marketing of particular points of view to particular audiences raises an interesting point. Although all of Michael Moore's films and all of the right-wing responses to them contain some kernel of truth, none of them are really concerned with truth; they are about restating and reaffirming a political identity that transcends any mere truth, in the service of which all is permitted. This is why right-wing internet saboteur Matt Drudge can admit to professional respect for *Fahrenheit 9/11*. His acknowledged jealousy over the manipulative power of Moore's technique is telling: 'I give [Moore's work] major props as a piece of art. I was filled with steamy jealousy throughout… It's all about the close-up… One reason *American Idol* does so well is the close-up; they announce who lost and zoom in to the eyes. When I saw [*Fahrenheit 9/11*] – even the opening three minutes of the movie, [when] you see his love of close-up – I said, "Aw, he's got it." You put that with a Harvey Weinstein campaign ad and you're good to go; Palme d'Or, baby… Nixon said history belongs to those who write it. That's what it is. You see things through your own prism. I feel what I do on the internet is just one guy's outlook on the world.' The medium is the message, in a way that Marshall McLuhan only partially comprehended.

Commenting on the phenomenon, RJ Cutler, the producer of 1993 documentary on Bill Clinton's campaign *The War Room*, remarked, 'What complicates it now is that at this point, if you look at Condoleezza Rice on the *Today* show and you take her at her word when she says something, it's almost like you're naïve. It's your own fault if you're not a sophisticated-enough viewer. To that extent, the blurring…the distance between the word and its meaning has grown very far apart, and that's something that television has accelerated dramatically. And, of course, that's been exploited by those who are controlling the message out of government administrations.'[145]

9 Moore Abroad

Michael Moore is the same phenomenon in Europe that he is in the United States, but differently. In America there are two sets of lines drawn, and they're more complicated than pro or con: there is the line between those who see patriotism as defined by support for the President and those – both left and right – who see patriotism in principled dissent; and then there is the line between those who are eager to believe Moore's view of the world and those who question his evidence and his logic. Call them 'right patriots', 'dissenting patriots', 'conspiros' and 'left sceptics' respectively. These categories break down in different ways, and there are overlaps. Some left sceptics are also dissenting patriots who have contempt for both Moore and Bush but who understand the seriousness of the war on terror. The conspiros are Moore's base, the right patriots Bush's.

In Europe it's a bit simpler, and it comes down to the question of whether the United States is a force for good or evil in the world – a way of putting it that already reduces the scope of argument considerably.

Moore's star quality was imported early and caught on in a big way, at least in Britain. I spoke with Alan Fountain, Professor of Television Studies and Programme Leader in Television Production at Middlesex University, who knows the medium inside and out: he's worked in all aspects of the film and television industry since the 1970s as director, writer and producer. In the 1980s he was a commissioning editor with Channel 4, where he specialised in independent film and video. On a trip to the US, he was invited to see a rough cut of Moore's *Roger & Me*, was impressed and put up some money for its completion, in effect pre-buying it for the channel. Warner Brothers' eventual buyout brought it to UK cinemas first. A major release for a leftish documentary in the UK was extraordinary; *Roger & Me* did very well and Moore's reputation was solidly launched in Europe. Beyond that, the film opened the door for a resurgence of interest in documentary film, and Moore established a particular style.

'The success of [Moore's] films has – not single-handedly, but near-single-handedly – turned around the prospects for new mainstream releases of documentaries in Britain and perhaps Europe,' Fountain told me. 'It's not unusual now for there to be five or six documentaries going around in the art houses and in mainstream release, and most of them are somewhat politically left... I teach a "history of the documentary" course to young people who are about 21. Moore is one of the few documentary makers they've ever heard of when they start. Many students really like his films. One of the things I ask them to do as part of their assessment is to choose a documentary and write a case study about it, and probably a third of the class has chosen one of his films. Most of these kids haven't heard of indigenous filmmakers like Nick Broomfield; Michael Moore is the name that they all recognise.'

Moore has been lambasted by the American right for criticising the US abroad in a time of war, but at that time he already had a cultural base in the UK. And it's not as if the Brits need Moore to educate them about the war in Iraq; the situation itself is highly instructive, and the BBC, unlike the American media, has done a good job of presenting the facts, so there is a political environment in which Moore's presentation will resonate. 'The whole situation with the war is another dimension,' said Fountain. 'There's a very intricate tie-in with American culture, media culture, television culture. The vast majority of the people who live here are very uncritical of the American mass media. There's a minority that are more critical. As the war continues, most of the people are now opposed and see Blair as doing what Bush tells him to do. Moore is seen as someone who is offering a different analysis, a different viewpoint from the official American view.'

On the Continent, it is different again. The British share a language with Americans, and in the satellite age US media are readily available to the UK. Consequently, they have many sources for ideas and impressions about American politics and culture. Beyond that, the basically Anglo-Saxon American cultural tradition – modified by a myriad of other influences, just as Britain's own culture has been – is familiar and transparent in the UK. Certainly many Europeans speak at least some English and can read it quite competently, but American broadcasts and American news and culture are not ambient in non-English-speaking societies in the same way that they are in Britain. Consequently, while Michael Moore is perhaps a popular representative of one part of the American political reality in Britain, on the Continent he is more likely to be seen as the single antidote to the Bush administration, a kind of orthodox counter-orthodoxy.

There are other elements. Europeans are angry at the international role of the US and at Bush's insistence on the American right to act unilaterally, and this has given Moore a strong platform. The Europeans' anger has some complicated roots; for a start, their demographic profile is aging alarmingly, meaning that a shrinking tax base and a growing non-working population leave little left over from social needs to invest in

European militaries (or, as now seems increasingly possible, a European military). Unwilling and increasingly unable to invest in their own military capacities, and weighed down by the baggage of an explicitly colonial past in ways that Americans are not, Europeans have become humiliatingly dependent on and subordinate to US policies in the world arena, and this of course feeds resentment.

With American military subsidies having largely paid for their welfare states, Europeans are unaccustomed to taking responsibility for security threats (viz the Yugoslav wars) and many in Europe therefore see the war in Iraq – and even that in Afghanistan – as purely and simply imperial aggression.

It is also true that long-standing ties to much of the developing world dating from the colonial era mean that Europeans often have a better sense of what's going on, sociologically, in their former colonies. It's unlikely that the French, say, would have been so blindsided by the genuine sociological power of Saddam Hussein's hold on Iraq's people; they would have realised that it was based on tribal and ethnic clientalism seen as legitimate by many if not most Iraqis, and would not have just barged in, expecting to be welcomed as liberators.[146] This more subtle knowledge of how the world works can lead to contempt, at best, for the American approach, especially in its most narrow-minded Texan manifestation. It can also lead to deeper suspicions. It is worthy of note that Thierry Meyssan's *L'Effroyable Imposture* ('The Shocking Deception'), in which Meyssan claims that 9/11 was a hoax perpetrated by the US government, has been a huge seller in Europe.

There may be other factors that make Moore an effective messenger in Europe. I suspect that Europeans are secretly pleased by Moore's personal slovenliness, which allows them to patronise him and, in a certain way, all Americans: 'Look, he's an honest American, but a reassuringly ugly American too.' It's like the French solemnly anointing Jerry Lewis as the greatest American comedian: it confirms something about the order of the universe.

All of this means that many Europeans respond to an American who apologises for being such. Moore is the anti-Bush and he plays up the image of America as a rapacious imperium inhabited by ignorant, holy-rolling fools whenever he speaks in Europe. An invariable part of his routine before any audience, at home or abroad, is to talk about how little Americans know, how dangerously isolated we are. Eighty-five per cent of Americans can't find Iraq on a map. Eleven per cent can't find the United States. He likes to face off non-Americans against Americans in his audiences and have them compete in pop quizzes on their respective countries' geography, history and politics, and he usually finds that the non-American knows more about America than the other way around. Strictly speaking, this is not surprising, since non-Americans have many more good reasons to study America than Americans have to study other countries, but the routine does what it is designed to do.

Fahrenheit 9/11 opened different political fissures abroad than those it created domestically, and sometimes surprising ones. In doing so, it brought the debate over American political reality to the whole world.

There was the predictable, uncritical reaction in certain quarters. The novelist John Berger wrote that Moore is 'a people's tribune', speculated as to whether the film could 'change the course of civilisation' and, most astonishingly, claimed that it 'appeals to people to think for themselves and make connections'.[147] But there were less-than-glowing responses, too, even from the left – even from the French, despite that 20-minute standing ovation at Cannes.

The French showed some real objectivity and Gallic intellectual engagement in criticising the film, and often came to the conclusion that it was manipulative and poorly made. Thomas Sotinel, writing in mainstream newspaper *Le Monde*, was soberly assessing what was true and untrue in the film as early as 19 May (Bush–Saudi connections, yes; Afghan pipeline, no). The critic Jean-Luc Douin called it 'effective but simplistic and sometimes demagogic… By its avowed objectives, by its tone, *Fahrenheit 9/11* appears as a militant film, a propagandistic film…such as those of [Soviet Stalin-era hack propagandists] Dziga Vertov, Mikhail Kalazatov or Joris Ivens.' Intelligent criticism grounded in a knowledge of the political history of film was probably more than mainstream American audiences were capable of, and certainly more than they would expect from the stereotypically perfidious French. '*Fahrenheit 9/11* is just another symptom of the way in which American cinema uses spectacle as an art, as a way to denounce Axes of Evil,'[148] Douin went on. Does the American right object to French snobbery when it is directed against the American left?

The French cultural critic Pascal Bruckner had an interesting view on why some French people embrace Moore while many can't respect him. As Bruckner sees it, Moore allows the French to remember two of their proudest traditions: their early discovery of American talent – Faulkner, Miller, Hemingway, Stein, many of the jazz greats who couldn't be served a cup of coffee at whites-only lunch counters in the America of their times – and their solidarity with the political visionaries of the world. 'Moore became our very own dissident, somewhere between Vaclav Havel and Andrei Sakharov, freed from the clutches of a totalitarian administration, protected by the good people of the French hexagon and honoured by the Palmes in Cannes…' Bruckner wrote. 'Through Moore, the French could grab a piece of the good America and use it to exorcise the bad – the predators of Wall Street and Washington, the rich, the super-rich and their lackeys.'[149]

Moore's status was a symptom of that most banal and overly remarked-upon French paradox: that of simultaneously loving and hating America. But the French are smarter than that, and while they might have little sense of Moore's place in the American debate, they know how to apply intellectual rigour. 'The audience felt cheated by the director – under the guise of making them laugh, he had treated them as idiots,' Bruckner went on. 'It wasn't simply that Moore uses blatant caricatures, dramatically oversimplifies and makes a cheap play for tears; rather, it is because, to draw voters away from Bush, he uses precisely the same weapons as those used by the Republican propaganda machine: disinformation, shortcuts, omissions... This mimicking of conservative propaganda reduces *Fahrenheit 9/11* to a simplistic militant manifesto...but people, including French people, do not like to be manipulated like this. The hatred that Bush engenders on this side of the Atlantic alone is not enough to make Moore lovable. The French feel that Moore doesn't teach them anything new and that his arguments are aimed at their gullibility rather than their intelligence. In other words, the French people don't like being treated as though they are American voters.'[150]

Fahrenheit 9/11 had pushed a much more worthy anti-Bush film – William Karel's *Le Monde Selon Bush* ('The World According To Bush') – out of contention at Cannes; the organisers thought that it would be bad form and would smack of anti-Americanism to have two anti-Bush films up for awards. Karel's film covers much of the same ground as Moore's but without the childish stunts and cheap, paranoid manipulations. Karel put it like this: 'Michael Moore has the phenomenal gall to take a position. He's an American, engaged in the campaign on the side of the Democrats. My conception of the documentary is that commentary plays no part; it deals with facts and figures. I would have loved to say that Rumsfeld and Bush are crazy and dangerous, that their unconditional support of [Israeli Prime Minister Ariel] Sharon is the worst service that one could render to Israel, but I would never do that, not in any film of mine... I have tried to strike a balance when talking about Bush's 1,000 days, to assemble his errors and the horrors he's committed. There are no noisy revelations but, taken all together, everything adds a bit of force to the argument.'[151] It's very unlikely that Karel's film would ever have made more than $200 million in independent circulation in the United States.

Criticism for *Fahrenheit 9/11* came from strange places. Back in the US, the Republicans made much of the fact that the film was popular in the Arab world, allowing many to insist darkly that it was 'helping the terrorists'; rumour had it that, when it played in Beirut, it was the first film since the invention of cell phones for which the Beirutis actually turned theirs off. But even in Lebanon, Moore's methods were suspect. The *Lebanese Daily Star* ran a long piece by Ibish Hussein,[152] head of the Arab-American Anti-Discrimination Committee, on something that I noticed about the film the first time I saw it: how the exoticised Saudis are portrayed as inherently evil, money-loving, war-profiteering, an entire nationality tainted by the sins of its plutocratic princes. As a member of a related Semitic people too often similarly rendered in propaganda as dark-eyed, hook-nosed exotics obsessed with money and addicted to conspiracy, this made me uncomfortable. No matter how much the Lebanese dislike Bush and the war in Iraq, they aren't blind to some of the nastier aspects of Moore's American populism and the larger implications that this has for his credibility.

Fahrenheit 9/11 had an ambivalent reception in the new European democracies formerly dominated by the Soviet Union, many of them – in one of the most astonishing changes of my lifetime – now NATO members; some of them – Poland, for example – contributors of not-insignificant contingents to the Iraq War. Here, reaction to Moore is, in a different way than in the West, a profound matter of political identity.

Western-style capitalist democracy has been revived quickly in these mostly Catholic countries far more easily than in the historically Orthodox and Muslim parts of the Soviet Empire, mainly because it has roots that pre-dates the Soviet period. During the Cold War, a sentimental sense of the unlimited virtues of the West reigned in this part of the world, but the nations liberated in 1989 have had plenty of opportunities to get over that one-dimensional belief over the past 16 years, during which time they have seen their job security evaporate, learned to fight for health care and social security and come to understand the agonising decisions involved in having to direct their own foreign policies in a world in which they must respond to pressure from both East and West. Many Poles, Czechs, Slovaks and Hungarians feel the tension in the philosophical differences between, say, an ideological capitalist politician like the Czech President Vaclav Klaus – who never had time for social democracy – and his predecessor, Vaclav Havel, the playwright and moral philosopher who led Czechoslovakia's 'Velvet Revolution' and who is essentially a Western democratic progressive shaped by the Western counter-culture. Havel was a friend of Frank Zappa and Bill Clinton. Klaus most definitely was not.

Then again, the last 16 years have also seen another kind of political development entirely, led by Central and Eastern European politicians who merely transformed the Soviet style into a new nationalist populism: Vladimir Meciar in Slovakia, Leonid Kuchma in Ukraine, Ion Iliescu in Romania and Belarus's Aleksandr Lukashenko, who is a dictator in the full Soviet mode. So, in the former Soviet satellite states – some of them in NATO, some of them also in the European Community and some of them preparing to join these institutions – reaction to Moore and *Fahrenheit 9/11* takes on a different burden. In these countries, it is an argument about the interpretation of the political past, the economic present and the multilateral future, all at once.

Poland is a particularly interesting case, since it was consistently one of the more restive Soviet satrapies. Its Catholicism meant that it always maintained close cultural ties with the West, and it had a long history of revolt against its Soviet rulers going back beyond the Solidarity movement that arose in the 1980s to the Committee for the Defence of Workers (Komitet Obrony Robotników, or KOR) in the 1970s, and even to the 'Polish Home Army' that resisted both the Nazis and the Soviets in the 1940s. Since the Catholic Church was tolerated and influential, and since most of Poland's farm-based economy remained in private hands, it was always a bit of an anomaly in the Soviet Bloc. It was so culturally disposed to be pro-Western that union-busters Margaret Thatcher and Ronald Reagan could afford to ignore the contradictions of an alliance with the union leader, Lech Walesa, and vice versa. Of all the former Bloc countries, Poland is most closely aligned with the policies of George W Bush, and he has some Polish popular support. There is the inevitable reaction to this support, too.

These feelings unfold with some urgency, because Poland is not neutral in Iraq and this has consequences. Recently, several Arabs were arrested in Warsaw possessing detailed plans of the city's central railway station. It is not surprising that Poles take a particular interest in *Fahrenheit 9/11*.

In Warsaw, screenings of the film had an almost festive feeling as members of the diverse anti-war counter-culture took their seats and excitedly encountered each other as family, nodding and chatting in agreement at each new subtitled revelation of an American conspiracy. Websites for Polish film fans had a more mixed reaction, expressing the national ambivalence about close military ties with the United States. Some comments called it manipulative propaganda, 'a shitty product…and only a product'. Others expressed a more sophisticated post-communist point of view: 'To use the word "propaganda" in a completely negative sense is just a mistake, a confused way of thinking. Yes, this is a propagandistic film, because the filmmaker is trying to bring the viewer to certain conclusions that he has already reached. But how beautiful, how suggestive, how powerful and passionate this propaganda is! Propaganda films aren't necessarily bad; they are only bad for people of the "old times" who still think in terms of categories from more than 15 years ago. I feel embarrassed when I hear someone say that a film is "hideously propagandistic"; this Polish way of understanding film is just stupid.'[153] The movie did seem to strike a chord. In July 2004, *Fahrenheit 9/11* took over $110,000 in its opening weekend on 28 screens in Poland, which put it in fourth place nationally.

However, no place in Europe – and therefore no place in the world – is Moore more popular than in Germany. It's easy to speculate about this. Germany was a front-line state of the Cold War and, as such, had an enormous American military presence for many years, something that never wins the affection of the locals. Germans were appalled at the Vietnam War and felt abused and manipulated when, in the 1980s, Ronald Reagan – with the consent of European leaders – distributed Pershing missiles throughout Western Europe, most of which, due to the logic of the Cold War confrontation, ended up in Germany.

Germans are also highly sceptical of American adventurism; in 2002, Gerhard Schroeder's party won re-election in a very tight race by promising not to send troops to Iraq under any circumstances whatsoever, even if such action was authorised by the United Nations. Germans have their own homegrown version of Thierry Meyssan's theory, as expressed in Andreas von Bülow's *The CIA And The Eleventh Of September*. Unlike Meyssan, however, von Bülow once held a position in his country's government (he is a former Minister of Technology).

There is the complex psychology of a country that was twice conquered and was once occupied in large part by American soldiers but cannot legitimately complain about this fact. Perhaps all of this contributes to the cult of Moore in Germany.

And a cult it is. Over 1 million copies of *Stupid White Men* were sold in Germany – almost a third of the book's total global sales and far more than the 630,000 copies sold in the United States – and in 2003 it resided simultaneously at both Number One and Number Six on the German bestseller lists, for the German and English editions. Moore's other books also sell enormously well in Germany. 500,000 Germans saw *Bowling For Columbine*; 1 million saw *Fahrenheit 9/11*. His status in Germany has been favourably compared to that of Jerry Lewis in France[154] – an interesting observation that suggests the essentially clownish nature of his popularity.

Moore is even less subtle in German translation, too, and this seems to reflect some craving on the part of the German market. The English-language title of one of his bestselling books is *Stupid White Men...And Other Sorry Excuses For The State Of The Union*. It's understandable that the 'State Of The Union' part of the title, with its phraseological formality, might not translate literally into German, but this doesn't quite explain the actual title of the German translation: *Stupid White Men: Settling The Score With America Under Bush*.

Moore, speaking in Germany and releasing articles in German translation, never fails to deliver the message that America is a crazy and dangerous place and to urge Germans to reject American social and foreign policy. The following is typical: '[The Bush administration] would not hesitate to destroy anything that got in its way, especially if they are on the way to make more money. And they will punish even old allies if you don't kneel by the side of the road and bow your head as they march by on their way to the next regime change (preferably in a country which has some promising oil fields)...' Moore goes on to say that 85 per cent of Americans can't find Iraq on a map – as if this is relevant to the debate about the necessity for the Iraq War – and cautions Germans not to give in to right-wing arguments against their welfare state. 'Don't go the American way when it comes to economics, jobs and services for the poor and immigrants. It is the wrong way.'[155]

The combination of flattery of Europeans with anger at America does seem to have won Moore many friends in Germany and in much of the rest of the world, and this is an interesting phenomenon in its own right, but when this kind of attitude was picked up at home – and in the age of the internet and with the help of enthusiastic bloggers, it was, and to a very great extent – it tended to marginalise Moore's domestic appeal. Most Americans don't like to be called fools to outsiders, even those who don't like their government. The condescension in Moore's own simplistic presentation of the issues is at least as bad as that issuing from the Republican platform, and the anger at one's own countrymen is an unorthodox approach on the part of someone who presumably still needs and wants their support. Moore's antics in Europe have handed his opponents a stick to beat him with – a rather irresponsible move for a man who says that he wants to rally the American left as a powerful force.

Part 4

The Road Ahead

10 Populism

Despite his failure to unseat George W Bush, Michael Moore has a large following and great popular appeal, and he's not going away any time soon. A chastened Hollywood, perhaps remembering how *Bowling* and *Fahrenheit* had unravelled on inspection, offered him no Oscars for the 2004 film year, not even any nominations,[156] but in 2004 *Fahrenheit* won the Peoples' Choice Award for Favourite Film, an award that is determined in an egalitarian, popular fashion: by public voting on the www.pcavote.com web page. Moore hasn't lost his base.

When I heard him speak near the end of 2004 at a private reception for people in the film industry – an event designed to tout *Fahrenheit 9/11* among potential Academy voters for the Best Picture slot – Moore was in his element, and he perhaps unconsciously revealed this confusion of politics and showbiz.

In front of an adoring crowd, a crowd still deeply wounded and angered by Bush's November victory, he climbed some steps at the back of the room and gave a brief summation of where we found ourselves at that point in political time: 'Well, we got out of bed on November third...

'Here's what happened. Four years ago, Karl Rove said that there were 4 million evangelicals who didn't vote and that he wanted to turn them out next time – and he did. Here's the good news: 70 million people – poor people, women, African-Americans, Hispanics – didn't vote this time. And they don't have 70 million evangelicals.

'They won because they had a storyline. It didn't matter that it was fiction. Here's their story: Bush stands at Ground Zero, megaphone in hand, and says, "I hear you. We're going to get the people who did this and no one will ever attack you again." And the people weren't attacked again. What was Kerry's story? Can anyone tell me? His story was, "I'm not Bush." And we still got 49 million people out to vote.

'Bush has been working on his storyline for four years. Crawford? That was Karl Rove's idea; he got him the ranch, the hat, the wardrobe. Americans love the movies; they love movie characters. Republicans understand Hollywood and the Democrats don't. Republicans don't run policy wonks like Gore, Rumsfeld or Condi; they run movie stars. Americans like to vote for movie stars – Reagan, Arnold, Sonny Bono. We win when we run rock stars – Bill Clinton. Kerry was trying to tell his story in 17 paragraphs. Doesn't work. You have to tell your story in 17 seconds. Karl Rove is a master at that.

'What's happened in America? What's changed? When I was a kid, we went to the weekly union meeting and we talked to each other about our lives and the issues, and we had a sense of solidarity in that. Nowadays, what do working people have? Where do we get that sense? The mall? What do the Republicans have? Church on Sunday. That's where they get that sense of community and fellowship.

'Americans are liberals. They support liberal positions. The latest CNN/Gallup poll shows that 59 per cent of Americans – 59 *per cent* – are outraged at the possibility of the overturn of *Roe vs Wade*. A majority of Americans want gun control; a majority think the war in Iraq is a bad idea. In fact, the only major areas in which Americans are not liberal are the death penalty and gay people marrying each other.

'That's what the Democrats have to understand. The Democrats can win, but not with the watered-down republicanism of the Democratic Leadership Council. Given the choice between real Republicans and fake Republicans, leather or pleather – does anyone remember pleather? – of course people will take the real Republican! Who would choose pleather when they could have real leather? But I note that *Fahrenheit* was nominated for Best Picture in the People's Choice Awards. That's not the Academy; that's not *USA Today* or Fox News. That's where the American people are at.

'We need better candidates! Who's our rock star? Well, who wouldn't vote for Tom Hanks? Who wouldn't vote for Paul Newman or Robert Redford? Who wouldn't vote for Melissa Gilbert, the president of the Screen Actors' Guild? Hey, you can't vote against *Little House On The Prairie*!

'What about [Senator Barack] Obama? I'm back in Michigan now, full-time, and a guy back at home who probably never used the phrase "African-American" in his whole life told me, "I like Obama." Why? "I like his story." His story! It's that kind of narrative that appeals to people.

'What we need is a front man who surrounds himself with the right people. When we run a wonk, we lose.'

At the Q&A session that followed a screening of *Fahrenheit*, Moore followed up on the idea that showbusiness trumps policy in a sort of self-referential circle. He did it so well that the crowd hardly noticed when he crossed the line into silliness. Shuffling out on stage, head down, in his trademark jeans and baseball cap and a black sweater draped over his enormous belly, he appeared modest and ill at ease as he took questions, but he soon warmed to his subject and said quite sensible things about why the Democrats lost: 'I know James Carville. I called him up before the debates and told him, "When Bush goes after Kerry for being a flip-flopper, here's what he has to say: 'Mr President, I only had one position on the war, ever. I believed you. And you betrayed my trust and the trust of the American people.'" And Kerry just could not do it. He could not go for the kill.' Moore's proposed solution? He again called for the Democrats to nominate Tom Hanks – but only if his first choice, Oprah Winfrey, was unavailable. He insisted that he was serious.

Moore's analysis of the problems of the Democrats is trenchant, his solution less so. There is something simultaneously naïve and cynical about his view of American politics as a scene of competing entertainments: 'We'll vote for whoever is most convincing in the role.' This cynicism is only slightly ameliorated by the cold hard fact that American voters – at least, those since Reagan and very likely long before – tend to bear out Moore's estimate of them. It's precisely this gap between governance and entertainment that gets Americans into so much trouble, and in a distinctly American way. Reagan enjoyed being a cowboy; he enjoyed being George Gipp and that guy who lost both his legs to a crazed surgeon in *King's Row*. And he undoubtedly enjoyed playing the role of President of the United States. Bush the elder was a one-termer because he was a 'policy wonk' (a frightful expression) trying to look like a cowboy. Clinton was equal parts playboy and wonk, but he caught the collective imagination of US voters as a playboy, a smart playboy. No one has been better at the cowboy role than Bush the younger.

Did any of these roles really deliver good governance? Perhaps the American people should think about that, and think hard, before putting too much faith in developing their character actor. Would they really want Tom Hanks as President? Would Tom Hanks want Tom Hanks as President? Would he surround himself with the right people? How would the American people know that they were the right ones? How would he know? It's a clever tag line – it plays well in 17 seconds – but Moore can't quite separate the real business of politics (the business of governance) from what politicians have to do to get there (the business of entertainment). This confusion also offers Moore a great device for avoiding responsibility; as he once put it on the CNN show *Lou Dobbs' Moneyline*, 'How can there be inaccuracy in comedy?'[157]

Moore starts out by making a populist argument: Americans are good, decent, hardworking people who want to do the right thing but are kept powerless by the machinations of Republican mandarins like Rove and the Bush family who find actors to front for them. A populist agitator of a previous age might have cast his lot with a smart, talented, theatrical candidate who understood the broad needs of ordinary people and who wanted to serve them – William Jennings Bryan, say, or in a different way (and very differently from each other) both of the Roosevelts. But Moore wants a front man who can *entertain* the people. He can't see the problem because he inhabits the world of popular culture so completely. Ironically, he *is* a rock star, as anyone who has seen him in front of a sympathetic audience can attest. When he asks the crowd for names of those who might win one for the left, his charisma calls forth the inevitable response: 'YOU!' No, he hangs his head modestly: I'm just a filmmaker.

If there is one consistent theme in Moore's work, it is his attempt to reclaim the language of working-class identity and working-class values for the *actual* working class and its interests. That's the reason for the trademark look; that's why Flint and his uncle who was a founding member of the UAW and took part in the great sit-down strike of 1937 are never far from Moore's political discourse. As his old friend and associate Sam Riddle told me, 'It's not like he's some naïve, aw-shucks, working-class bumpkin who's trying to get into politics. This guy was on the debate team in high school; he prepped himself to do everything he's doing now.' Unlike George W Bush's carefully cultivated image as an ordinary guy, this is not entirely disingenuous because, unlike Bush – who has always lived in a bubble of extreme privilege, although he never seems to notice – Moore comes by it honestly, even if his life has gone in a different direction for many years.

Todd Gitlin, a former president of Students for a Democratic Society and nowadays a professor of journalism and sociology at Columbia University and a prolific writer on politics and culture, recently shared some thoughts with me on the populist style and its tendency to veer into demagoguery and on how this relates to Michael Moore. He put it like this: 'Populism is nothing other than a prejudice on behalf of the ostensible common sense of the ordinary person, and the potential for demagoguery is always built into it, since the demagogue is always, almost by definition, the person who mobilises sentiment that other people can recognise as theirs... The point is to generate a Pavlovian response rather than a reasoned one.'

Moore's timing is good. Gitlin puts the Moore phenomenon in perspective: 'Today there's a sense of predicament that lends itself to the demagogic pseudo-solution: "They" have it in for "us", whether "they" means the terrorists or the ruling class... Intellectually, there's nothing new about that. What's new is the weird hybrid fact-and-entertainment combo that Moore has worked out for it. Whenever he's in intellectual trouble, he dances away by saying that he's just an entertainer – something Bush can't do, by the way. This way of avoiding taking full responsibility for political engagement no doubt happens somewhere near the threshold of consciousness, although he's clearly intellectually unscrupulous.

'Moore branded himself. In our culture, being the outsider can be a brand, a calling card, a badge of recognition. It opens up the tube of cement that can lock the outsider into an entourage. Early new-left iconography featured the gang, an affinity that linked *West Side Story* with the Cuban Revolution with the Civil Rights movement. At some deep level – although obviously the moralities are very different – it was the idea of a tightly knit band of brothers who were going to explode the world and change everything... The '60s, by elevating youth culture to a standard of value, took Nietzsche away from the intellectuals and elevated the long-haired, grunting, drug-crazed rebel – Jim Morrison, say. The culture turned the "born to be wild" mystique into an affirmation. Then, in the mid-'70s, Moore is in the backwash when this thing reaches the blue-collar Midwest. De-industrialisation, revival of blue-collar militancy, wildcat strikes, farm foreclosures – that was real. It was part of this wild insurgency, the Midwest against the banks. Obviously, it is full of fertile metaphors.'

There's a truth here about Moore the cultural outlaw, but it is very far from General Motors, the union meeting, the Boy Scouts and baseball. Moore's a paradoxical outsider in that a big part of his whole presentation is that he's an ordinary guy who's figured out some things and is loyal to his roots.

To help explain Moore's romantic outsider status, Gitlin directed me to a little-known cultural critic of the 1940s and 1950s, Robert Warshow, who died in 1955 at the age of 37, and specifically to his essay 'The Gangster As Tragic Hero'. Warshow, unlike many intellectuals of his time, was deeply interested in popular culture, although at times his interest is rather condescending. Only a half century later, his outlook already seems a bit antique, and his words often serve as a measure of how much American politics have changed; when we hear, 'The avowed function of the modern state...is not only to regulate social relations but also to determine the quality and the possibilities of human life in general,'[158] we realise that the voice of Warshow – who was an anti-Communist, and who was making an observation, not a statement of principles – is coming from very far away indeed. Likewise, when he writes of the gangster as the individual who must assert his identity and his need, the antisocial hero who seeks total freedom and is doomed to failure by the logic of both film and society, we understand the romantic attraction but not the weight of the observation. In Warshow's time, the trope of the gangster had been absorbed into cinematic convention; in ours, the trope of analysis of the trope of the gangster has been absorbed into intellectual convention. But in Warshow's collection of essays in which 'The Gangster...' appears, there is one piece that I thought quite relevant to Moore: the essay on Julius and Ethel Rosenberg, who came to represent – for Warshow and others – a generation of American communists.

The Rosenbergs were arrested in 1950 for spying. They were charged with having persuaded Ethel's brother, David Greenglass, who worked in the weapons lab at Los Alamos, to give them classified information on atomic tests and of passing this information to the Soviet Union. The Rosenbergs were sentenced to death and, like Niccola Sacco and Bartolomeo Vanzetti a generation before them, became public martyrs for the American left, many of whose members, as a matter of deep belief about the world, insisted that they were framed.

Unlike Sacco and Vanzetti, however, the Rosenbergs actually were guilty. The archive of intercepted and decrypted Soviet spy communications known as the Venona Project, released by the National Security Agency in 1995, refers to their spying, and in his posthumous memoirs, published after the fall of the Soviet Union, Nikita Khrushchev said, 'I heard from both Stalin and Molotov that the Rosenbergs provided very significant help in accelerating the production of our atomic bomb.'[159]

Warshow looks at the Rosenbergs' letters and journals, published as a propagandistic effort to win sympathy for their cause while their death-penalty appeals were under way. He notes how the Rosenbergs claim all sorts of popular and politically acceptable elements of American culture. Yet none of this do they own or understand, and, as Warshow quotes from their journals, their pretentious righteousness becomes pathetic and almost unbearable.

Warshow points out what is so false and wrong about their self-conscious affiliation with various American traditions: 'We need not doubt that Julius was strengthened by singing "Kevin Barry" or "United Nations" or that Ethel was cheered by hearing "Ballad For Americans" or, making allowances for her language, that she was "enraptured" by the NBC *Summer Symphony*. It is even possible to imagine that Ethel was actually excited at the "trouncing" administered by the Dodgers to the Giants...and that her excitement was related to the Dodgers' "outstanding contribution to the eradication of racial prejudice". We know how easily these responses could have been changed: if "Old Man Tosc" had slighted Paul Robeson, if the Dodgers had fired one of their Negro players, if *Gentleman's Agreement* had been unfavourably reviewed in the *National Guardian*. But the initial responses and their contradictories would have been equally real, and equally unreal.'[160]

The Rosenbergs are pathetic because they have committed to a course in which they cannot be themselves; their whole world is false, dictated by whatever is expedient from the point of view of a determining set of precepts, and they cannot escape it or even know that they are lost. As Warshow notes, they cannot conceive that they are guilty because it is impossible that serving their cause could be a crime; if the world thinks so, the world fails to understand the meaning of crime. The grotesquerie lurking behind this delusion is that what the Rosenbergs were guilty of was helping a foreign power to acquire the means to kill millions of Americans. There is both a tremendous negation of the self involved in their service to the Soviet Union and a pathological egotism.

In their dogged adherence to a particular ideological identity, the Rosenbergs reminded me, just a little, of Michael Moore. No, I don't think Moore would pass weapons secrets – he's a pacifist, after all, and his attitude towards politics is different and of his time – but he is committed to seeing good and evil in the world in the same ideological, one-dimensional way that the Rosenbergs did, and he doesn't hesitate to use whatever sentimental and cultural hooks are handy to make his points. To understand the game he is playing, you need only think of how Moore castigates Bush for attacking Afghanistan – and then castigates him some more for not being worried enough about the murderous Osama bin Laden. But in fact it's not a game; if you think so, you miss something important about Moore. He believes in his role and his cause, just as the Rosenbergs did, and he completely believes every point he makes at the time he makes it. His arguments lack discipline, but his outlook does not. Orwell would have understood Moore very well.

The damage that this sort of split vision can do was described to me by Peter Ross Range, a veteran journalist, former Vietnam correspondent for *Time* magazine and White House correspondent for *US News & World Report* and who is now the editor of *Blueprint*, the online magazine of the centre-right Democratic Leadership Council.[161] On Moore's approach to filmmaking, he said, 'That kind of sloppy and tendentious and hilarious attack on political enemies was not necessarily good for the Democratic Party and not good for the country, even though it was highly entertaining. The man is a master of certain things – the comic moment, the tendentious allegation very cleverly presented. I think *Columbine* is a better movie than *Fahrenheit*, especially if one doesn't have the tools or information to deconstruct it, and most people don't. Seeing it a second time, I began to see the games that he was playing, like having the Flint sheriff comment on the welfare-to-work system as though he knew something about sociology. There are plenty of experts that one could interview on that subject, but instead he interviews the sheriff, because the sheriff thinks it's a bad thing. It's especially powerful and problematic when this stuff is shown to our friends in Europe, where they really don't know the details of what's going on here. It has a very big impact on people who have no way of judging the veracity or proportionality or appropriateness of what he's doing.'

Range brings up a problem that he's written about in articles on Moore,[162] something that might be called paranoid lowbrow political post-modernism: 'What's not fine about *Fahrenheit* is what I would call the Oliver Stone effect: to distort history and put it out there among people who are not in a position to judge it, like the young, the uninformed and the foreign.' As with Stone's bizarre – and apparently quite sincere – conviction that Lyndon Johnson and a vast array of government agencies successfully conspired to kill Kennedy and kept their secret for 40 years, an undisciplined, highly partisan take on history finds its way into the cultural bloodstream and is embraced by many as fact, with that extra frisson of a *secret* fact known and accepted only by the truly hip and aware. Moore is far from the first person to use this technique, but credit (if that's the word) him with this: he greatly stimulated the production of reality-denying propaganda on all sides.

11 Terrorism

There is a serious problem – the *most* serious problem – with Moore as spokesman for a vital, popular and forward-looking left, and this is his failure to grasp the meaning of the war on terror. As a defining issue of the times, this failure deserves some special consideration.

There are thoughtful leftists in the US that believe that the reasons the American people were given for war in Iraq were bogus, the goals blatant lies and the means chosen incapable of achieving those goals, even if they had been the real goals. But some of these people are startled and horrified when Moore insists (and too many on the left agree) that the war in Iraq was about 'nothing'; that, because Bush lied, Saddam was no threat, Iraq was irrelevant to the war on terror and the whole thing was just an enormous ploy to get pipelines for the oil companies, contracts for Halliburton, the Patriot Act for John Ashcroft and Bush elected in 2004.

Many who are not of the American right – Christopher Hitchens, Peter Beinart, Jonathan Chait, Kenneth Pollack,[163] along with many genuine Iraqi democrats such as Barham Salih, Adnan Pachachi and Kanan Makiya, and even, to some extent, British Prime Minister Tony Blair – have made serious and legitimate arguments for the war with Iraq.

Most notably in his book *Dude, Where's My Country?* and in

Fahrenheit 9/11, but also in public speeches and articles and on his website, Moore has insisted that the war is just a shield for a domestic clampdown, and that the most salient fact about terrorism is that it is a useful tool to manipulate the people: 'They know that *real* Americans are not into dominating anyone, so they have to sell it to us in fancy packaging – and that package is FEAR. In order to properly scare us, they need a big, bad enemy.'[164]

What's so terribly frustrating about this argument is that it's true, but it's not the whole truth. Bush and his people have shamelessly used 9/11 for political gain and to further their agenda of elitist domination at home and American hegemony abroad, but that doesn't mean that the US doesn't need to take the threat of terrorism seriously and act on that threat. It doesn't mean that al-Qaeda isn't an organisation that wants to kill as many Americans as possible, one that has the desire and the means to procure a nuclear device.

In December 2004, Peter Beinart wrote a long piece in *The New Republic* that will be remembered as one of the seminal articles to come out of the period of the war on terror. Beinart compares the liberal anti-Communists of the 1950s with the stalwarts in the war on terror today and points out that the anti-Communists were the saviours of liberalism. Those who were willing to see and to speak and act on the evils of Stalinism gave the liberal agenda power and credibility, and those who were willing to work alongside the Stalinists in American life – if not actually condoning or agreeing with them – were doing the opposite: discrediting and neutralising liberalism.

Beinart says that the anti-war-on-terror factions today – most notably Moore and MoveOn – are the 'softs' of this generation's most important battle, and that they threaten the prospects and credibility of liberalism as a movement: 'Today, most liberals naïvely consider Moore a useful ally, a bomb-thrower against a right wing that deserves to be torched. What they do not understand is that his real casualties are on the decent left. When Moore opposes the war against the Taliban, he casts doubt upon the sincerity of liberals who say they opposed the Iraq war because they wanted to win in Afghanistan first. When Moore says terrorism should be no greater a national concern than car accidents or pneumonia, he makes it harder for liberals to claim that their belief in civil liberties does not imply a diminished vigilance against al-Qaeda.

'Moore is a non-totalitarian, but, like [Henry] Wallace, he is not an anti-totalitarian. And when Democratic National Committee Chairman Terry McAuliffe and Tom Daschle flocked to the Washington premiere of *Fahrenheit 9/11*, and when Moore sat in Jimmy Carter's box at the Democratic Convention, many Americans wondered whether the Democratic Party was anti-totalitarian either.'[165]

Beinart's argument has some flaws. American communism of the 1950s was not wholly, completely and inherently orientated toward Moscow, although much of it was. And in characterising the enemy as 'totalitarian Islam' and ascribing primarily religious rather than primarily political goals to this enemy, Beinart comes close to endorsing Bush's unhelpful tautology 'They attacked us because they are evil.' Beinart thus amplifies the fundamental errors of the neo-conservative view of the war on terror: the complete lack of recognition of the importance of colonial and neo-colonial relationships in shaping the mad doctrines of Islamic fundamentalism. These points and others have been very ably addressed in responses to Beinart, especially those expressed by John Judis[166] and Eric Alterman.[167]

But Beinart's central point is very real and true, and it should be taken to heart by liberals who want to succeed in American politics and by those who, much more importantly, are not 'soft' on fundamentalist terror and who truly believe in a free, open, liberal, socially inflected political and cultural environment. Beinart raises issues that Moore, with his hodgepodge of ill-disciplined, contradictory and ideological anti-war positions, cannot begin to resolve. The fact that Moore is so profoundly unsatisfying when it comes to taking on these vital issues in the real world – as opposed to the play world of entertainment and the emotionally satisfying world of incitement – is a measure of his ultimate failure to offer a stable and effective pole of attraction in American politics.

Ultimately, Moore's position on the Iraq War is as serious as the solutions to intractable world conflicts that he offers in *Stupid White Men*: a page or so apiece on how to handle Northern Ireland, Israel/Palestine, the former Yugoslavia and North Korea (Moore recommends that the North Korean dictator Kim Jong Il should 'watch better movies' and that Hollywood should sponsor his film proposals.[168]) As far as the reader can tell, Moore seems to sincerely believe that these problems can be solved with a few flippant bullet points.

It appears that Moore wants to have it both ways: to get laughs for his humour and to be respected for his world vision. As Larissa MacFarquhar astutely noted in her *New Yorker* profile of Moore,[169] Moore finesses his credentials as a thinker by casting issues in such a way that the conspiracists can experience the shock of recognising a truth and the non-conspiracists can comfort themselves with the idea that, 'Hey, it's just satire' – and Moore picks up the support of both groups. There's an emptiness here, and in the long run it counts. People will always pay to see his movies – as Moore says, they're entertaining – but, as the 2004 election showed, millions of tickets sold do not translate into millions of votes against the radical right.

Beinart's article, no matter how flawed in its details, was a call for seriousness in the debate about the war in Iraq. If Moore is to address Islamic terrorism at all, and do it in a way that will not isolate him from political influence, he will have to address it seriously. There is a serious anti-war position; Moore hasn't found it yet. If he continues to be anti-war, he must find it or become slowly irrelevant – and take much of the left with him.

12 Prospects

Michael Moore's work will continue to unfold in the context of his political times. There isn't much left of the American liberal movement, if one defines modern liberalism as guarding and expanding the social ideals and public commitments of the New Deal. Meanwhile, Republicans have used savvy political organisation to completely marginalise Democrats in government, in ways both traditional and quite novel. They control both Houses of Congress, the presidency, the courts. Their majority gives them control of the House and Senate Rules Committees, which they have used in unprecedentedly partisan ways. They control a majority of the statehouses, which allows them to control redistricting and to cement a majority in Congress. Tom DeLay, the Majority Leader of the House of Representatives, has informed lobbying firms that they should employ only Republicans. This kind of monopoly on power is something that will be sure to feed the frustrations of the liberal left and lead people to the uncompromising and sometimes childish polemics of a figure like Moore.

In the wake of its losses in 2004, the Democratic Leadership Council, a group of centrist Democrats that has been trying to steer the party to a more conservative Democratic consensus since the early 1990s, and many prominent Democrats (Harry Reid, Max Baucus, Evan Bayh, Joe Lieberman) have been calling for the party to abandon more of its liberal principles, even – in a particularly disastrous suggestion – to 'get religion'.[170] *The New Republic* – once a liberal publication but under the recent editorships of Andrew Sullivan and Michael Kelly, and presently that of Peter Beinart, skewing unpredictably right and centre – has castigated Democratic attempts to return to liberalism. The magazine even endorsed Joe Lieberman – whose politics are somewhat to the right of the Republican Party's centre and who piously injects religion into public discourse – in the Democratic primaries. In the wake of the election, *The New Republic* lobbied hard against Howard Dean assuming the role of Democratic Party chairman.[171] The editors were horrified by the selection of liberal Nancy Pelosi as House Minority Leader, noting that she has the full support of groups such as the AFL-CIO, Americans for Democratic Action and Planned Parenthood.

Moore frequently inveighs against the shift to the right every time he talks about the Democratic Party, but the louder he gets, and the more public attention he gets, and the more he provokes mainstream America by insulting Americans while abroad and minimising the threat of Islamic fundamentalism, the more he encourages the shift and the more the Democratic Party shrinks from the principles he enunciates. It's a terrible dynamic for which both Moore and the Democrats share responsibility. Saying this is not to blame Moore when he tells the truth; it is to blame him for not cleaning up his act and being more respectful of facts.

Moore is committed to some good things. He wants to expand the wealth and power of the working class, being highly sceptical of the return to capital that its controllers arrogate to themselves and insisting that much of this is rightly owed to labour. He defends women's rights, gay rights, abortion rights, national health care. He believes in fairly distributing the burden of taxation. He believes in public ownership of vital public services.

Faced with all of this, many on the left try to take the good with the bad. Todd Gitlin wrote as much in a piece on Moore and his political role, 'Michael Moore, Alas' (echoing André Gide on Victor Hugo). After slamming Moore's irresponsible and inconsistent approach to facts, Gitlin writes, 'Benighted democracy needs the contention that Moore provokes because the newspapers don't provoke it, television doesn't, the Democrats didn't, Congress didn't, judicious folks didn't. No one who didn't get worked up about the administration's distortions re WMD, al-Qaeda and mushroom clouds has the right to pure rage against Michael Moore. He's not running for President, after all. (More good news…) Moore is the master demagogue an age of demagoguery made… Still, Moore could be a better version of Moore and still be Moore. He could show us that war kills and Bush is appalling, and yet be more scrupulous. But Moore is the only Moore we have – alas. Moore is the anti-Bush, and damn if we didn't need one.'[172]

Deirdre English told me something similar, something that captures much of the ambivalence that thoughtful people on the left feel about Moore as a public advocate: 'He's done some good things in bringing things into the media that weren't there. I think one of the most important things he did in *Fahrenheit* was to bring attention to the victims of the war, to show people what it's like to be a believer, a patriot, and to have your child die for a cause that was so wrongly constructed in the first place. There are things that can only be shown effectively from the perspective of working-class Americans. As I go through my ordinary day here in San Francisco…well, I'm a professor at UC; I don't meet people whose children are in Iraq. But the woman who runs the little cafe I had dinner in last night, her son is there and she knows one person who lost an eye and another who lost a leg there. The carpenter who plugged a leak in my ceiling knows a lot of people who are there. But these people aren't getting into the media because the media is out of touch with them. But Moore is in touch with them; he can get their stories out. The media do a bad job of reaching out to those people, do a bad job of understanding them, of representing their interests, writing about them, and Moore does a good job of that. To the extent that he's representing them, that's a good thing; to the extent that he becomes a paranoid, demagogic voice himself, or begins to push his own opinions down people's throats, I think that's a bad thing.'

It is true that Moore identifies a grievous gap in the presentation of reality that the mainstream media has been derelict in filling, but how responsible has he been himself? This question is connected to the problem of Moore as a person: someone who has, in the past, had no qualms about fudging the facts for his greater purposes or betraying people who trusted him, someone who claims the right to intrude on and interrogate others and yet does not allow himself to be intruded on and interrogated in the same way. Someone who has repeatedly threatened legal action – against at least Glen Lenhoff, Adam Hochschild and the Foundation for National Progress, Alan Edelstein, and the online magazine *Salon* – and then withdrawn his claim. Someone who has been known to treat his staff badly, who demands special concessions for himself, who offers grand theories that incite without really explaining. Someone who, like Bush, sees the world in simple black and white, and who admits no mistakes.

Mark Dowie pointed out to me that Moore has used his anger to appeal to a lowest-common-denominator comedic tribal rage that satisfies the human needs for symbolic bloodshed and a good laugh, just as the rants of Ann Coulter do. Sophisticated people may shun this sport – *The New York Times*'s public editor, Daniel Okrent, in charge of editorial oversight, wrote in his introductory column, 'I'd rather spend my weekends exterminating rats in the tunnels below Penn Station than read a book by either Bill O'Reilly or Michael Moore'[173] – but this might mean only that sophisticated people will continue to be increasingly marginalised in politics, and this cannot fail to help the right. Dowie rightly laments the harm that the success of Moore and Coulter (and Limbaugh and Imus, Stern and Springer before them) have done, but he sees more of it on the way, and sadly it is hard to argue with this prediction. In culture, as in markets, good coinage is driven out by bad.[174]

In the wake of November 2004, Moore seems unable to distinguish between the power of public attention and real power. What are we to make of his post-election makeover, the business suit and carefully trimmed goatee with which he now greets the late-night talk-show hosts? Is he making an ironic showbusiness statement, or does he believe himself to be ironically dressing for power? Either way, only the irony counts.

In the end, you can't really separate the man from his politics. As Laura Fraser – the freelance journalist whom Moore once accused of supplying drugs to the editors of *Mother Jones* – put it, 'I support the politics of [*Roger & Me*], but politics are…personal and a social conscience has to be based on personal credibility.'[175] If the left gives Moore a pass, however reluctantly and with however many qualifications and notes on the extenuating circumstances, is it not collectively confirming James K Glassman's view, expressed in the wake of the election, that Moore is all the left has got?

Moore could still be effective if he decided to play it straight and buckle down to work. His next movie is going to be about the broken American healthcare system, a serious and adult subject that eschews the egotistical grandstanding involved in trying to single-handedly take down an illegitimate President. This is a good sign.

'I don't consider Moore a major voice of the left, because his voice is so fucked up,' Mark Dowie told me. 'I think one of the reasons that there isn't an effective, vocal left is because of people like Moore, who've spoiled it by taking the Ann Coulter approach to politics, just slamming and bamming and tossing around unsubstantiated points in an irresponsible way. I think he's a leftish-leaning voice of the culture, but I don't think he's a voice of the left…and I wish he was! Because he's got what it takes; he's got the background and the credentials to do it. And maybe he will grow up now that he's got 28 million bucks in the bank and do something of real value that doesn't set itself up for the kind of trashing his previous work has received from the right and the centre.'

There's a real longing on the left for someone who can articulate its issues in an honest and powerful way and who can harness the traditional tools of populism in their service. Moore would have to grow up a lot and think a lot more deeply if he wanted to be that person. He'd have to accept Albert Maysles' challenge to research his material without fear of what he'd discover or create. Can he do it?

We'll have to wait and see.

Notes

INTRODUCTION

1   James K Glassman, 'Will Michael Moore's *Fahrenheit 9/11* Defeat A President?', *Capitalism Magazine*, 25 June 2004 (http://www.capmag.com/article.asp?ID=3760).

2   David Bossie, *The Washington Times*, 8 November 2004.

3   One of its founders, Howard Kaloogian, was active in the 1970s California tax revolt, whose legacy has been such a disaster for California's fiscal health. Mr Kaloogian is proud of this association in MAF's posted bio, although the affect on the revenue that California has ever since been able to collect for its schools, fire departments and ever-burgeoning prisons is not discussed. One result, however, was that rich people did get to keep more of 'their' money.

4   George F Will, *The Washington Post*, 4 November 2004

5   The name comes from an acronym for the Youth International Party, but the Yippies were members of a political party in only the broadest possible sense.

6   The pig was purchased from a farmer on the outskirts of Chicago by folk singer Phil Ochs. Yippie Jerry Rubin read the pig's public declaration of candidacy for him. It is unlikely that the pig – given the name Pigasus – met the age requirements for the office, although he was certainly native-born. At the subsequent trial of the Chicago Seven, radical lawyer William Kunstler asked Ochs, 'Were you informed by an officer that the pig had squealed on you?' (From Phil Ochs' testimony, compiled as part of Professor Douglas O Linder's Famous Trials Project at the University of Missouri, Kansas City [http://www.law.umkc.edu/faculty/projects/ftrials/Chicago7/chicago7.html].)

7   Part of Moore's charm – and a big part of his effectiveness – is that he is capable of self-mockery. One example is an episode of his television show *The Awful Truth* in which he pretends to be hawking Michael Moore role-playing kits for kids, superhero-style. There is a Moore mask, a corporate CEO mask, a security-guard badge and a microphone, and kids in his ad take turns playing Muckraking Mike and Corporate Creep. The 'advertisement' closes with the words 'You'll be fighting for justice and also helping me, Michael Moore, make enough money to choke a horse.'

CHAPTER 1

8   Michael Moore, *Downsize This!* (HarperPerennial, 1997), p142.

9   The quote shown in the University of Michigan's Flint library is from the Dudley C Lunt abridgement of George Wilson Pierson's *Tocqueville And Beaumont In America* (Gloucester, Maine; Peter Smith, 1969), p197. The original is from Tocqueville's *A Fortnight In The Wilderness*, begun on 1 August 1831 and written on the steamboat *Superior*.

10   Michael Moore and Kathleen Glynn, *Adventures In A TV Nation* (HarperPerennial, 1998), p8.

11   Press release, 'Michael Moore Meet Up Group', 13 January 2005.

12   Michael Moore, *Stupid White Men*, p100.

13   Michael Moore, 'Who Is "Brian"?', *The Flint Voice* vol. 1 no. 1, December 1977.

14   Politics, philosophy and economics have all greatly suffered from the persistence in Western intellectual life of both kinds of romantic theories of human nature. Jean-Jacques Rousseau, Friedrich Hayek, Karl Marx and Ayn Rand can share the blame equally.

15   Moore did help get at least one black female artist's project onto the big screen; Leslie Harris's 1997 debut, *Just Another Girl On The IRT*, made history in this way and was partially funded by a grant from Moore's foundation.

16   Ben Hamper, *Rivethead*, p103.

17   Ben Hamper, *Rivethead*, p2.

18   According to NPR's news director at the time, Robert Siegel, Moore lost this position when, in a segment on child abuse, he suggested that it was the fault of parents who taught their children to obey. (See Laurence

Jarvik, 'Will The Real Michael Moore Please Stand Up', *Montage* magazine, February 1990.)

CHAPTER 2

19   Michael Moore, 'Ronnie's Kids', 'Backstage' column, *Mother Jones*, September 1986.

20   Michael Moore, 'A Room With A View', 'Backstage' column, *Mother Jones*, October 1986.

21   *Mother Jones* was and is far from uncritical of Israel and ran articles on the Palestinian issue both before and after Moore's tenure as editor.

22   This incident is discussed in a piece by Alex S Jones in the 27 September 1986 edition of *The New York Times*.

23   Moore in fact did this while he was the editor at *Mother Jones*. It didn't seem to be a problem.

24   *San Francisco Chronicle*, September 7, 1986.

25   Adam Hochschild, 'A Family Fight Hits The Headlines', 'Backstage' column, *Mother Jones*, December 1986.

26   Deposition of Paul Farhi in the case of *Michael Moore and Kathleen Glynn vs Foundation for National Progress and Adam Hochschild*, Oakland, California, 25 February 1987.

27   Quoted in Paul Berman, 'Nicaragua 1986', *Mother Jones*, December 1986.

28   Although conservatives often credit Reagan with creating the unrelenting pressure that drove the Sandinistas from office, they miss the fact that their manner of leaving (they lost an election) completely belied Reagan's thesis that they were inherently anti-democratic. The Sandinistas honoured election results that they could quite legitimately have disputed; despite tremendously adverse conditions, they had still won more than 40 per cent of the vote – more than any single party in the opposition coalition – in the face of constant war, economic embargo and the open political and financial support (\$11 million's worth) of the United States for their opponents, something that would have been illegal under US law if the Nicaraguans had tried to interfere in a US election in this way.

The electorate knew that the only way to prevent further US-sponsored attacks on Nicaraguan civilians was to vote against the Sandinistas. Even under these very questionable circumstances, and even though they still fully controlled their large military, the Sandinistas gave up power when they lost the election. How well does that square with the right's claim that they hated democracy? It makes as much sense as Reagan's UN ambassador, Jeane Kirkpatrick, blaming the dismal state of the Nicaraguan economy on Sandinista mismanagement, which certainly was a factor. It might have occurred to Kirkpatrick, however, that constant terrorist attacks and a trade embargo from the country's formerly largest trading partner might also have played a role.

29   *Nicaragua vs United States*, ICJ 14, 149.

30   It is worth noting that the significance of this old battle of the American left is not isolated to the 1980s, and that it is not merely a formative but now dated event in the political life of Michael Moore. The most ardent supporters of Ronald Reagan's policies of arming Latin American allies who had terrible human rights records in the 1980s are in power again in the Bush administration. Most provocatively, Bush has hired Elliott Abrams, Reagan's Assistant Secretary of State for Human Rights and for Inter-American Affairs, in which position he was one of the masterminds of the Nicaraguan Contra war. Under George W. Bush he first held the equally Orwellian title of Special Assistant to the President and Senior Director for Democracy, Human Rights and International Operations and then, more recently, that of Special Assistant to the President and Senior Director for Near East and North African Affairs, including Arab/Israel relations, in which capacity he has been unsympathetic to the idea that the Palestinians have any legitimate claims against Israel.

Bush also rehabilitated John Negroponte, who was Reagan's ambassador to Honduras from 1981 to 1985. Because of his conduct in this position, Negroponte has been accused of turning a blind eye to politically sponsored death squads in that country and in El Salvador, and working hard to build logistics and support for the Nicaraguan Contra forces. Negroponte worked closely with General Gustavo Alvarez, the Honduran military commander who founded Battalion 316, which has been linked to many types of human rights violations, including kidnapping, torture and murder. Under his stewardship, the US embassy was accused of withholding information about Honduran repression from the official human rights reports compiled by the embassy, because such actions, if widely known, could endanger military aid to Honduras, an important part of Reagan's war on Nicaragua. Bush appointed Negroponte as his ambassador to the United Nations, and since July of 2004 he has served as ambassador to

Iraq – although a word that is used to describe the envoy of one sovereign state to another hardly seems to fit the United States–Iraq relationship at present. And just before this book went to press, Bush named Negroponte as the nation's first Director of National Intelligence, a new post designed to unify intelligence-gathering in the wake of September 11. This is a man who claimed that there were no death squads, not even any political prisoners in Honduras in the 1980s.

Abrams' and Negroponte's roles in Central America in the 1980s have led some commentators to link their names with crimes against humanity. The following pieces are just the tip of a very large iceberg. For a good summary of Abrams' complicity in atrocities, see 'Elliott Abrams: It's Back!,' *The Nation*, June 14, 2001, by David Corn. For a review of Negroponte's complicity in atrocities committed in Honduras, see 'Our Man In Honduras,' *New York Review of Books*, September 20, 2001, by former *New York Times* Honduras correspondent Stephen Kinzer, written on the occasion of Bush's nomination of Negroponte as American ambassador to the United Nations. The article can be found online at http://www.nybooks.com/articles/14485. Kinzer makes the point, among many others, that '[o]ne of [Negroponte's] first tasks would be to try to regain the seat the United States recently lost on the UN Human Rights Commission. Presumably he would have to argue that the United States is a faithful defender of human rights, not one of those hypocritical nations that observe principles only when it suits them.' There is more than a little irony in the fact that it was Negroponte, after he secured the post of Ambassador, who announced that the United States 'can never in good conscience permit Americans to become subject to [the International Criminal Court's] authority.' (Remarks by Ambassador John D. Negroponte, United States Permanent Representative to the United Nations, following the vote on UN Security Council Resolution 1422 on the International Criminal Court, July 12, 2002; these remarks can be found online at www.un.int/usa/02_098.htm.).

31 Paul Berman, 'Nicaragua 1986', in *Mother Jones*, December 1986.

32 Alexander Cockburn's introduction to *Snowball's Chance*, an anti-Orwell 'sequel' to *Animal Farm* by the serendipitously named John Reed (Roof Books, 2002).

33 Cockburn agreed to take some questions by email but did not write back when I asked him about the events at *Mother Jones* and about how he would respond to criticism that he is soft on leftist totalitarians.

34   Alexander Cockburn, *The Nation*, 20 September 1986.

35   Moore's note, quoted in Paul Berman's analysis of the incident in 'Me And Mother Jones', *The Village Voice*, 16 September 1986.

36   See, for example, writer and former Vice-President Sergio Ramirez's memoir, *Adios Muchachos* (Santillana USA Publishing, 2000).

37   Alexander Cockburn, *The Nation*, 13 September 1986.

38   Not least in his very powerful books *King Leopold's Ghost*, which is an exploration of the historical and continuing damage done to the Congo by King Leopold of Belgium's brutal personal rule; and in *Bury The Chains*, a stunning and inspiring history of the British abolitionist movement.

39   Guy T Saperstein, *Civil Warrior: Memoirs Of A Civil Rights Attorney* (Berkeley Hills Books, 2003), pp204–5.

CHAPTER 3

40   The period uniforms are somehow less chilling than the nametags that claim social normalcy ('HELLO, my name is…') that are worn by other neo-Nazis as they gather at a Michigan retreat to talk about 'mud people' and white power.

41   Bureau of Labor Statistics (www.bls.gov).

42   In fact, Moore originally thought of calling his film 'Pets Or Meat' on that very analogy, but he saved the title for his followup project.

43   There is a perhaps apocryphal story of an exchange between a GM manager and a UAW representative regarding Poletown that captures some of the dead-end quality of this kind of thinking. 'These machines don't go on strike,' observes the manager with satisfaction. 'Yes,' replies the UAW rep, 'and how many cars do they buy?'

44   See Maryann Keller's *The Rise, Fall, And Struggle For Recovery Of General Motors* (HarperCollins, 1990).

45   Ben Hamper, *Rivethead*, p47.

46   I am not so naïve as not to realise that this tradition is probably more symbolic than actual; undoubtedly the Japanese executives had all kinds of non-paycheque compensation.

47   Doron P Levin, *The New York Times*, 19 January 1990.

48   Rob Medich, 'Look Who Talked', *Premiere*, May 1990.

49   Pauline Kael's review of *Roger & Me* in *The New Yorker*, 8 January 1990.

50   Michael Moore, 'Roger And I: Off To Hollywood And Home To Flint', *The New York Times*, 15 July 1990. Far from being the willing tool of the moneyed interests behind the Lincoln Center, Jacobson was in fact fired soon after his interview with Moore appeared in *Film Comment*. Jacobson did not attribute his firing to the interview, or at least not entirely, but he did say that 'the interview was the last and most visible expression of an editorial policy that the Film Society did not like and could not support'. For those so inclined, a different and opposite conspiracy theory than Moore's is at least as plausible in explaining why Jacobson was fired: the Film Society of Lincoln Center was a sponsor of the New York Film Festival, where *Roger & Me* was a big hit.

51   David Armstrong, *The San Francisco Examiner*, 12 January 1990.

52   Andrea C Basora, 'Michael & Me', *Newsweek*, 20 April 1998.

53   Harlan Jacobson, 'Michael and Me', *Film Comment*, vol. 25, no. 6, November–December 1989.

CHAPTER 4

54   *Adventures In A TV Nation* (HarperPerennial, 1998), pp4–5.

55   That's not the only lesson, though. This former resident of Canada also noticed that actor Wallace Shawn, who plays Canadian Prime Minister Clark MacDonald, in fact bears a slight resemblance to former Canadian Prime Minister (1896–1911) Sir Wilfrid Laurier.

56   *Adventures In A TV Nation*, p12.

57   Ben Hamper, 'No Suck, No Pay: *New York Journal*, Part 2' (http://www.michaelmoore.com/hamper/nyc_part2_pg01.html).

58   For the exchange between Moore, Talbot and Radosh, see 'Michael Moore Fires Back At *Salon*', *Salon*, 4 July 1997 (http://dir.salon.com/july97/moore970703.html). Radosh's original piece on Moore: 'Moore Is Less', *Salon*, 6 June 1997 (http://www.salon.com/june97/media/media970606.html).

59   Larissa MacFarquhar, 'The Populist', *The New Yorker*, 16 and 23 February 2004.

CHAPTER 5

60   See Osha Gray Davidson, *Under Fire: The NRA And The Battle For Gun Control*, p44.

61   There is an enormous bibliography of medical and statistical studies available from the Help Network, 'an international network of medical and allied organisations dedicated to reducing firearm injuries and deaths', which is affiliated with the Children's Memorial Hospital of Chicago. The bibliography can be found online at http://www. helpnetwork.org/pdf/publications/HELP%20biblio%20web%2012.03. 2004.pdf.

62   See *Presser vs Illinois*, 1886; *United States vs Miller*, 1939; and *Lewis vs United States*, 1980. In addition, the Supreme Court has upheld various lower federal court rulings that interpret the Second Amendment as a collective rather than individual right, as described in *United States vs Tot*, 1942 (in which the Third Circuit Court of Appeals ruled that 'weapon-bearing was never treated as anything like an absolute right by the common law'); *Farmer vs Higgens*, 1991; *United States vs Warin*, 1976; *Quilici vs Morton Grove*, 1982, in which the Seventh Circuit Court of Appeals ruled that 'the possession of handguns by individuals is not part of the right to keep and bear arms'; and *Hickman vs Block*, 1996, in which the Ninth Circuit Court of Appeals ruled that, 'Because the Second Amendment guarantees the right of the states to maintain armed militia, the states alone stand in the position to show legal injury when this right is infringed.'

63   Charter of the National Rifle Association.

64   Pierce, a former physicist, wrote under the pseudonym 'Andrew MacDonald'. For some reason, many American white supremacists consider the Scots to be the finest flower of pure Aryan development.

65   Postulating the existence of such a thing is, of course, a gross generalisation, but not an unrealistic one.

66   In an odd connection, Michael Moore had donated the school's computer equipment.

67   What Moore did is recounted by the bank employees themselves in Michael Wilson's film *Michael Moore Hates America*.

68   Andrew Collins' interview with Michael Moore in *The Guardian*, 11 November 2002 (http://film.guardian.co.uk/interview/interviewpages/ 0,6737,841083,00.html).

69 Current statistics show that Americans have more guns than Canadians, and both have more guns than the Swiss. Thirty-nine per cent of US households possess firearms, compared to 29 per cent in Canada and 27.2 per cent in Switzerland (including Army and Reserve households), according to the article 'International Violent Death Rates' at www.guncite.com, a pro-Second Amendment site (www.guncite.com/gun_control_gcgvintl.html).

70 It is a fact, however, that there are military assault rifles in many Swiss households and that the Swiss homicide rate is far lower than those of the US or Canada (Switzerland has 1.32 deaths per 100,000 compared with Canada's 2.16 and 5.70 in the US [source: *International Journal Of Epidemiology*, UK, 1998]). Here, I believe that we do have to look for cultural explanations; does any person seriously believe that, were there to be a military assault rifle in every US household, the homicide rate in America would be as low as that of Switzerland? But whether Moore's *particular* cultural explanation is or is not correct is an entirely different question.

71 Actually, at the plant to which Moore refers here, Lockheed produced rockets for launching television communication satellites.

72 *The Boston Globe*, 27 October 2002.

73 The speech is included on the bonus disc for the DVD release of *Bowling For Columbine*.

74 Dave Kopel, 'Bowling Truths', *National Review Online*, 4 April 2003 (http://www.nationalreview.com/kopel/kopel040403.asp).

75 A white supremacist who shot and killed the civil-rights leader Medgar Evers in 1963, acquitted by all-white juries several times but finally convicted – 31 years after the fact – in a federal court of violating Evers' civil rights.

76 See, for example, Kay S Hymowitz's 'This Family Shouldn't Have Been Saved' in *The Wall Street Journal*, 3 March 2000.

77 Rob Nelson interview with Michael Wilson, 'The Last Patriot Standing', *City Pages* (http://citypages.com/databank/25/1241/article12459.asp. 9/15/2004).

78 Joel Bleifuss, 'Michael Moore Stars At Academy Awards', *In These Times*, 24 March 2003.

79 Michael Moore, interviewed on *The Charlie Rose Show*, 14 January 2004.

CHAPTER 6

80   Robert Welch, *The Politician* (Western Islands, 1975), p266.

81   On the grounds of respect for states' rights, that classic argument of the civil-rights era that sprang from the Tenth Amendment and that was so often deployed against the equal rights of citizenship guaranteed by the 14th Amendment.

82   See Karen Rothmeyer, 'Citizen Scaife', in *Speak Out Against The New Right*, edited by Herbert F Vetter (Beacon Press, 1982).

83   Undoubtedly many on the right will object to my characterisation of Bork as a 'phony scholar' in the same class as Dinesh D'Souza and the insufferable Michael Novak. Yes, Bork really is a brilliant intellectual. Unfortunately, he's also become a moralistic zealot who has written books with titles like *Slouching Towards Gomorrah: Modern Liberalism And American Decline* (Regan Books, 2003), and this orientation has considerably corrupted his powers of logic.

84   See Eric Alterman, 'The Right Books And Big Ideas', *The Nation*, 22 November 1999.

85   Leftists of small-D democratic sympathies easily detect something sinister and dishonest in this. Cockburn has defended Castro and the Soviet Union in print, and in the 1980s he supported – or, at best, did not support opposition to – the Soviet invasion of Afghanistan. In presenting him as the voice of the left, *The Wall Street Journal* can be strongly suspected of using him to tar all leftists of any stripe as extremists while demanding credit for its own broad-mindedness.

86   This description of the genesis and extent of the right's control of the American media is, necessarily, shallow and cursory. Readers who desire more detail on this very important subject can look – among many other sources – to several hugely important and necessary books: Eric Alterman's *What Liberal Media?* (Basic Books, 2003), Joe Conason's *Big Lies* (Thomas Dunne Books, 2003), David Brock's *The Republican Noise Machine* (Crown Books, 2004) and Sheldon Rampton and John Stauber's *Banana Republicans: How The Right Wing Is Turning America Into A One-Party State* (Jeremy P Tarcher, 2004). A very useful online source – again, one among many – is www.disinfopedia.org.

87   The BBC's Board of Governors will soon be abolished, following concerns raised in an inquiry about an inherent conflict of interest in its dual role

as advocate and manager of the corporation. It will most likely be replaced by a system that avoids this situation comprising a BBC Trust (to set policy) and a BBC Executive Board (to carry it out).

88 The use of the word 'public' in the names of these organisations is somewhat misleading. Both declare themselves private corporations on their websites. The Public Broadcasting Service gets about 35 per cent of its revenue from public sources, including both state (18.3 per cent) and federal (16.4 per cent) grants. National Public Radio gets 1–2 per cent of its $100 million annual budget from federal grants and has to fight for every penny of this against conservative lawmakers who would love to cut it off entirely, just on principle.

89 There are big differences, however, between the methods and practices of Moore and those of a sober news-gathering organisation like the BBC, differences as big as those between the BBC and Fox News. Most significantly, the BBC has an established protocol for fact-checking and institutional oversight.

90 Michael Kazin, *The Populist Persuasion*, p11.

91 In a time of war in the Middle East, unstable oil supplies and terrorism that derives some of its funding from oil profits, one could make the argument that wasting fuel is unpatriotic, but you won't hear this from a Republican elite firmly allied with the US energy industry.

92 Think, for example, of Newt Gingrich's new book, *Winning The Future: A 21st-Century Contract With America* (Regnery Publishing, 2005), in which this man who has never shown much personal religious devotion urges even greater penetration of the institutions of State by the agenda of 'people of faith'.

93 *The New York Times*, 29 October 2000.

94 See Thomas Frank, *What's The Matter With America?*

95 Quoted in David Brock's *The Republican Noise Machine*, p123.

96 Kevin Phillips, 'The Future Of American Politics', *The National Review*, 22 December 1972.

97 Richard Hofstadter, *The American Political Tradition* (Vintage Books, 1989), p62.

98 Michael Kazin, *The Populist Persuasion*, p22.

99 Coughlin eventually retreated to a form of right-wing populism that

seems to thrive from time to time in the Catholic Church: a corporatist social doctrine claiming the lead role for the Church and its traditions and an insistence that respect for these things among both workers and employers would usher in a golden era of justice and godliness and respect for properly constituted authority, such as that which supposedly reigned under the Church in the Middle Ages. The abuses of the capitalist class would be punished and the working man would be taken care of, as long as he honoured the proper relationships between the Church and the larger society.

Think of Mel Gibson's Catholic chauvinism and love for authority merged with Pat Buchanan's social agenda and populist economics. If the imagined polity that results seems vaguely familiar, there's a reason for that, and it's no surprise that Coughlin expended considerable political capital in a defence of Spanish dictator Francisco Franco's authoritarian, romantic view of the traditional Spanish social order.

100   Indeed, while many non-conservatives recognised the damage that mixing sex and governance was doing to the republic, few would deny a certain satisfaction in the sex scandals that broke over the heads of Newt Gingrich and his presumed successor as Speaker of the House, Robert Livingston, in the aftermath of the Clinton impeachment. Indeed, there was little criticism from the left of pornography publisher Larry Flynt for 'outing' Livingston's affair and threatening to out other Republicans, even though it was hard to find anyone on the left who thought that Flynt had done a good or honourable thing. The refrain 'Live by the sword, die by the sword' was much bandied about.

101   'John Ellis' is a Bush family name. 'Jeb', commonly given as the first name of the Governor of Florida, is actually an acronym for John Ellis Bush.

102   The office of State Secretary of State is quite different from the federal office of the same name. The State Secretary of State oversees state civic matters, such as elections.

103   There is a picture of these rioting Republican staffers, each of them tagged and identified by name, in John Nichols and David Deschamps's *Jews For Buchanan: Did You Hear The One About The Theft Of The American Presidency?* (New Press, 2001).

104   Jeffrey Toobin, *Too Close To Call: The 36-Day Battle To Decide The 2000 Election* (Random House, 2002), p156.

105   For details on these conflicts of interest, see Richard K Neumann Jr's

'Conflicts Of Interest In *Bush v. Gore*: Did Some Justices Vote Illegally?', *Georgetown Journal Of Legal Ethics*, spring 2003.

CHAPTER 7

106 Every time I come across this attitude, I think of the net redistribution differential between the East and the Central and Western states. Those honest, hard-bitten citizens of the red states take in, on average, about $1.25 worth of revenue from the federal government for every dollar they pay in federal taxes, and this difference comes right out of the pockets of those effete, elite, parasitical blue-state loafers and academics, who, as it happens, actually produce most of the wealth of the nation. The 'heartland' could not maintain anything like its present population without these massive transfers of wealth from the Northeast in the form of net tax subsidies, federal farm subsidies, grazing subsidies and mining and water concessions.

107 An arm of the ultra-conservative Concerned Women For America.

108 Move America Forward tries to pass itself off as a grassroots organization, but it shares offices with a high-powered Republican consulting firm, Russo Marsh & Rogers. Sal Russo, who has worked with a long string of right-wing Republicans, including Ronald Reagan, George Deukmeijan, Jack Kemp and Orrin Hatch, is its chief strategist. Howard Kaloogian, a former Assistant Republican Leader in the California State Assembly and a leader of the movement to recall elected Democratic Governor Gray Davis and of California's fiscally disastrous Proposition 13 'tax revolt', is a co-chairman.

109 Christopher Hitchens, 'Unfairenheit 9/11' (http://slate.msn.com/id/2102723/).

110 *Newsweek*, 'Teaming Up', 15 November 2004. This election wrap-up story was reported by Eleanor Clift, Kevin Peraino, Jonathan Darman, Peter Goldman, Holly Bailey, Tamara Lipper and Suzanne Smalley and written by Evan Thomas.

111 For example, on *The Charlie Rose Show*, 1 July 2004.

112 See Andrew Gumbel's 'Moore Accused Of Publicity Stunt Over Disney "Ban"', *The Independent*, 7 May 2004.

113 Louis Menand, 'Nanook And Me', *The New Yorker*, August 2004.

114 For a detailed overview of the failed negotiations involving Unocal, the Taliban and the US State Department, see Ahmed Rashid's fascinating book *Taliban: Militant Islam, Oil and Fundamentalism in Central Asia*, especially Chapter 13, 'Romancing the Taliban 2, The battle for Pipelines 1997-99: the USA and the Taliban'.

115 Mary Ann Poust, *Catholic New York*, 26 October 2000.

116 Regular viewers of the Fox Network are also statistically much less likely to have an accurate understanding of how American political institutions work and of what the Constitution says, as David Brock points out in *The Republican Noise Machine*.

117 See Christopher Hitchens, 'Unfairenheit 9/11' (http://slate.msn.com/id/2102723/).

118 Limbaugh's serial mendacity has been extensively documented, most notably in *Logic And Mr Limbaugh: A Dittohead's Guide To Fallacious Reasoning* by Ray Perkins Jr (Open Court Publishing Company, 1995); *Rushed To Judgment* by David Barker (Columbia University Press, 2002); *The Great Limbaugh Con* by Charles M Kelly (Fithian Press, 1994); and *The Way Things Aren't: Rush Limbaugh's Reign Of Error* by Fairness and Accuracy In Reporting (New Press, 1995), which also keeps a running tally of Limbaugh's lies on its website at www.fair.org. You can browse FAIR's enormous archive of documented Rush lies at http://www.fair.org, where a search on 'Limbaugh' will yield an enormous amount of material.

Written in a more breezy, populist style, but no less accurate, are comedian Al Franken's books on the media: *Rush Limbaugh Is A Big Fat Idiot And Other Observations* (Dell, 1999) and *Lies And The Lying Liars Who Tell Them* (Dutton Books, 2003). Additionally, almost every serious media watchdog organisation that is concerned with truth in broadcasting maintains its own Limbaugh file.

119 A professional comedian has exposed her as an expert in the manipulation of context and the abuse of footnotes. See Al Franken's *Lies And The Lying Liars Who Tell Them*.

120 From www.michaelmoore.com (no longer posted).

121 David Boaz, 'Attacks On American Values', posted at http://www.cato.org/dailys/10-01-01.html.

122 Boaz also clearly has no understanding of democratic socialism (I've

never seen any evidence that Michael Moore favours any other kind) if
he thinks that respect for the individual is in opposition to it.

123 Ann Coulter, 'Put The Speakers In A Cage' (http://anncoulter.com/columns/
2004/072604.htm).

124 Ann Coulter, 'This Is War', *The National Review Online*, 13 September
2001 (http://www.nationalreview.com/coulter/coulter091301.shtml).

125 Unpublished fragment quoted in *Washington Monthly Online* at
http://www.washingtonmonthly.com/features/2001/0111.coulterwisdom.
html.

126 Jonah Goldberg, 'L'Affaire Coulter', *The National Review Online*, 3 October
2001 (http://www.nationalreview.com/nr_comment/nr_comment100301.
shtml).

127 http://www.nationalreview.com/thecorner/2002_10_20_corner-archive.asp.
As it turns out, John Muhammad is not gay, as far as anyone knows.

128 McCain had won in New Hampshire and Bush desperately needed to
win an important contest – and soon – in order to stay in the race. Just
at this point, a shadowy 'polling group' began to call up voters in the
South Carolina Republican primary and ask them the question, 'Would
it affect your vote if you knew that John McCain had a non-white child?'
(McCain and his wife have an adopted Bangladeshi daughter, Bridget.)
McCain, who had been ahead in the polls, lost the primary to George
W Bush, and Bush never looked back.

129 Michael Moore, *USA Today*, 1 September 2004.

130 From a transcript of Giuliani's speech to the convention posted on CNN's
website at http://www.cnn.com/2004/ALLPOLITICS/08/30/giuliani.
transcript/.

CHAPTER 8

131 Those who stand to lose out due to this arrangement are never idle,
however. It is worth mentioning that the first reactions of Donald
Rumsfeld and George W Bush to the Abu Ghraib pictures was to blame
those who took them; the problem was not the abuse, it was the pictures
of the abuse. In memos and orders, Bush and Rumsfeld immediately set

about confiscating as many pictures as they could find rather than addressing the genesis of this shameful crisis.

132 David Bossie, interviewed on CNBC's *Capital Report*, 29 September 2004.

133 *The Washington Times* is published by Korean billionaire Sun Myung Moon, of Moonie cult fame, who is a major contributor to right-wing causes and who wields such influence in the capitol that he was crowned the new Messiah in a ceremony in the Dirksen Senate Office Building on 23 March 2004, with Congressmen Tom Davis III, Philip Crane, Eddie Johnson, Curt Weldon, Danny Davis, Harold Ford Jr, Roscoe Bartlett, Sanford Bishop and Chris Cannon attending, along with Senator Lindsey Graham and former Senator Larry Pressler. Moon somehow got a Shofar-blowing rabbi to declare him 'possibly the Messiah'. Who says politics is boring? (Thanks to John Gorenfeld's website at http://www.gorenfeld.com for these juicy details.)

134 David N. Bossie and Christopher M. Gray, Bin Laden's Rage: Why He and His Followers Hate the United States. 'Policy Paper' posted on www.citizensunited.com.

135 David N. Bossie, Blame America First: College Campuses Respond the War on Terror. 'Policy Paper' posted on www.citizensunited.com.

136 In 1954, the CIA commissioned a secret report, since declassified, that was written by Dr. Donald N. Wilber, a participant in the coup; the report is entitled Clandestine Service History: Overthrow of Premier Mossadeq of Iran, November 1952-August 1953. This report can be read online at http://www.nytimes.com/library/world/mideast/iran-cia-intro.pdf.

137 See David B Ottaway, 'Democratic Fundraiser Pursues Agenda On Sudan', *The Washington Post*, 29 April 1997.

138 In the film, Michael Ledeen of the American Enterprise Institute says that terrorism directed against America all started with the Ayatollah Khomeini, forgetting that it was the America-installed Shah who crushed dissent and pushed Iranian politics into the one corner of society he could not control or co-opt: radical Islam. It's unclear whether Ledeen is even aware that al-Qaeda considers Shia Islam (the kind practised in Iran) a heresy and that the Iranians have nothing to do with bin Laden's particular Islamic terrorist group.

139 For a thorough debunking of Emerson's work even before 9/11, see

John F Sugg's 'Steven Emerson's Crusade', 4 December 2000, at http://www.mediamonitors.net/whoisemerson.html.

140 Moore has this on film in *Fahrenheit 9/11* in a scene that cannot be taken out of context.

141 Perhaps this is due to a technicality – Hawaii was a US territory but not a state in 1941 – but it seems to be a technicality invoked in order to reduce the status of one of America's greatest wartime leaders, a man who rarely invoked religion.

142 As someone who tried very hard to get an interview with Moore, I have a great deal of sympathy for Wilson's frustration.

143 This film focuses on those perennial shibboleths of the right: leftist censorship and campus speech codes. These things are not defensible, and few thoughtful leftists try – or want – to defend them. Of course, it's easy to cherry-pick particularly egregious and bizarre violations of the letter and spirit of the First Amendment on America's thousands of college campuses, and of course the right never addresses its own far more egregious historical and contemporary violations that come from far more powerful and influential institutional sources. To take just one example, anyone who cares to can rent Robert Greenwald's film *Outfoxed! Rupert Murdoch's War On Journalism* and see Bill O'Reilly declare that those who oppose the Iraq War will be expected to 'shut up' once the shooting starts. This incident, and 1,000 others like it, disseminated by one of the nation's most powerful media outlets, did not elicit cries of outrage from the right.

144 Jim and Ellen Hubbard, interview with Liane Hansen on *Weekend Edition*, National Public Radio, 5 September 2004.

145 Comments from Drudge and Cutler in Joe Hagan's 'Amanpour Says Saddam TV Was Distorted... Drudge Says Moore's 9/11 Is Pure – Drudge!', *The New York Observer*, 12 July 2004.

CHAPTER 9

146 The question of why the British, who also have Middle Eastern colonial experience, did not realise this is an interesting one. It is true, however, that the British occupying forces in Iraq have had significantly more success than the American forces in navigating the cultural perils. It might simply be that the pull of the 'special relationship' with their cousins across the Atlantic is more powerful than their former colonial relationships.

Then again, British and French colonial patterns were always different. While the British system of indirect rule might have given many colonial subjects more day-to-day control of their own lives – and kept the British out of sight in many colonial matters – the French were more willing to assimilate their subjects, in the process perhaps getting to know them better. Starting in 1834, French colonial subjects under certain circumstances could acquire French citizenship, and in 1848, when universal male suffrage was introduced, colonial men who had citizenship could vote and sit in the French parliament. It's hard to imagine Indians in the parliament of Victoria, or that of George VI, the monarch at the time of Indian independence in 1947. In many ways, French colonialism was more intimate than the British version, if no more legitimate.

147 John Berger, 'The Beginning Of History', *The Guardian*, 24 August 2004.

148 Jean-Luc Douin, *Le Monde*, 7 July 2004 (my own translation).

149 Pascal Bruckner, 'Paris Dispatch: Tour de Farce', *The New Republic*, 19 July 2004.

150 Ibid.

151 William Karel, interviewed in *Le Monde*, 12 June 2004 (my own translation).

152 Huseein Ibish, '*Fahrenheit 9/11* misses mark on conspiracies', Lebanon's *The Daily Star*, 12 July 2004.

153 Comment posted on the website of Polish film society Stopklatka, 25 July 2004 (my own translation).

154 Stephen Zeitchik, 'Michael Moore In Germany: Better Known Than JFK?', *Publishers Weekly*, 22 October 2003.

155 'Nicht Ganz Amerika Ist Verrückt' ('Not All Americans Are Crazy'), www.zeit.de/2003/46/AbdruckMoor, September 2003 (my own translation).

CHAPTER 10

156 Moore had taken *Fahrenheit 9/11* out of contention in the documentary category, so as to be eligible for the Best Picture Award. Had *Fahrenheit* been nominated, it would have been competing in this category against an unusually strong field that included *Sideways*, *Hotel Rwanda*, *Million Dollar Baby* and *Ray*.

157 Michael Moore, interviewed on CNN's *Lou Dobbs' Moneyline*, 12 April 2002.

158 Robert Warshow, 'The Gangster As Tragic Hero' (1949), in *The Immediate Experience* (Harvard University Press, 2001), p97.

159 Nikita Khrushchev, *Khrushchev Remembers: The Glasnost Tapes*, edited by Jerrold L Schecter and Vyacheslav V Luchkow (Little, Brown, 1991), p194.

160 Robert Warshow, 'The "Idealism" Of Julius And Ethel Rosenberg' (1953), in *The Immediate Experience* (Harvard University Press, 2001), p47.

161 Range also contributed an article to the harshly partisan *Michael Moore Is A Big Fat Stupid White Man*, a fact about which he seems to be just slightly uncomfortable; the book is a rather shoddy production, although his article is not. Range, pressed for a quick decision by the book's publisher, figured that it was better to get it out there and that his piece could speak for itself.

162 For example, 'Michael Moore's Truth Problem', *Blueprint* (http://www.ndol.org/ndol_ci.cfm?contentid=252483&kaid=127&subid =177).

CHAPTER 11

163 Although Chait's and Pollack's arguments rested primarily on the threat of Saddam's weapons of mass destruction, they worked from the best information available to them at the time, and they did so honestly (unlike the Bush administration, which let it be known what kind of information it wanted), and both have made other arguments, too.

Furthermore, it would be shallow and callow to suggest that the WMD argument has been completely discredited. An important part of Pollack's thesis was that the post-1991 sanctions regime on Iraq was falling apart and that it could not be sustained much longer. In the absence of sanctions, there would have been no effective way of keeping Saddam from fulfilling his long-held ambition of acquiring these weapons. Would this have been an acceptable scenario? There were legitimate arguments against overthrowing Saddam, and there were legitimate arguments for lifting sanctions, which were clearly hurting the Iraqi people more than they were hurting Saddam's power structure, but liberals who argued at the time – as many did – both against war *and* against sanctions were indulging in irresponsible moral grandstanding.

164 Michael Moore, *Dude, Where's My Country?*, p101.

165 Peter Beinart, 'A Fighting Faith: An Argument For A New Liberalism', *The New Republic*, 13 December 2004.

166 John B Judis, 'Purpose Driven', *The New Republic Online*, 8 December 2004.

167 Eric Alterman, 'A Reply To Peter Beinart', *The Nation*, 10 January 2005.

168 *Stupid White Men*, p195.

169 Larissa MacFarquhar, 'The Populist', *The New Yorker*, 16 and 23 February 2004.

CHAPTER 12

170 Why the Democratic Leadership Council believes that this would be seen as anything other than the cynical, condescending ploy that it in fact would be is an interesting question.

171 'Scream 2', *The New Republic*, 13 December 2004, by the editors.

172 Todd Gitlin, 'Michael Moore, Alas', on *OpenDemocracy.net*, 1 July 2004 (http://www.opendemocracy.net/themes/article-3-1988.jsp).

173 Daniel Okrent, 'The Public Editor: An Advocate For *Times* Readers Introduces Himself', *The New York Times*, 7 December 2003.

174 Mark Dowie, 'A Nation Of Minds' (unpublished, courtesy of Mr Dowie).

175 Laura Fraser, 'In *Roger & Me*, Michael Moore Plays Fast And Loose With The Facts', *San Francisco Bay Guardian*, 17 January 1990.

Sources

BOOKS

ANDERSON, JACK: *Inside The NRA: Armed And Dangerous.* (Dove Books, 1996)

BARNARD, JOHN: *Walter Reuther And The Rise Of The Auto Workers* (Little, Brown & Co, 1983)

BROCK, DAVID: *The Republican Noise Machine: Right-Wing Media And How It Corrupts Democracy* (Crown Books, 2004)

BUGLIOSI, VINCENT: *The Betrayal Of America: How The Supreme Court Undermined The Constitution And Chose Our President* (Nation Books/Thunder's Mouth Press, 2001)

CONASON, JOE: *Big Lies: The Right-Wing Propaganda Machine And How It Distorts The Truth* (Thomas Dunne Books, 2003)

COULTER, ANN: *Treason: Liberal Treachery From The Cold War To The War On Terrorism* (Crown Forum, 2003)

DERSHOWITZ, ALAN: *Supreme Injustice: How The High Court Hijacked The Election Of 2000* (Oxford University Press, 2001)

DIZARD, JAN E; MUTH, ROBERT MERRILL; and ANDREWS, STEPHEN P, JR (eds): *Guns In America: A Reader* (New York University Press, 1999)

EFRON, EDITH: *The News Twisters* (Nash Publications, 1971)

FRANK, THOMAS: *What's The Matter With Kansas? How Conservatives Won The Heart Of America* (published in the UK as *What's The Matter With America?*) (Metropolitan Books, 2004)

FRANKEN, AL: *Lies And The Lying Liars Who Tell Them: A Fair And Balanced Look At The Right* (Dutton Adult Books, 2003)

FRIEDLANDER, PETER: *The Emergence Of A UAW Local, 1936–1939* (University of Pittsburgh Press, 1975)

GRAY DAVIDSON, OSHA: *Under Fire: The NRA And The Battle For Gun Control* (University of Iowa Press, 1998)

HAMPER, BEN: *Rivethead: Tales From The Assembly Line* (Warner Books, 1992)

HANNITY, SEAN: *Deliver Us From Evil: Defeating Terrorism, Despotism, And Liberalism* (Regan Books, 2004)

HARDIE, DAVID and CLARKE, JASON: *Michael Moore Is A Big Fat Stupid White Man* (Regan Books, 2004)

HITCHENS, CHRISTOPHER: *A Long Short War: The Postponed Liberation Of Iraq* (Slate Books/Plume Books, 1998)

HOFSTADTER, RICHARD: *The American Political Tradition* (Vintage Books, 1989)

HOFSTADTER, RICHARD: *The Paranoid Style In American Politics And Other Essays* (Harvard University Press, 1996)

KAZIN, MICHAEL: *The Populist Persuasion: An American History* (Cornell University Press, 1998 [revised edition])

KELLER, MARYANN: *The Rise, Fall, And Struggle For Recovery Of General Motors* (HarperCollins, 1990)

LAWRENCE, KEN (ed): *The World According To Michael Moore* (Andrews McMeel Publishing, 2004)

MICKLETHWAIT, JOHN and WOOLDRIDGE, ADRIAN: *The Right Nation: Conservative Power in America* (Penguin Books, 2004)

MOORE, MICHAEL and GLYNN, KATHLEEN: *Adventures In A TV Nation* (HarperPerennial, 1998)

MOORE, MICHAEL: *Downsize This!* (HarperPerennial, 1997)

MOORE, MICHAEL: *Dude, Where's My Country?* (Warner Books, 2003)

MOORE, MICHAEL: *Stupid White Men...And Other Sorry Excuses For The State Of The Nation* (Regan Books, 2002)

NASH, GEORGE H: *The Conservative Intellectual Movement In America Since 1945* (Intercollegiate Studies Institute, 1998)

NICHOLS, JOHN and DESCHAMPS, DAVID: *Jews For Buchanan: Did You Hear The One About The Theft Of The American Presidency?* (New Press, 2001)

PACKER, GEORGE: *The Fight Is For Democracy: Winning The War Of Ideas In America And The World* (Perennial, 2003)

PHILLIPS, KEVIN: *The Emerging Republican Majority* (Arlington House, 1969)

PIERSON, GEORGE WILSON: *Tocqueville And Beaumont In America* (Peter Smith, 1969)

POLLACK, KENNETH: *The Threatening Storm: The Case For Invading Iraq* (Random House, 2002)

RAMIREZ, SERGIO: *Adios, Muchachos* (Santillana USA Publishing, 2000)

RASHID, AHMED: *Taliban: Militant Islam, Oil and Fundamentalism in Central Asia* (Yale U Press, 2001)

REED, JOHN: *Snowball's Chance* (Roof Books, 2002)

SAPERSTEIN, GUY T: *Civil Warrior: Memoirs Of A Civil Rights Attorney* (Berkeley Hills Books, 2003)

SCHECTER, JERROLD L and LUCHKOW, VYACHESLAV V (eds): *Khrushchev Remembers: The Glasnost Tapes* (Little, Brown & Co, 1991)

STEIN, BEN and DEMUTH, PHIL: *Can America Survive? The Rage Of The Left, The Truth, And What To Do About It* (New Beginnings, 2004)

SUGARMAN, JOSH: *National Rifle Association: Money, Firepower And Fear* (National Press Books, 1992)

TAPPER, JAKE: *Down And Dirty: The Plot To Steal The Presidency* (Little, Brown & Co, 2001)

TOOBIN, JEFFREY: *Too Close To Call: The 36-Day Battle To Decide The 2000 Election* (Random House, 2002)

VETTER, HERBERT F (ed): *Speak Out Against The New Right* (Beacon Press, 1982)

WARSHOW, ROBERT: *The Immediate Experience: Movies, Comics, Theater, And Other Aspects of Popular Culture* (Harvard University Press, 2001)

WELCH, ROBERT: *The Politician* (Western Islands, 1975)

FILM AND TELEVISION

ABBOTT, JENNIFER and ACHBAR, MARK (dirs): *The Corporation* (2005)

GREENWALD, ROBERT (dir): *Outfoxed: Rupert Murdoch's War On Journalism* (2004)

KAREL, WILLIAM (dir): *Le Monde Selon Bush* (2004)

KNOBLOCK, KEVIN (dir): *Celsius 41.11* (2004)

MOORE, MICHAEL (dir): *Bowling For Columbine* (2002)

MOORE, MICHAEL (dir): *Canadian Bacon* (1995)

MOORE, MICHAEL (dir): *Fahrenheit 9/11* (2004)

MOORE, MICHAEL (dir): *Pets or Meat: The Return to Flint* (1992)

MOORE, MICHAEL (dir): *Roger & Me* (1989)

MOORE, MICHAEL (dir): *TV Nation* (television show, 1993 and 1994)

MOORE, MICHAEL (dir): *The Awful Truth* (television show, 1998 and 1999)

PETERSON, ALAN (dir): *FahrenHYPE 9/11* (2004)

RIDGWAY, JAMES (dir): *Blood In The Face* (1991)

SELLIER, CHARLES (dir): *Faith In The White House* (2004)

WILSON, MICHAEL (dir): *Michael Moore Hates America* (2004)

JOURNALS, NEWSPAPERS AND MAGAZINES
See 'Notes' for exact articles referenced, where applicable.

Boston Globe, The (US)
Capitalism magazine (US)
Catholic New York
City Pages (US)
Detroit Free Press, The (US)
Die Zeit (Germany)
Film Comment (US)
Flint Journal, The (US)
Flint Voice, The (US)
Free To Be (US)
Guardian, The (UK)
The International Herald Tribune
In These Times (US)
Le Monde (France)

Lebanon Daily Star, The (Lebanon)
Media File
Metro
Michigan Voice, The (US)
Mother Jones magazine (US)
Nation, The (US)
National Review, The (US)
New Republic, The (US)
New York Observer, The (US)
New York Post, The (US)
New York Sun, The (US)
New York Times, The (US)
New Yorker, The (US)
Newsweek (US)
Premiere magazine (US/UK)
Publishers' Weekly (US)
San Francisco Bay Guardian, The (US)
San Francisco Chronicle, The (US)
San Francisco Examiner, The (US)
San Francisco Weekly (US)
USA Today (US)
Village Voice, The (US)
Wall Street Journal, The (US)
Washington Post, The (US)
Washington Times, The (US)

WEBSITES

See 'Notes' for exact articles referenced, where applicable.

The American Enterprise Institute (www.aei.org)
Ann Coulter's web site (www.anncoulter.com)
Blueprint (www.ndol.org)
British Broadcasting Corporation (www.bbc.co.uk)
Cable News Network (www.cnn.com)

The Cato Institute (www.cato.org)
Citizen's United (www.citizensunited.com)
Dave Kopel's "59 Deceits in Fahrenheit 9/11"
(www.davekopel.com/Terror/Fiftysix-Deceits-in-Fahrenheit-911.htm)
Free Republic (www.freerepublic.com)
Greg Palast's web site (www.gregpalast.com)
Help Network (www.helpnetwork.org)
The Heritage Foundation (www.heritage.org)
Media Monitors (www.mediamonitors.net)
Michael Moore's web site (www.michaelmoore.com)
Move America Forward (www.moveamericaforward.org)
National Review Online (www.nationalreview.com)
Open Democracy (www.opendemocracy.net)
Salon (www.salon.com)
Slate (www.slate.com)
Stopklatka (Poland) (www.stopklatka.pl)

Index